DEMOCRACY

PROBLEMS AND PERSPECTIVES

Roland Axtmann

EDINBURGH UNIVERSITY PRESS

Edinburgh University Press Ltd
22 George Square, Edinburgh

Typeset in Linotype Sabon by
Iolaire Typesetting, Newtonmore, and
printed and bound in Great Britain by
Athenaeum Press, Gateshead

A CIP record for this book is available
from the British Library

ISBN 978 0 7486 2009 8 (hardback)
ISBN 978 0 7486 2010 4 (paperback)

Contents

Acknowledgements

Without the support, understanding and generosity of my editors at Edinburgh University Press, Nicola Ramsey and James Dale, I could not have finished this book. I was lucky that they were my editors.

The section on 'Globalisation and democracy' in Chapter 5 incorporates my revised contribution to Nigel Dower and John Williams (eds), *Global Citizenship. A Critical Reader* (Edinburgh University Press, 2002), which was published under the title 'What's wrong with cosmopolitan democracy?'. With the permission of Continuum Publishers, I have used some passages of my contributions in Roland Axtmann (ed.), *Balancing Democracy* (2001) in Chapters 3, 4 and 5 of this book.

The Leverhulme Trust awarded me a Research Interchange Grant which allowed me to organise three international conferences between 2003 and 2005 on 'Global democracy, the nation-state and global ethics' under the auspices of the Centre for the Study of Globalisation at the University of Aberdeen, Scotland. I should like to thank my former colleagues, Professor Roland Robertson and Dr Nigel Dower, who co-hosted the events, as well as the conference participants for creating an intellectual environment which challenged me to sharpen my arguments.

The Department of Politics and International Relations at the University of Wales Swansea, with its long and distinguished tradition in political theory and the theoretical approach to understanding democracy, proved to be an intellectually congenial environment in which to revise my thoughts and finish this book. My special thanks go to Mark Evans and Alan Finlayson as well as to the 'theorists' among our postgraduate community: none of them, I dare say, would agree with many of the arguments put forward in this book.

My family supported work on this book immeasurably by agreeing to move with me from Scotland to Wales. They cheered me up whenever necessary, but more importantly they never complained when I shut myself away in the study. My affectionate thanks to Gerti, Lauren and Tim.

Swansea, August 2006

Preface

Democracy is a regime type in which citizens, who are united for giving law, rule themselves. Such self-rule must be exercised by globally-oriented citizens who combine local and global patriotism. This Kantian position is developed in Chapter 1 of this book and provides both the starting-point and the foundation of the arguments put forward in this study. Such patriotic cosmopolitanism is quite distinct from the 'new liberal cosmopolitanism' (Peter Gowan) that aims to promote capitalism, human rights and democracy around the world. 'Human rights' have become the new 'standard of civilisation' whose enforcement – if necessary by violent means in the form of humanitarian intervention – the 'liberal' West has accepted as its new burden in the name of humanity. The same holds true for the promotion of democracy and the enforcement of the (alleged) right to democratic governance. What is being promoted under the heading of 'good governance' is liberalism as a comprehensive doctrine. It sees the individual person as being prior, and morally superior, to community; capitalism in its neo-liberal version as being intrinsically and inevitably congenial and conducive to liberty; and pluralist, representative democracy as being the only feasible form in which 'free' political communities can organise themselves. The net result of this attempt at the globalisation of democracy and human rights is a 'liberal anti-pluralism' (Gerry Simpson) which denies the principle of the sovereign equality of states and marginalises as 'rogue' or 'outlaw' states those countries which (it is alleged) fall short of the required standard of liberal civilisation – a shortcoming all the more serious in those cases where such states also interfere with the power-political interests of the 'great powers' of the West. While there have been attempts to utilise Kant's writings for a philosophical, and possibly even moral, justification for such a policy, my own reading of Kant's cosmopolitanism does not support such a view.

A critical discussion of the uses to which the idea of 'human rights' are put in the international arena must not prevent us from reflecting upon the intricate relationship between liberal democracy and human rights. At issue is here the relationship between 'private' and 'public' autonomy

– a theme we shall pursue through a consideration of arguments presented by Jürgen Habermas – and that between 'negative' and 'positive' liberty. Are there any limits to the self-rule of the citizens – and are these limitations 'pre-given' in the form of inalienable rights of the individual? Are human rights 'external' to popular sovereignty and do they provide protection for the individual and for minorities against the potential tyranny of the majority? Furthermore, whereas at the international level the human rights discourse is frequently truncated as a result of the hegemony of the liberal-individualist doctrine, within Western liberal states the human rights discourse is still informed by concerns about the appropriate relationship between civil, political, and social rights and their respective institutionalisation.

One other theme that is running through the chapters of this book is the relationship between sovereignty and democracy. There is not just the liberal anti-pluralist denial that 'outlaw' states possess sovereignty and, in this connection, a reinterpretation of sovereignty as a duty to protect (rather than a right to control). The assumption of 'liberal' democracy since its inception in the late eighteenth century has been that democratic rule is exercised in the sovereign, territorially consolidated nation-state. In a bounded territory, people's sovereignty is the basis upon which democratic decision-making takes place; and 'the people' are the addressees, or the constituents, of the political decision. The territorially consolidated democratic polity, which is clearly demarcated from other political communities, is seen as rightly governing itself and determining its own future through the interplay between forces operating within its borders. Only in a sovereign state can the will of the people command without being commanded by others. Chapter 4, in particular, teases out the political and institutional significance of this assumption. Yet, as we know, the capacity of the state for sovereign control within its territory has been affected by the forces of 'globalisation'; and the idea of 'the people', the *demos*, in the singular has lost its purchase as a result of the realisation, and the political acceptance, of the multinational and multi-ethnic composition of many so-called 'nation-states'. I address some aspects of these developments in the final chapter. Rather than accept that these developments will (or ought to) usher in the institution of post-national citizenship and lead to the establishment of a cosmopolitan democracy, I emphasise the need to retain a commitment to strengthening democracy at the level of the nation-state – while, at the same time, endorsing Bhikhu Parekh's idea of the globally-oriented citizen who combines local and global patriotism and embraces a Kantian 'enlarged thinking' as a patriotic duty and a cosmopolitan virtue.

Kant's Republicanism and the Cosmopolitan Persuasion

A constitution providing for the *greatest human freedom* according to law that permit *the freedom of each to exist together with that of others* (not one providing for the greatest happiness, since that would follow of itself), is at least a necessary idea, which one must make the ground not merely of the primary plan of a state's constitution but of all laws too.

Immanuel Kant, *The Critique of Pure Reason*
(Kant [1781] 1998: 397 [A 316; B 373], emphasis in original)

Kant's Republicanism and the 'Moral Personality' of States

Immanuel Kant's theory of political republicanism pinpoints succinctly key elements of modern political rule. First, Kant endorsed the idea of the sovereignty of the people that manifests itself in constitution-making and law-making: 'The legislative power can belong only to the united will of the people' (Kant [1797] 1996, hereafter MM, 457 [6: 313]).[1] Citizens as the members of a society uniting for the purpose of legislating are said to have the lawful freedom to obey only those laws to which they have given their consent; to enjoy equality before the law so that they possess perfectly symmetrical rights of coercion relative to each other; and to be their own master, dependent on no other person's will, but only on themselves, and this 'civil independence' includes the material means to secure their existence and sustenance.

Secondly, Kant conceptualised freedom as 'negative' liberty, defining 'every restriction of freedom through the arbitrary will of another party' as coercion:

No one can coerce me to be happy in his way (as he thinks of the welfare of other human beings); instead, each may seek his happiness in the way that seems good to him, provided he does not infringe upon that freedom of others to strive for a like end which can coexist with the freedom of every one in accordance with a possible universal law (i.e., does not infringe upon this right of another). (Kant [1793] 1996, hereafter TP, 290–1 [8: 290–1])

By rejecting the paternalist idea of happiness which a benevolent state might want to impose on its subjects, Kant, thirdly, rejected the notion of substantive state-objective and declared that individuals as citizens know for themselves what they want to will. It is they, and only they, who have the right and competence to decide what laws are right and just so that 'the action of one can be united with the freedom of the other in accordance with a universal law' (MM, 387 [6: 230]). It is their will, and their will alone, that is the source of the law. Law is no longer seen as manifesting a concordance with a transcendent idea or 'natural law'; the *'summus imperans'* is not bound, or restricted, by *a* law, but bound to give laws (Maus 1992: 158–9).

But where, or in what, does the legitimacy of this positive law reside? From where does it receive its justification and coercive validity if not from an extra-legal source? For Kant, the legitimacy of the law is dependent upon the legitimacy of the law-maker. Legitimacy of the law issues out of a procedure of deliberation in which free individuals (as citizens) participate on an equal footing with each other and in which 'each decides the same thing for all and all for each' (MM, 457 [6: 314]). The authorisation of the legislator to obligate others through his mere will is thus grounded in the procedural sovereignty of the people that manifests itself in individuals who, as citizens, deliberate in public with the intent to formulate universal laws (Maus 1992: chapter 8). Self-legislation is the hallmark of a people's sovereignty.

Finally, in rejecting the state's objective to provide for 'common welfare' and 'happiness', Kant also denied that a state could coerce its citizens to enter an ethical community, or that a legislator could found a constitution directed towards ethical ends through coercion. Through politics, human beings cannot become moral beings. Kant's refusal of any moral *telos*, or purpose, of the political community was complemented by his view that there was also a disjunction between a republican government and the 'virtues' of individuals:

> Now the *republican* constitution is the only one that is completely compatible with the right of human beings, but it is also the most difficult one to establish and even more to maintain, so much so that many assert it would have to be a state of *angels* because human beings, with their self-seeking inclinations, would not be capable of such a sublime form of constitution. But now nature comes to the aid of the general will grounded in reason, revered but impotent in practice, and does so precisely through those self-seeking inclinations, so that it is a matter only of a good organisation of a state (which is certainly within the capacity of human

beings), of arranging those forces of nature in opposition to one another in such a way that one checks the destructive effect of the other or cancels it, so that the result for reason turns out as if neither of them existed at all and the human being is constrained to become a good citizen even if not a morally good human being. The problem of establishing a state, no matter how hard it may sound, is *soluble* even for a nation of devils (if only they have understanding) . . . (Kant [1795] 1996, hereafter PP, 335 [8: 366])

Kant thus proposed an institutional arrangement that counteracts interest with interest and passion with passion. Even if we presuppose the existence of only self-interested rational individuals, a republican polity could still be established.

According to Kant, a republican polity has two key characteristics. First, it bestows citizenship status on the autonomous, property-owning individual. As a citizen, the individual must obey only those laws to which he has given his prior consent and to which all citizens are equally subject. Since he owes his existence and support entirely to himself, the citizen enjoys civil independence as he is not dependent upon the will of another member of society. Coercion to which he may be subjected is considered legitimate only if it is derived from the general will of the people. In the institution of citizenship, the public use of reason goes hand-in-hand with the development of economic self-interest.

The second feature emerges out of Kant's conceptual distinctions. According to Kant, the forms of a state (*civitas*) 'can be divided either according to the different persons who have supreme power within a state or according to the *way* a people *is governed* by its head of state, whoever this may be' (PP, 324 [8: 352]). The first classification concerns the form of sovereignty (*forma imperii*) and distinguishes between autocracy, aristocracy, and democracy, or the power of one: the prince; the power of some: the nobility; and the power of all those who together constitute the civil society: the people. The second classification concerns the form of government (*forma regiminis*), 'the way a state, on the basis of its civil constitution (the act of the general will by which a multitude becomes a people), makes use of its plenary power' (PP, 324 [8: 352]). The *forma regiminis* is either republican or despotic:

> *Republicanism* is the political principle of separation of the executive power (the government) from the legislative power; despotism is that of the high-handed management of the state by laws the regent has himself given, inasmuch as he handles the public will as his private will. Of the

3

three forms of state, that of *democracy* in the strict sense of the word is necessarily a *despotism* because it establishes an executive power in which all decide for and, if need be, against one (who thus does not agree), so that all, who are nevertheless not all, decide. (PP, 324 [8: 352])

It is on the basis of this distinction that Kant can conceive of autocratic monarchical rule where, nevertheless, the ruler may govern 'in a *republican* (not a democratic) manner'; in other words, the people are treated 'in accordance with principles akin in spirit to the laws of freedom which a people of mature rational powers would prescribe for itself, even if the people is not literally asked for its consent' (Kant, [1798] 1970: 187). It is on the same basis that, instead of a democratic system, Kant advocated a form of 'aristocratic republicanism', that is, 'rule by the few, guided and restraint by the many, through the legislature . . . [with] the few always be[ing] answerable to the community in a representative legislature . . .' (Williams, 1983: 276–7; MM, 481 [6: 341]). Indeed, any form of government which is not representative is without form, 'because the legislator cannot be in one and the same person also executor of its will' (PP, 324 [8: 352]). To put it differently, a republican autocrat is in conformity with the *spirit* of a representative system; but a democrat is of necessity 'despotic' because there is no representation. In addition to these 'formal' aspects, the republican constitution is based on the freedom of every member of society as a human being; the equality of each individual with all the others as a subject; and the independence of each member of a commonwealth as a citizen (TP, 291 [8: 290]). The republican constitution, therefore, underlies as far as law is concerned, any kind of civil society and ensures uniquely the recognition of the moral personality of human beings.

The following qualifications need to be kept in mind, however. Kant's concept of equality refers to individuals as members of a commonwealth who are subjected to coercive right equally with all the other members of the state: whoever is subject to laws is a subject within a state and as such has coercive rights against every other citizen. This uniform equality of human beings as subjects of a state is, however, quite consistent with the greatest inequality in terms of the quantity and degree of their possession: equality under the law can go hand-in-hand with socio-economic inequality (TP, 292 [8: 291–2]). Yet, according to Kant, this idea of the equality of human beings as subjects within a commonwealth also implies that 'every member of a commonwealth must be allowed to attain any level of rank within it (that can belong to a subject) to which his talent, his industry and his luck can take him; and his fellow subjects may not stand in his way by means of a *hereditary* prerogative . . . so as to keep him and his descendants forever beneath the rank' (TP, 293 [8: 292]). In other words, an aristocracy may not prevent the formation of a bourgeoisie. Furthermore, for Kant it was self-evident that not all subjects were qualified to be co-legislators; there is a distinction between active citizens and passive subjects:

> He who has the right to vote in this legislation is called a *citizen* (*citoyen*, i.e., *citizen of the state*, not of a town, *bourgeois*). The quality requisite to this, apart from the *natural* one (of not being a child or woman), is only that of *being one's own master* (*sui generis*), hence having some *property* (and any art, craft, fine art, or science can be counted as property) that supports him. (TP, 295 [8: 295])

Hence, for Kant 'republican' citizenship is both exclusive (excluding women, children, and those individuals without property) – thus explicitly excluding notions of substantive equality and universal suffrage – but also inclusive to the extent that it constitutes a citizenry that comprises not only the landed class but also the (economic) bourgeoisie and the professional middle class. As property owners – notwithstanding the size of their respective property – they all possess the right to the same number of votes. Since it cannot reasonably be expected that the citizens will reach unanimity in their decisions, but only to show a majority of votes (and, indeed, not even of direct votes but only of those who are delegated to do so as representatives of the people), 'the very principle of letting such a majority be sufficient, adopted as with universal agreement and so by contract, must be the ultimate basis on which a civil constitution is established' (TP, 296 [8: 296–7]).

How does Kant arrive at this conceptualisation of political community? There is, first, Kant's definition of the person as 'a subject whose actions can be *imputed* to him. *Moral* personality is therefore nothing other than the freedom of a rational being [*vernünftiges Wesen*] under moral laws . . . From this it follows that a person is subject to no other laws than those he gives to himself (either alone or at least along with others)' (MM, 378 [6: 223]). Only those laws of a society are compatible with the moral personality of human beings to the making of which individuals as citizens have contributed. Secondly, Kant further claims that human beings have an 'innate' right to freedom: '*Freedom* (independence from being constrained by another's choice), insofar as it can coexist with the freedom of every other in accordance with a universal law, is the only original right belonging to every man by virtue of his humanity' (MM, 393 [6: 237]). This right should be backed up and protected by the coercive power of a just state that enforces the laws that delimit a person's external freedom. This just state is a 'republic'.

For Kant, this 'innate' freedom is a manifestation of the most fundamental human faculty, reason: it is a peculiarity of reason 'that, aided by the imagination, it can create [*erkünsteln*] artificial desires which are not only unsupported by natural instinct but actually contrary to it' (Kant [1786] 1963: 56). Reason is positively liberating, as it releases the individual from the clutches of instinct and natural propensities, opening up for him an infinite range of objects and enabling him to choose his own way of life without being tied to any single one 'like the other animals'. Reason provides the capacity for human beings to give themselves laws and set themselves ends that are not determined by nature, but that draw upon their imagination, their memory, their values and their experiences. Edmund Burke expressed this thought well when he wrote that 'art is Man's nature' (Burke 1791/1887). It is on the basis of this argument that Sanku Muthu suggests that Kant's conception of freedom implies a theory of cultural agency:

> [A] being with culture is one who can create desires, values, and ideals, a being who can inscribe meanings and idealizations of beauty on to the world, and one who can anticipate the future . . . 'humanity', as a set of distinguishing and constitutive capabilities and powers, consists of 'cultural agency'. (Muthu 2003: 130)

The idea of reason, for Kant, is not to isolate itself but to converse: reason needs community and the discursive intercourse with other rational beings (Kant 1913: 392, no. 897: '*Die Vernunft ist nicht dazu gemacht, dass sie sich isoliere, sondern in Gemeinschaft setze*'). Kant's famous argument that enlightenment, understood as the emergence of human beings from their self-incurred minority (or immaturity), is premised on making public use of one's reason in all matters, is the best-known statement to that effect: '. . . by the public use of one's own reason I understand that use which someone makes as a *scholar* before the entire public of the *world of readers*' (Kant [1786] 1991: 18 [8: 37]). This statement leads to the notion of a reasoning political public as the necessary means of enlightenment. The public exercise of reason is, in turn, premised on the freedom of expression, and the thoughts that are expressed depend on the freedom to communicate:

> Opposition to freedom of thought comes firstly from *civil coercion*. We do admittedly say that, whereas a higher authority may deprive us of freedom of *speech* or of *writing*, it cannot deprive us of freedom of *thought*. But how much and how accurately would we *think* if we did not think, so to speak, in community with others to whom we *communicate* our thoughts and who communicate their thoughts to us! We may therefore conclude that the same external constraint which deprives people of the freedom to *communicate* their thoughts in public also removes their freedom of *thought*, the one treasure which remains to us amidst all the burdens of civil life, and which alone offers us a means of overcoming all the evils of this condition. (Kant [1786] 1991: 247)

There is, moreover, a kind of silent dialogue that underpins the public use of reason. Thinking depends on 'enlarged thought' that enables us to think in the position of everyone else. A person of a broad-minded way of thinking 'sets himself apart from the subjective private conditions of the judgment, within which so many others are as if bracketed, and reflects on his own judgment from a universal standpoint (which he can only determine by putting himself into the standpoint of others)' (CJ, 175 [5: 295]). It is through an act of imagination that we can take the standpoint of other rational beings and engage in critical thinking. As James Bohman has argued:

> Each of Kant's 'maxims of common human understanding' captures some necessary condition for the public use of reason: that each individual abstract from his or her point of view and adopt the viewpoints of others; that each think consistently in revising shared beliefs in light of new reasons offered. Reasons offered in reflective judgments employing these maxims will be convincing so long as each participant also offers his or her own reasons to others, while at the same time anticipating the collective outcome of such a process as a whole. (Bohman 1997: 185)

However, there is yet another aspect to Kant's notion of discursive intercourse. When discussing aesthetic judgement, Kant points out that, for instance, conceptions of taste rely upon communicating our feeling of pleasure or displeasure to others, 'and includes a susceptibility, which this very communication affects pleasurably, to feel satisfaction (*complacentia*) about it in common with others (socially)' (Kant [1797] 1974: 111 [7: 244]). In this view, (aesthetic) judgments are embedded in patterns of intersubjective communication, indeed, are only possible within a structure of sociability. As such, it is conducive to moral development: 'Making a man *well-mannered* as a social being falls short of forming a *morally good* man, but it still prepares him for it by the effort he makes, in society, to please others (to make them love or admire him). – In this way we could call taste morality in one's outward appearance' (Kant [1797] 1974: 111–12 [7: 244]). For Kant, then, thinking and judging are necessarily dependent upon communicability and sociability and, hence, on a public sphere.

Secondly, we cannot understand Immanuel Kant's political philosophy unless we appreciate the pivotal role that the concept of 'state of nature' plays in it. In *The Metaphysics of Morals* (1797), Kant argues that it is not

> some deed that makes coercion through public law necessary. On the contrary, however well disposed and law-abiding men might be, it still lies a priori in the rational idea of such a condition (one that is not rightful) that before a public lawful condition is established, individual human beings, peoples, and states can never be secure against violence from one another, since each has its own right to do *what seems right and good to it* and not to be dependent upon another's opinion about this. So, unless it wants to renounce any concepts of right, the first thing it has to resolve upon is the principle that it must leave the state of nature, in which each follows its own judgment, unite itself with all others (with which it cannot avoid interacting), subject itself to a public lawful external coercion, and so enter into a condition in which what is to be recognized as belonging to it is determined *by law* and is allotted to it by adequate *power* (not its own but an external power); that is, it ought above all else to enter a civil condition. (MM, 456 [6: 312])

Two main arguments stand out in this passage. First, in the state of nature conflicts arise over differential judgements on what is 'good and right' and there are no protections of the individuals from the coercive imposition of one person's will upon that of another. Such an imposition denies that which is essential to our humanity: autonomous self-determination of those ends we wish to pursue. We are therefore beholden to leave this state of nature. Secondly, that which is allotted to the individual 'by right' must be guaranteed and protected by a sovereign power. After all, 'if he lives among others of his own species, man is *an animal who needs a master*' (Kant [1784] 1970, hereafter IUH, 46). His self-seeking animal inclinations mislead him into exempting himself from the law wherever he can: 'He thus requires a *master [Herr]* to break his self-will and force him to obey a universally valid will under which everyone can be free' (IUH, 46). The coercive power is acceptable and legitimate to the extent that it secures for the individual freedom under the law. The state of nature is thus truly left behind when a union of individuals has been established for the purpose of being under common, self-given, rightful laws secured and protected by a coercive power.

While Kant accepts the right of individuals to force others into a state of 'civil society', he does not grant a similar right to states in relation to other states. According to Kant, the 'state of nature' in which individuals find themselves and the 'state of nature' which obtains between states must be kept analytically separate. This means that the transition out of the 'state of nature' must be conceived as quite different for individuals and states respectively:

> what holds in accordance with natural rights for human beings in a lawless condition, 'they ought to leave this condition', cannot hold for states in accordance with the right of nations [*Völkerrecht*] (since, as states, they already have a rightful constitution internally [*eine rechtliche Verfassung*] and hence have outgrown the constraint of others to bring them under a more extended law-governed constitution in accordance with their concepts of right [*nach ihren Rechtsbegriffen*]). (PP, 327 [8: 355])

To coerce unwilling states into an international 'state of civil society' would violate the fundamental principle of the autonomy of the citizens of a state who, after all, formed a union in order to be free under the law. As Richard Tuck (1999: 221) has observed: 'If states did not voluntarily recognize the principles of international and cosmopolitan right, there was nothing which other states could do to compel them, nor could the other state treat them *as if* they had acceded to the principles.' We should look in greater detail at how Kant arrives at this position; along which lines he distinguishes between international and cosmopolitan right; and what this means for the constitution of domestic and international order.

The Sovereign Equality of States, Peaceful Coexistence and the International Constitution

In *The Metaphysics of Morals*, Kant develops his theory of the right of nations:

> The right of *states* in relation to one another (which in German is called, not quite correctly, the *right of nations* [*Völkerrecht*], but should instead be called the right of states, *ius publicum civitatum*) is what we have to consider under the title of the right of nations. Here a state, as a moral person, is considered as living in relation to another state in a condition of

natural freedom and therefore in a condition of constant war. (MM, 482 [6: 343])

This statement contains at least four assumptions. First, the idea of a right of nations is premised upon the existence of many states which are independent of each other. Secondly, the *status naturalis*, in which states find themselves in this pluriverse, is a state of war, not a state of peace. Hence, 'a condition of peace must therefore be *established*' (PP, 322 [8: 349]). Thirdly, the character of the state as a 'moral person' bestows autonomy on the state, and the interference of outside powers would thus constitute a trespass on the rights of an independent people (PP, 319–20 [8: 346]): all states, not only those constituted as republics are protected against intervention. Kant's definition of the state as a moral person underpins his notion of right of nations: only those laws conform to the moral personality of states which have been formulated by all the states bound by them. Consequently, fourth, states exist in a condition of equality. Hence, no war between independent states can be a punitive one (*bellum punitivum*). This is for the simple reason that a punishment can occur only in the relation of a superior (*imperantis*) to those subject to him (*subditum*). But such a relation does not obtain between states (MM, 485 [6: 347]).

We must qualify this last statement. As we have seen, Kant assumes that there obtains a sovereign equality of states that grounds the right of self-determination and of non-interference. States are of equal standing, and war between such states cannot take on the character of a punitive war, as we have seen above (MM, 485 [6: 347]). Yet, Kant also uses the concept of the 'unjust enemy' that he takes from Achenwall's and Pütter's handbook *Elementa iuris naturae* (1750) (Schmitz 2003). By an 'unjust enemy' he means someone 'whose publicly expressed will (whether by word or deed) reveals a maxim by which, if it were made a universal rule, any condition of peace among nations would be impossible and, instead, a state of nature would be perpetuated' (MM, 487 [6: 349]). As we shall see presently, in the context of Kant's overall position, this can be understood to mean that an unjust enemy is he who undermines or violates that contract through which a federation of states is founded that guarantees to its members autonomy and non-interference as well as the right of self-defence. Yet, we may note that Kant does not clearly state under what circumstances it is that freedom of the community of states is threatened or who *in concreto* decides about the presence of such a threat (and thus authorises war against the unjust enemy).

Kant maintains that, considered empirically, the will to subjugate other states or to grow at their expense is always present (TP, 309 [8: 312]). The differences of language and religion also keep peoples apart and incline them towards mutual hatred and the excuse of war. Indeed, their very propinquity inclines them towards hostilities (PP, 336 [8: 367]). Under those circumstances, Kant asks: How can peace be founded? Pragmatically, what is required is for states to commit themselves to the following six principles (PP, 317–20 [8: 343–7]):

1. Only those peace treaties are valid which are made without secret reservation of the material for a future war.
2. No independently existing state, whether it be large or small, may be acquired by another state, through inheritance, exchange, purchase, or gift.
3. Standing armies shall gradually disappear.
4. No national debt shall be contracted in connection with the foreign affairs of the state.
5. No state shall forcibly interfere in the constitution and government of another state.
6. No state at war with another shall permit such acts of hostility as must make mutual confidence impossible in time of future peace.

In Kant's estimation, there are a number of empirical socio-political developments that are congenial to international pacification. Kant claims that the spirit of commerce, and thus mutual self-interest, cannot coexist with war; the rising cost of warfare and the devastating effects of war would propel states away from warfare and compel them to seek peace. This would be the case above all in those states whose republican constitution would enable the citizens to resist the war efforts by their government. According to Kant, the republican constitution offers the prospect of peace for the following reason:

> When the consent of the citizens of a state is required in order to decide whether there shall be war or not (and it cannot be otherwise in this constitution), nothing is more natural than that they will be very hesitant to begin such a bad game, since they would have to decide to take upon themselves all the hardships of war (such as themselves doing the fighting and paying the costs of the war from their own belongings, painfully making good the devastation it leaves behind, and finally – to make the cup of troubles overflow – a burden of debt that embitters peace itself, and that can never be paid off because of new wars always pending) . . . (PP, 323–4 [8: 350–1]; also MM, 483–4 [6: 344–6])

Yet, Kant's analysis goes well beyond narrow empirical observations. As Kant argues in *Idea for a Universal History with a Cosmopolitan*

Purpose, the powers and capacities of the human species belong to humanity collectively more than they do to individuals. They develop over the entire historical succession of human generations. According to Kant, there is a mechanism to be found in nature that allows for the development of these capacities, and, eventually, also for overcoming the condition of unrestricted freedom. This mechanism is the unsocial sociability of human beings, their propensity to enter into society, on the one hand, and a constant mutual resistance, on the other, which threatens to dissolve this society:

> Man has an inclination to *live in society*, since he feels in this state more like a man, that is, he feels able to develop his natural capacities [*Naturanlagen*]. But he also has the tendency to *live as an individual*, to isolate himself, since he also encounters in himself the unsocial characteristics of wanting to direct everything in accordance with his own ideas. He therefore expects resistance all around, just as he knows of himself that he is in turn inclined to offer resistance to others. It is this very resistance which awakens all man's powers and induces him to overcome his tendency to laziness. Through the desire for honour, power or property, it drives him to seek status among his fellows, whom he cannot *bear* yet cannot *bear to leave*. (IUH, 44)

It is this desire for greater self-worth than that of our fellow human beings, our 'self-conceit' [*Eigendünkel*] (Kant [1788] 1996, hereafter CPR 199 [5: 73]), that 'provokes an unsociably social state of discontented competitiveness among human beings, and this competition, in turn, while making us both evil and unhappy, promotes the collective development of our species-capacities' (Wood 1996: 69). But their quarrelsomeness, their competitive vanity, their insatiable desire to possess or to rule – all these traits eventually make human beings also conceive of the need to formulate and embrace a civil constitution as a condition of peace (IUH, 47–9).

With regard to the external relationship of a state with other states, unsocial sociability plays a pivotal role also:

> The same unsociability which forced men to [work for a law-governed civil constitution] gives rise in turn to a situation whereby each commonwealth, in its external relations . . . is in a position of unrestricted freedom. Each must accordingly expect from any other precisely the same evils which formerly oppressed individual men and forced them into a law-governed civil state. Nature has thus again employed the unsociableness of men, and even of the large societies and states which human beings construct, as a means of arriving at a condition of calm and security through their inevitable *antagonism*. (IUH, 47)

For Kant, this 'quarrelsomeness' was most forcefully expressed in wars, tense and unremitting military preparations and the resultant social, political, and economic distress which inevitably would befall each state. An international constitution was needed to obtain a more peaceable condition. But what would this international constitution look like?

Kant argued that in this international constitution, as in the civil constitution, freedom, equality, and independence of the parties to the contract must be assured. According to reason, states must give up 'their savage (lawless) freedom' and 'accommodate themselves to public coercive laws' (PP, 328 [8: 357]). In theory, this would mean the creation of a republican *civitas gentium* which would eventually embrace all peoples of the world. Yet, states do not wish to lose their freedom, equality, and independence in a 'world' state. Here, Kant's argument that there is a disanalogy between the idea of 'the state of nature' with regard to individuals and 'the state of nature' with regard to states becomes pertinent again. Kant regards the ideal state as a union of individuals for the purpose of being under common, self-given laws. To coerce unwilling states into a 'state of states' violates the basic idea of the political autonomy of the citizens as well as the autonomy of the people collectively (Kleingeld 2004). This argument, which underpins Kant's principle of non-intervention, also defends the right of states not to be forced to join a 'world republic'.

Hence, Kant must look out for an alternative institutional solution:

> [S]o (if all is not to be lost) in place of the positive idea *of a world republic* only the *negative* surrogate of a *league* [*Bund*] that averts war, endures, and always expands can hold back the stream of hostile inclination that shies away from right, though with constant danger of its breaking out. (PP, 328 [8: 357])

What is necessary for this idea of a federal convention [*Föderalität*] to take hold is for a powerful and enlightened people to embrace a republican constitution and thus provide 'a focal point of federative union of other states (PP, 327 [8: 356]: '*einen Mittelpunkt der föderativen Vereinigung für andere Staaten*'). While a federative union is second-best compared with a world republic, it is certainly far better than the complete merging of all states in one of them, that is, the creation of a universal monarchy. Having done away with independent states, a universal monarchy would indeed be a 'soulless despotism' (PP, 336 [8: 367]). Indeed, a universal commonwealth under a single ruler may itself lead to 'the most fearful despotism', as history has shown more than once with states that have grown too large. A federation according to a commonly agreed right of nations is therefore preferable (TP, 308 [8: 311]).

This union or alliance of several states is best defined as a permanent congress of states. This congress merely signifies a voluntary gathering of various states which can be dissolved at any time and which, therefore, is in need of periodical renewal. This alliance [*Verbündung*] must not embody a sovereign authority as in a civil constitution, but only a partnership or sodality [*Genossenschaft*] (MM, 483 [6: 344]). Hence, it is quite unlike 'a federation (like that of the American states) which is based on a constitution and can therefore not be dissolved' (MM, 488 [6: 351]). This congress is charged with protecting its members against external aggression while refraining from interference in one another's internal disputes (MM, 438 [6: 344]): it punishes aggression, not regime type (Cavallar 2001: 246). It is a body that enables states to settle their disputes in a civilised manner by legal proceedings. Importantly, however, it does not possess coercive power.

We should be clear about the reasons for Kant's favouring a league of states. Pauline Kleingeld has summed up Kant's position succinctly:

> Citizens and politicians ought to work practically towards the establishment of a league, but the ultimate goal they should have in mind in doing so is a situation in which all states have become republics and their citizenry has become enlightened enough to *want* to submit to the public and enforceable laws of a republican state of states. This ideal of a fully realised perpetual peace may well remain out of reach – indeed Kant thinks it will – yet it remains for him an ideal that one can and ought to strive for and that can be approximated. (Kleingeld 2004: 318; also: 321)

But it is also important not to misinterpret Kant's statement that 'the right of nations shall be based on a *federalism* of free states' (PP, 325 [8: 354]). Lutz-Bachmann (1997: 69), for example, understands Kant's statement to mean the creation of a 'federation of free republics', so that 'only republics are eligible for membership in this league of states'. Garrett Brown (2005), too, reads Kant along those lines. He uses this interpretation to make two additional claims: first, that 'only republican states that uphold Kantian principles of domestic justice can be considered sovereign in the true sense'; and, secondly, that membership of the league 'demands conformity to universal principles that directly reduce claims of absolute state sovereignty and suppress international policies based on self-interest alone' (Brown 2005: 509,

517; see also Teson 1992). We shall see in the final section of this chapter how Kant is deployed in order to problematise sovereignty – and we shall pursue this theme more fully in Chapter 4.

However, an interpretation that narrows down membership of a Kantian federation to 'republics' is not without problems. First, we have already encountered Kant's argument that republics tend towards peace. Being republics, they recognise and respect each other's autonomy, territorial integrity, and political sovereignty. It is this claim that has given rise to a huge literature in International Relations on 'democratic peace'. If republics tend towards peace anyway, what does a federation composed exclusively of republican states contribute to peace? Secondly, the historical context of Kant's *Perpetual Peace* is the struggle of republican, revolutionary France with the 'absolutist' monarchies of Europe. Only a federation of these different regime types would contribute to a peaceful stabilisation of the European order. Furthermore, a federation of republican states would have united only a very small number of states in the late eighteenth century (and well into the nineteenth century as well). There is also the conceptual distinction to which we referred above that allowed Kant to distinguish between autocratic and aristocratic republicanism – while denying that there could be a 'democratic' republicanism.

Yet, if one accepted these considerations as valid, how then are we to understand the expression 'free states'? We have seen that one of Kant's key concerns has been to theorise the overcoming of lawlessness through legitimate public coercion. Arguably, for Kant 'all empirically existing states are compatible with freedom insofar as they are a bulwark against lawlessness' (Franceschet 2000: 220). We have also seen that Kant conceptualises the state as an independent moral-legal person with whose autonomy no outside power is entitled to interfere. It is in these two senses that states are 'free'. It is this 'freedom' that gives a world federation its extreme diversity and plurality (Bohman 1997: 187). To put it succinctly: not the 'homogeneous' League of Nations that was founded after the First World War, but the 'heterogeneous' United Nations established after the Second World War are the best approximation to Kant's federation. (We shall return to this topic in Chapter 4.)

Kant's Cosmopolitanism

For Kant, this 'rational idea of a *peaceful*, even if not friendly, thoroughgoing community of all nations on the earth that can come into relations affecting one another' is a principle having to do with rights (MM, 489 [6: 352]). Given the spherical shape of the earth, all states were *originally* in a community of land in the sense of a community of possible physical interaction (*commercium*):

> that is, in a thoroughgoing relation of each to all the others of *offering to engage in commerce* [*Verkehr*] with any other, and each has a right to make this attempt without the other being authorised to behave toward it as an enemy because it has made this attempt. – This right, since it has to do with the possible union of all nations with a view to certain universal laws for their possible commerce, can be called *cosmopolitan right* (*ius cosmopoliticum*). (MM, 489 [6: 352])

In another passage, Kant also derives cosmopolitan right as a right for a state of nations (*ius gentium*) from the fact that 'the earth's surface is not unlimited but closed' (MM, 455 [6: 311]). As a result of this proximity and the intercourse between states, 'the community of the nations of the earth has now gone so far that a violation of right in one place of the earth is felt in all', and that, therefore, the idea of cosmopolitan right is neither fantastic nor exaggerated (PP, 330–1 [8: 360]).

However, this is not the only sense in which Kant speaks of cosmopolitan right. He recognises that there are not only the relations of one state towards another as a whole – the subject-matter of the right of nations – there is also the relation of individual persons of one state towards the individuals of another state as well as towards another state as a whole (MM, 482 [6: 343–4]). In this context, cosmopolitan right is more narrowly defined as a right possessed by an individual when he or she comes accidentally or voluntarily to the territory of other states: it is a right of hospitality. Hospitality means:

> the right of a foreigner not to be treated with hostility because he has arrived on the land of another. The other can turn him away, if this can be done without destroying him, but as long as he behaves peaceably where he is, he cannot be treated with hostility. What he can claim is not the *right to be a guest* (for this a special beneficent pact would be required, making him a member of the household for a certain time), but the *right to visit* . . . to present oneself for society. (PP, 328–9 [8: 357–8])

The cosmopolitan right enables individuals and peoples to attempt to develop intercourse with each other: 'In this way distant parts of the world can enter peaceably into relations with one another, which can eventually become publicly lawful and so finally bring the human race closer to a cosmopolitan constitution' (PP, 329 [8: 358]). It does not, however, give the right of conquest and interference to any nation or people. This view grounds Kant's pronounced critique of Western colonialism. Only if the cosmopolitan right of hospitality is upheld – including the obligation of a state not to turn away strangers if such a rejection were to cause their death (an 'imperfect' duty since it can be overridden by a state's legitimate grounds of self-preservation) – 'can we flatter ourselves that we are continually approaching perpetual peace' (PP, 360 [8: 331]). Arguably, the contemporary rights regime for refugees and asylum seekers may be perceived as being grounded in the cosmopolitan right of hospitality and the correlating 'imperfect' duty of admission in a case of 'life or death'.

That individuals will 'present themselves' is not just an inevitable effect of the 'spherical shape' of the earth, but it is also a result of a moral duty:

> It is a moral duty to oneself as well as to others not to *isolate* oneself (*seperatistam agere*) but to use one's moral perfections in social inter-course (*officium commercii, sociabilitas*). While making oneself a fixed center of one's principles, one ought to regard this circle drawn around one as also forming part of an all-inclusive circle of those who, in their disposition, are citizens of the world – not exactly in order to promote as the end what is best for the world [*das Weltbeste*] but only to cultivate what leads indirectly to this end: to cultivate a disposition of reciprocity – agreeableness, tolerance, mutual love and respect (affability and propriety, *humanitas aesthetica et decorum*) and so to associate the graces with virtue. (MM, 588 [6: 473])

We see here Kant's notion of cosmopolitanism conceptually linked to his notion of sociability, whose importance for Kant's political phi-losophy we have discussed before. But to be drawn out of oneself in social intercourse and to cultivate a disposition of reciprocity makes sense only if one accepts the challenge of the encounter with the unfamiliar. And the actuality of the unfamiliar is grounded in human freedom as cultural agency that results 'in diverse mores, practices, beliefs and institutions of different peoples' (Muthu 2003: 8). To put it differently: when we physically present ourselves for society in another country or when we take our bearings from the idea of being a world citizen (or rather, act upon the moral duty of understanding ourselves as world citizens), we encounter, and are reciprocally beholden to reflect upon, different standpoints and value them out of respect for the human beings who have taken them. Kant insists in his *Anthro-pology*, as Martha Nussbaum points out, that 'we owe it to other human beings to try to understand their ways of thinking, since only that attitude is consistent with seeing oneself as a "citizen of the world"' (Nussbaum 1997: 36–7). Nussbaum's reference is to Kant's statement that sees an individual's egoism as being transcended through pluralism: 'The opposite of egoism can be only pluralism, that is, the attitude of not being occupied with oneself as the whole world, but regarding and conducting oneself as a citizen of the world' (Kant [1797] 1974: 12). Yet, we would do well not to push the interpretation of this statement too far. Arguably, Kant's concern here is with the individual who ought to transcend their egoism by seeing themselves in the company of fellow human beings: 'world' in an almost 'phenomenological' sense. Still, in doing so, we engage, of necessity, in 'enlarged thinking'; and the abolition of war and the right of universal hospitality are the necessary conditions for the greatest possible enlargement of the enlarged mentality (Arendt 1982: 73–7).

Kant does not assume that we share fundamental norms, values or principles. Indeed, diversity as a result of cultural agency does not just bring about pluralism but often incommensurable individual and collective ways of living in the world, and living a meaningful life. There is inevitable conflict over 'what seems right and good' to each of them (MM, 456 [6: 312]). To respect, often incommensurable, pluralism is to respect our shared humanity (Muthu 2003: 209). The cosmopolitan right is violated if there is a lack of appropriate respect shown by foreigners for the ways of life of a society. But a disposition of reciprocity as a core aspect of 'enlarged thinking' also imposes clear expectations on the 'native' population. 'We' must present 'our' way of being in the world in a form that is intersubjectively communicable. Jeremy Waldron expresses this aspect of cosmopolitan right supremely well:

> If we take a tradition or practice of our culture seriously, then we should treat it . . . as a standard which does some normative work in the life of one's community . . . work . . . which might (in principle or at least as a matter of logical possibility) have been performed by other norms, alternative standards, and which therefore cannot be understood except in terms of its association with an array of reasons that explain why in fact it is *this* norm rather than *that* – monogamy, for example, rather than polygamy – which is the standard we happen to uphold. (Waldron 2000: 243)

Presenting one's *initial* allegiance to one's cultural practices and institutions in this spirit opens up the possibility of presenting it to others of different cultures 'as a first move in a complicated business – involving bargaining, deliberation, compromise, voting, authority – of coming to terms with those with whom we need to come to terms' (Waldron 2000: 243).

Waldron's reading of Kant's position opens up a final line of inquiry, the link between cosmopolitanism and patriotism. Kant was adamant that national delusion [*Nationalwahn*], the illusion that one's own nation is inherently superior to others should be 'eradicated' and replaced by 'patriotism and cosmopolitanism' (Kant 1913: 590–1, no. 1353). In another passage, Kant remarks that 'global patriotism' and 'local patriotism' are proper to the cosmopolite, 'who in fealty to his country must have an inclination to promote the well-being of the entire world' (Vigilantius 1997: 406 [27: 673–4]). The reasons that Kant offers in support of this view are as follows.

Kant believed that every individual should be a 'friend of human beings as such (i.e., of the whole race)' (MM, 587 [6: 472]); but, in his view, such sentiments are usually not sufficient in motivating humane behaviour:

> Now the benevolence present in love of all human beings is indeed the greatest in its *extent*, but the smallest in its *degree*; and when I say that I take an interest in this human being's well-being only out of my love for all human beings, the interest I take is as slight as an interest can be. I am only not indifferent with regard to him. (MM, 570–1 [6: 451])

It is more likely that people act morally in local settings. However, such engagements at the local level should be informed by the 'enlarged thinking' that arises out of the recognition of one's membership of a global community to which one belongs simply in view of the fact that one is human. The reality of our cosmopolitan existence ought to inform our actions. Of necessity, local and global patriotism are, therefore, intertwined.

There is, furthermore, yet another intricate link between patriotism and cosmopolitanism. Kant calls patriotic that way of thinking where:

> everyone in a state (its head not excepted) regards the commonwealth as the maternal womb, or the country as the paternal land, from which and on which he sprang and which he must leave behind [to his descendants] as a cherished pledge. Each regards himself authorised to protect its rights by laws of the common will but not to subject the use of it to his unconditional discretion. (Gemeinspruch 8: 291 [own translation])

In such a commonwealth, the state (*civitas*) treats its subjects as members of one family; but it also treats them as citizens of the state, as the citizens who 'are united for giving law' (MM, 457 [6: 314]). To treat subjects as citizens is the sign of a 'patriotic' government. The citizen, in turn, has the duty of civic patriotism which comes down to promoting the functioning and improvement of the *civitas* as a just state (Kleingeld 2003: 309; see also Kleingold 1998; 2000). In line with Kant's 'First Definitive Article for Perpetual Peace', one can identify the cosmopolitan significance of this duty of civic patriotism: 'The more civic patriots of the Kantian sort there are in the world, the more people there are who support republican forms of government, and the closer this will get us to global justice' (Kleingeld 2003: 310) – and a more peaceful world.

Cicero's Republicanism and Stoic Cosmopolitanism: Kant in Comparison

Kant's attempt to combine republicanism, patriotism, and cosmopolitanism has a long pedigree. Indeed, to achieve such a combination was one of the goals of Roman Stoicism, and of Cicero in particular (Nussbaum 1997). There are a number of concerns shared by Cicero and Kant that are worth highlighting.

To start with, Cicero offered a philosophically informed account of republicanism (see Schofield 1999). He defined *res publica* as *res populi*: the republic is the property of the public – the common weal is the people's affair (Republic I: 39; III: 43).[2] But what is a 'people'? It is not any and every collection of human beings, herded together in any way whatsoever, but 'a numerous gathering brought together by legal consent and community of interest [*coetus multitudinis iuris consensu et utilitatis communione sociatus*]' (Republic I: 39). Weakness [*imbecillitas*] is not the primary reason for coming together, but a natural tendency to sociability. It is part of human nature to form communities; and the origins of political community thus do not lie in a contract for mutual protection. Whereas Plato (Republic II: 369b) and Aristotle (Politics I: 2) emphasised the utilitarian origins of community for securing one's own needs, Cicero upholds the Stoic view of man's natural sociability: 'It is not true, as some claim, that men embarked upon communal life and fellowship in order to provide for life's necessities just because we could not manage, without others, to provide ourselves with our natural requirements' (On Duties I: 158). Even if all needs of a human being were met, that human being 'would flee from loneliness, seeking a companion . . .' (On Duties I: 158; also: I: 12): 'for our species is not made up of solitary individuals or lonely wanderers' (Republic I: 39).

According to Cicero, mutuality and moral consensus binds a community together. Without a shared sense of justice that is institutionalised in the community, there can be no 'people'. For such a situation to obtain there must be no oppression: 'So who would call that a republic, i.e. the property of the public, when everyone was oppressed by the cruelty of a single man, and there was not one bond of justice nor any of that agreement and partnership which constitute a community' (Republic III: 43). Cicero argued the case in favour of 'aristocratic' republicanism. 'When everything is supposed to be done through the people and to be in the people's control, when the masses punish whoever they please, when they seize, carry off, hold on to, or squander whatever they like' – then such a state is not a 'republic': 'the rabble is just as tyrannical as one man'; and as we have already seen, when a tyrant is in charge, there is no 'republic' (Republic III: 45). Cicero then further suggests that 'every republic (which, as I said, is the property of the public) must be governed by some decision-making process [*consilium*] if it is to last' (Republic I: 41). Cicero advocates that the power of *consilium* be best entrusted to an aristocratic council: 'If . . . a free people chooses the men to whom it will entrust itself, and if, with a genuine desire for security, it chooses only the best men, then without a doubt the security of such states [*civitatium salus* – the welfare and safety of cities] depends on the policies of aristocrats' (Republic I: 51). 'Government as trust' is premised, however, on the appropriate, dutiful exercise of governmental power:

> In general those who are about to take charge of public affairs should hold fast to Plato's two pieces of advice: first to fix their gaze so firmly on what is beneficial to the citizens that whatever they do, they do with that in mind, forgetful of their own advantage. Secondly, let them care for the whole body of the republic rather than one part and neglect the rest. The management [*procuratio*] of the republic is like a guardianship [*tutela*], and must be conducted in the light of what is beneficial not to the guardians, but to those who are put in their charge. (On Duties I: 85).

This translates into the duties of a magistrate such that he realises that he represents the city and is expected 'to sustain its standing and its seemliness, to preserve the laws and administer justice, and to be mindful of the things that have been entrusted to his good faith' (On Duties I: 124). Kant's distinction between *forma imperii* and *forma regiminis* is as much present in Cicero's account of republicanism as is the emphasis on justice as integrating communities which owe their origins to the fact that human beings are sociable by nature.

For Cicero, there exists a fellowship among mankind which was established by the gods (On Duties III: 28), a fellowship of the entire human race whose 'bonding consists of reason and speech, which reconcile men to another, through teaching, learning, communicating, debating and making judgements' (On Duties I: 50). While '[t]he most widespread fellowship existing among men is that of all with others' (On Duties I: 51), there are several degrees of fellowship among men:

> To move from the one that is unlimited, next there is a closer one of the same race, tribe and tongue, through which men are bound strongly to one another. More intimate still is that of the same city, as citizens have many things that are shared with one another: the forum, temples, porticoes and roads, laws and legal rights, law-courts and political elections; and besides these acquaintances and companionship, and those business and commercial transactions that many of them make with one another. A tie narrower still is that of the fellowship between relations: moving from that vast fellowship of the human race we end up with a confined and limited one. (On Duties I: 53)

We encounter here the (widespread Stoic) idea of the 'circle' of obligations of which Kant has also spoken (as we saw above). Hierocles made probably the most famous statement in this respect:

> In general each of us is as it were circumscribed by many circles, some smaller, others larger, some enclosing and others enclosed, depending on their differing and unequal relations to one another. The first and nearest circle is the one which a person has drawn around his own mind as around a centre; in this circle is included the body and things got for the body's sake. This circle is the smallest and all but touches its centre. Second, further from the centre and enclosing the first one, is the one in which are placed parents, siblings, wife and children. Third is the one in which uncles and aunts, grandfathers and grandmothers, siblings' children and also cousins. Next the circle including other relatives. And next the one including fellow-demesmen; then the one of fellow-tribesmen; then the one of fellow-citizens and then in the same way the circle of people from towns nearby and the circle of people of the same ethnic group. The furthest and largest, which includes all the circles, is that of the whole human race. (Hierocles, quoted in Annas 1993: 267)

Which duties in this social field of the 'concentric circle' take precedence? Cicero was quite clear about the sequence of duties: they are owed 'first to the immortal gods, secondly to one's country, thirdly to one's parents and then down the scale to others' (On Duties I: 160). Of all the fellowships, so Cicero claimed, 'none is more serious, none dearer, than that of each of us with the republic. Parents are dear, and children, relatives and acquaintances are dear, but our country has on its own embraced all the affections of all of us' (On Duties I: 57). Cicero does not endorse the view that human beings, as 'citizens of the universe', do not owe any special loyalty to any particular *polis* or republic; that their true and only allegiance is to the governance of God – a view widely held by the Stoics, although Epictetus, for example, does recognise that man should assume his role as a citizen (*cf*. Epictetus [1946] 1952: I, ix, 1–6; II, x, 3; II, xxiii, 36–41; III, xxi, 6; Devine 1970; Hill 2000). Duties towards the republic override cosmopolitan duties towards 'mankind'. The protection and main-tenance of *res publica* demand our most dutiful service. After all, man is 'naturally' a citizen and active participation in the life of the city is his due. As 'Cato' said in *De Finibus* (3.37 and 68): no one is in such a backward society that they have no interest in public discussion for its own sake; after all, it is consistent with natural instinct 'that the Wise Man should desire to engage in politics and government'. It is this particular understanding of what it means to be a (virtuous) human being that Pericles expressed memorably in his famous funeral oration to his Athenian fellow-citizens – as recounted by Thucydides in his *History of the Peloponnesian War*: 'We do not say that a man who takes no interest in politics is a man who minds his own business; we say that he has no business here at all' (Thucydides 1972: 147).

We may develop this argument by looking at Cicero's treatment of friendship. Kant's scepticism regarding the idea of 'the friend of human beings as such' is also detectable in Cicero. For Cicero, the warm affections between friends and friendship with compatriots are stronger than our feelings towards humankind in general:

> This fact seems to me to be clear, that we come into the world under this condition, that there is to be a certain bond of fellowship among all, but increasing in strength according to the closeness of the connection. Hence fellow-citizens have more a claim on us than foreigners, and relations than strangers; for friendship with the latter is the creation of nature herself, but there is not enough certainty that it will last. The point in which friendship is superior to relationship is that goodwill can be removed from relation-ships, but not from friendship; for where there is no longer goodwill the word 'friendship' cannot be used, but 'relationship' can. How great the force of friendship is can best be seen from this, that starting from the unlimited association of all mankind, which nature herself has knit together, this feeling is so concentrated and is brought within such narrow

limits that the whole range of affection becomes a bond by which two individuals or a small group are united. (*De Amicitia*, quoted in Baldry 1965: 200)

It is, above all, in friendships that 'a shared life and a shared living, counsel and conversation, encouragement, comfort, and sometimes even reproofs, flourish most . . . and friendship is most pleasing when it is cemented by similarity of conduct' (On Duties I: 58).

Yet, Cicero also claims that 'nature prescribes that one man should want to consider the interests of another, whoever he may be' (On Duties III: 27). As Cicero asserts in *De Finibus* (3.67, 69): 'The nature of man is such that an individual is connected to the whole human race by a kind of civil law', and *societas, coniunctio* and *caritas* (fellowship, companionship and affection) are said to unite every human to every other, and even between generations (Wright 1995: 188–9). Wright summarises this aspect admirably – and with resonances of Kant's conceptual distinction between 'local' and 'global' patriotism:

> Civic friendship, appropriate to a city honouring in justice the status of all the members of the citizen body, gives the pattern for the universal benevolence in the world setting, which is based on due respect for the humanity of others. Co-operation within the state in the interests of the whole community enlarges into universal mutual assistance. Therefore, since loving kindness one to another is based on natural instinct and enjoined by natural law, the converse, an act of unkindness, becomes treason towards a fellow cosmopolitan . . . The interconnection of justice, law, reason, and nature is in the interest of both citizen and world-citizen . . . acting justly strengthens the civic ties to the advantage of all citizens, and acting kindly towards a fellow human being enhances all human life. (Wright 1995: 189–90)

We do thus have obligations towards 'mankind'. These obligations express themselves in a duty to share: 'one should not keep others from fresh water, should allow them to take fire from fire, should give trustworthy counsel to someone who seeks advice; for they are useful to those who receive them and cause no trouble to the giver' (On Duties I: 52). But there is a balance to be struck: our obligations towards 'mankind' must not undermine the pursuit of our own interests as long as this pursuit of one's interests does not harm others (On Duties I: 25, 52 and III: 42). Still, the fellowship among human beings imposes certain duties *vis-à-vis* the foreigner: there is a duty to hospitality. While it is the duty of the foreigner or resident alien 'to do nothing except his own business, asking no questions about anyone else, and never meddle in public affairs, which are not his own' (On Duties I: 124), it would be inhuman 'to prevent foreigners from enjoying the city' (On Duties III: 47, 28; I: 51). Kant's idea of cosmopolitan right as hospitality can clearly be aligned with this view (*cf.* also On Duties II: 64).

In my reconstruction of Kant's argument, and by highlighting the similarities of his position with that taken by Cicero, I have aimed to show how his republicanism informs, and in a way defines, his cosmopolitanism. Kant does propose that there exists a moral community made up by the humanity of all human beings – a thoroughly 'Stoic' understanding, as we saw (Nussbaum 1996a). And the discourse of 'universal' human rights, to which we shall refer presently in this chapter (but more particularly in Chapter 2), may be connected to this idea of humanity as a 'moral community'. But Kant's emphasis on the 'moral personality' of states and the importance of republicanism as well as a quite narrowly defined 'cosmopolitan right' gives his cosmopolitanism a rather 'realistic' or 'moderate' complexion. Would Kant really have endorsed the view, expressed by Drost von Müller in 1797 in a piece on 'cosmopolitanism and patriotism', that 'where it is a question of the welfare of humanity, there even his fellow citizens appear to him [the cosmopolite] as a negligible part in the sublime whole' – as Kevin Paul Geiman (1996: 520 [also for the quotation]) suggests?

In a debate about the limits of patriotism, Martha Nussbaum came close to formulating such a position:

> To count people as moral equals is to treat nationality, ethnicity, religion, class, race, and gender as 'morally irrelevant' – as irrelevant to that equal standing . . . What I am saying about politics is that we should view the equal worth of all human beings as a regulative constraint on our political actions and aspirations. (Nussbaum 1996b: 133)

In her argument, Nussbaum stressed the importance of Kant's 'global patriotism' (Nussbaum 1996a: 3–17). In her account, however, we do not get a glimpse of the Kant for whom the commonwealth was a maternal womb and the paternal land whose 'republican' traditions, achievements and memory must be tended to with care, cherished and handed over intact to future generations (Kant 1793, hereafter Gemeinspruch: 8: 291). We find in Kant a love of the 'patria' or, to put it differently, a patriotic love of the *res publica*, a respect for civic patriotism. Self-legislating citizens define for themselves what is 'right and good' for them. They take pride in their achievements and want to preserve them, but they also accept that people in other common-wealths have a right to do just the same themselves. The cosmopolitan 'moment' is instantiated when we accept these possibly divergent self-understandings and engage in a process of intercultural communication and 'enlarged thinking'. Yet, such intercultural communication is not without premises. For Bryan Turner (2002: 57), cosmopolitanism 'does not mean that one does not have a country or a homeland, but one has to have a certain reflexive distance from that homeland'. He argues that irony is the principal component of cosmopolitan virtue:

> [T]he understanding of other cultures is assisted by an intellectual distance from one's own national or local culture . . . cosmopolitan virtue . . . requires self-reflexivity with respect to both our own cultural context and other cultural values. Such an orientation of irony and reflexivity produces a humanistic scepticism towards the grand narratives of modern ideologies . . . Scepticism and distance from one's own tradition are the basis of an obligation of care and stewardship for other cultures. (Turner 2002: 57)

Turner is right that, what is at stake is the acceptance that there is no 'final vocabulary'. Yet, as Hilary Putnam remarked in the debate with Nussbaum, 'we all have to live and judge from within our particular inheritances while remaining open to insights and criticisms from outside' (Putnam 1996: 97). 'Enlarged thought' needs grounding and a 'home', a 'bounded' scepticism. The willingness to listen to, and reflect upon, different traditions is, in turn, premised on a degree of solidarity – with the interloper as either fellow-citizen or fellow human being – that establishes the legitimate membership of the interloper in a conversational community.

John Rawls and Jürgen Habermas: Alternative Ways of Understanding Kant's Cosmopolitanism

If the previous section on Cicero opened up a view on one of the traditions on which Kant could draw when he formulated his position on 'local' and 'global' patriotism, this section offers a brief glimpse at the use made of Kant's cosmopolitanism by two contemporary theorists. In their own ways, both John Rawls and Jürgen Habermas take leave of certain aspects of Kant's *cosmopolitan* argument as set out in the previous sections.

In *The Law of Peoples* (1999), John Rawls argues that 'a world government, understood as a unified political regime with the legal powers normally exercised by central government – would either be a global despotism or else would rule over a fragile empire torn by civil strife as various regions and peoples tried to gain their political freedom and autonomy' (Rawls 1999: 36). 'World government' is not the answer to the question as to how rational and reasonable peoples might live together peacefully in a just world. His solution is closer to Kant's idea of a *foedus pacificum* (Rawls 1999: 10).

Not dissimilar to Immanuel Kant in *Perpetual Peace*, Rawls (1999: 37) sets out principles of the 'Law of Peoples':

1. Peoples are free and independent, and their freedom and independence are to be respected by other peoples.
2. Peoples are to observe treaties and undertakings.
3. Peoples are equal and are parties to the agreements that bind them.
4. Peoples are to observe a duty of non-intervention.
5. Peoples have the right of self-defense but not the right to instigate war for reasons other than self-defense.
6. Peoples are to honor human rights.
7. Peoples are to observe certain specified restrictions in the conduct of war.
8. Peoples have a duty to assist other peoples living under unfavorable conditions that prevent their having a just or decent political and social regime.

We should note immediately that the 'Law of Peoples' gives to peoples, not to individual persons, the status of the moral actors in international politics. Peoples are not the same as states. For Rawls, states as traditionally conceived are organisations geared toward the increase and maintenance of their power capacities and always guided by their basic interests:

> If *rationality* excludes the *reasonable* (that is, if a state is moved by the aims it has and ignores the criterion of reciprocity in dealing with other societies); if a state's concern with power is predominant; and if its interests include such things as converting other societies to the state's religion, enlarging its empire and winning territory, gaining dynastic or imperial or national prestige and glory, and increasing its relative economic strength – then the difference between states and peoples is enormous. (Rawls 1999: 28)

For Rawls then, peoples are collectives politically organised into states with limited sovereignty. This limited sovereignty finds expression in the limitation on the right to go to war to instances of self-defence (as well as in the interest of collective security), and on internal sovereignty as a consequence of the restrictive force of human rights. The epitome of such a 'state' are liberal peoples who are both rational (in deploying instrumental reasoning in pursuit of their interests) and reasonable (in being reflexively concerned with the interests of others and acknowledging reciprocity as a basic requirement for establishing justice between peoples). For liberal peoples, the reasonable constrains the rational.

These principles of the 'Law of Peoples' apply, in the first instance, only to a society of well-ordered peoples. The 'Law of Peoples' must, therefore, not be confused with the *ius gentium*. There are two types of peoples which make up this society of well-ordered peoples. First, there are, as already mentioned, liberal peoples. They have three basic features:

> a reasonably just constitutional government that serves their fundamental interests; citizens united by what [John Stuart] Mill called 'common sympathies'; and finally, a moral nature. The first is institutional, the second is cultural, and the third requires a firm attachment to a political (moral) conception of right and justice. (Rawls 1999: 23–4)

Liberal peoples do, of course, seek to protect their territory, to ensure the security and safety of their citizens, and to preserve their free institutions and the liberties of their civil societies. They try to assure reasonable justice for all their citizens and for all peoples (Rawls 1999: 29).

The second type of a well-ordered society is 'decent peoples'. In its external relations with other political communities, a decent people do not have aggressive aims and use peaceful means to pursue their objectives. It is composed of a number of different (cultural) groups, 'and each group is represented in the legal system by a body in a decent consultation hierarchy' (Rawls 1999: 64). Furthermore

> its system of law must be such as to respect human rights and to impose duties and obligations on all persons in its territory. Its system of law must follow a common good idea of justice that takes into account what it sees as the fundamental interests of everyone in society. And, finally, there must be a sincere and not unreasonable belief on the part of judges and other officials that the law is indeed guided by a common good idea of justice. (Rawls 1999: 67)

One major difference between liberal and decent peoples is the fact that decent peoples privilege a comprehensive (political or religious) doctrine and accord more rights to persons who adhere to that doctrine than to those who do not. In the light of this inequality, for Rawls to be able to define decent peoples as falling into the category of well-ordered societies he must deploy a narrow definition of human rights. Indeed, for Rawls human rights include:

> the right to life (to the means of subsistence and security); to liberty (to freedom from slavery, serfdom, and forced occupation, and to a sufficient measure of liberty of conscience to ensure freedom of religion and thought); to property (personal property); and to formal equality as expressed by the rules of natural justice (that is, that similar cases be treated similarly). (Rawls 1999: 65)

Significantly, those rights that distinguish liberal political constitutional systems from other types of political systems – such as those pertaining to the liberal principle that demands respect of persons as free and equal citizens – are missing from his list of human rights, presumably because decent peoples would not accept those rights.

Rawls suggests that both types of well-ordered societies would agree the same 'Law of Peoples' (Rawls 1999: 5). They follow the 'Law of Peoples' among themselves 'since that law suits their fundamental interests, and each wishes to honor its agreements with the others and to be known as trustworthy' (Rawls 1999: 125). Rawls argues that the representatives of well-ordered peoples, who meet in the (hypothetical) original position at the second level, are not given a menu of alternative principles and ideals from which to select. Rather, they 'simply reflect on the advantages of these principles of equality among peoples and see no reason to depart from them or to propose alternatives' (Rawls 1999: 41) – which is hardly surprising given that it has been stipulated that only those peoples who embrace these principles of peaceful intercourse are well-ordered, and because only well-ordered peoples are party to the original position in the first place. This tautological argument then can be brought to a happy conclusion by declaring that '[a] Society of [well-ordered, RA] Peoples is reasonably just in that its members follow the reasonably just Law of Peoples in their mutual relations' (Rawls 1999: 5).

Having introduced the category of well-ordered peoples, Rawls – as a logical corollary – also speaks of disordered peoples: the normative argument in favour of moving away from the idea of sovereign equality of states – an idea espoused (as we saw) by Kant on the basis of the ascription of 'moral personality' to states – gathers pace. There are three types of disordered societies, of which only the last type shall concern us here. There are, first, societies burdened by unfavourable historical, economic, or cultural conditions which will vitiate against their becoming well-ordered on their own. Rawls claims there to obtain a duty to assist those burdened societies to develop liberal or decent institutions. Secondly, there are societies that are benevolent absolutisms: 'they honor human rights; but, because their members are denied a meaningful role in making political decisions, they are not well-ordered' (Rawls 1999: 4). Finally, there are outlaw states (*nota bene*: 'states', not 'peoples'). These are regimes which refuse to comply with a reasonable 'Law of Peoples' (or rather, with the reasonable law of the well-ordered peoples). They are aggressive and dangerous and 'think that a sufficient reason to engage in war is that war advances, or might advance, the regime's rational (not reasonable) interests' (Rawls 1999: 90). For Rawls, it is self-evident that 'all peoples are safer and more secure if such states change, or are forced to change, their ways. Otherwise, they deeply affect the international climate of power and violence' (Rawls 1999: 81). Hence, the right to independence and to self-determination holds only for well-ordered peoples, but not for outlaw states. These outlaw states may rightly and justifiably be subjected to coercive intervention (Rawls 1999: 37–8). Indeed, only those societies that are non-aggressive and honour human rights have the right of self-defence. Well-ordered peoples have

> a right to war in self-defense but not, as in the traditional account of sovereignty, a right to war in the rational pursuit of a state's rational interests; these alone are not a sufficient reason. Well-ordered peoples, both liberal and decent, do not initiate war against one another; they go to war only when they sincerely and reasonably believe that their safety and security are seriously endangered by the expansionist policies of outlaw states . . . When a liberal society engages in war in self-defense, it does so to protect and preserve the basic freedoms of citizens and its constitutionally democratic political institutions. (Rawls 1999: 90–1)

It is open to interpretation whether one should understand these sentences as normative exhortation, empirical observation, sheer wishful thinking, or pure ideology.

We may do well to be alert to the argument that Rawls puts forward. In Rawls's theory, 'well-ordered people' enjoy 'limited' sovereignty only. Or to put it more precisely: 'the legitimacy of sovereignty [is] conditional upon a state's recognition of certain principles of justice, among them respect for human rights and the commitment not to instigate war for reasons other than self-defense'

(Benhabib 2004: 78). But 'outlaw states' are not accorded any sovereignty at all. Rawls's treatment of human rights is pivotal to the defence of this view (Nickel 2006).

According to Rawls, '[l]iberal and decent peoples have the right . . . not to tolerate outlaw states' (Rawls 1999: 81). When outlaw states violate human rights (as specified by Rawls), then 'forceful intervention' by well-ordered peoples might be justified: 'If the offenses against human rights are egregious and the society does not respond to the imposition of sanctions, such intervention in the defense of human rights would be acceptable and would be called for' (Rawls 1999: 94fn). Hence, Rawls (1999: 79) argues that 'human rights . . . specify limits to a regime's internal autonomy':

> [N]o people has the right to self-determination, or a right to secession, at the expense of subjugating another people. Nor may a people protest their condemnation by the world society when their domestic institutions violate human rights, or limit the rights of minorities living among them. A people's right to independence and self-determination is no shield from that condemnation, nor even from coercive intervention by other peoples in grave cases. (Rawls 1999: 38)

Mark Evans (2005: 74) embraces this argument by succinctly asserting that '[s]tates matter morally . . . only because the people who live in them matter morally . . . "humanitarian intervention" asserts the right of other peoples to come to the aid of those whose states, in violating their [citizens'] rights, have consequently forfeited the right of inviolable sovereignty.' This is also the position that Teson upholds: '[T]he rights of states are merely derivative of the rights and interests of individuals who reside within them' (Teson 1992: 53). Teson claims this to be the essence of a Kantian (although not necessarily Kant's) theory of international law – thus disregarding the implications of Kant's notion of states possessing moral personality.[3] Such an argument justifies the move away from the notion of the sovereign equality of states through reference to the human rights discourse: a 'normative individualism' replaces the 'statist conceptualisation' of international law. Human rights, in this understanding, limit the tolerable pluralism of the interstate system. We shall discuss in Chapter 4 the political significance of such an understanding of state autonomy as being 'essentially' and 'existentially' qualified by the primacy of human rights. But we should note here that, rather than 'perpetual peace', the aim appears to be 'perpetual' hegemony of the 'well-ordered peoples' on the basis of 'perpetual' vigilance and the military coercion of 'outlaw states'.

Rawls does not wish his position to be misconstrued as cosmopolitanism. He assumes that 'every society has in its population a sufficient array of human capabilities, each in sufficient number so that the society has enough potential human resources to realize just institutions' (Rawls 1999: 119). It is domestic society which is ultimately responsible for the well-being of its people. Concerns with global redistribution and hence with global justice are outside the realm of the 'Law of Peoples'. The 'Law of Peoples' is indifferent with regard to the question as to whether the well-being of the globally worst-off person can be improved. Rather, its central concern is 'the justice and stability for the right reasons of liberal and decent societies, living as members of a Society of well-ordered Peoples' (Rawls 1999: 120). This stance contrasts with a cosmopolitan position that does not accord any moral privilege to domestic societies and regards the social cosmos as composed of persons, rather than collectivities like societies or peoples. In one reading of (Kantian) cosmopolitanism, the well-being of individuals is of greatest importance:

> We want to say that people are entitled to be treated in certain ways (partly) in virtue of their characteristics as human beings and independently of considerations that might be particular to their own institutions and political cultures. But these are essentially cosmopolitan considerations, and they do not register in an international original position in which the unit of representation is peoples rather than persons and agreement on principles is motivated by their corporate interests as social units rather than the interests of their members as individuals. (Beitz 2000: 686; also: Buchanan 2000; Brown 2002; Kuper 2000)

That Rawls should define human rights not more restrictively (and hence allow himself to consider 'decent hierarchical societies' to be well-ordered societies); and that he should refuse to develop a theory of global justice has been much criticised from within the community of Rawlsian international political theorists. His denial of the sovereign equality of states and his endorsement of arguments in favour of coercive intervention, both of these arguments embedded in his conceptualisation of an hegemonic liberal 'Law of Peoples', have not attracted a similar critique from within the congregation of Rawlsians.

Jürgen Habermas's engagement with Kant's cosmopolitanism, however, does indeed stress the importance of the individual and the institution of cosmopolitan citizenship. For him, the point of cosmopolitan law is 'that it goes over the heads of collective subjects of international law to give legal status to the individual subject and justifies their unmediated membership in the association of free and equal world citizens' (Habermas 1997: 128). Habermas sees a trajectory from Kant's writings to Woodrow Wilson's Fourteen Points, the foundation of the League of Nations as well as the 'outlawry of war' movement after the First World War, the Briand–Kellogg Pact of 1928 to the war crimes tribunals of Nuremberg and Tokyo, the establishment of the United Nations and the genocide and human rights conventions over the last fifty years or so. Habermas rejoices at three innovations since 1945: first, compared with the exclusiveness of the League of Nations with its membership restricted to states with a 'liberal' constitution, the United Nations is universal both with regard to its membership and the applicability of the international law generated by it; secondly, the UN Charter (Article 1, sections 1 and 2) has brought together the aim of maintaining peace with a politics of human rights protection. As a result, the 'international community' commits itself to realising constitutional principles which have hitherto been institutionalised only in (liberal-democratic) nation-states; and thirdly, the prohibition on using force other than for instances of clear self-defence has been complemented by a realistic threat of collective punishment and sanctions in case of violation of this rule.

As a result of these developments, the political importance of the United Nations has increased in that: first, the Security Council does not only get involved in interstate conflicts, but also intervenes in intrastate conflicts. With this development, we have moved away from a restrictive interpretation of the non-intervention norm and are moving towards the implementation of the idea of an international police force; secondly, in recent years, the United Nations has revived the institution of war-crimes tribunals to prosecute and sentence grave violations of international law; and thirdly, the recognition of states in international law has become dependent on states behaving in accordance with the security and human rights standards of the United Nations. If they do not, they will face ostracism from the 'international community' as 'rogue states' (Habermas 2004: 152–78). Habermas welcomes both the innovations and the increased political clout of the United Nations.

Habermas, too, does not embrace the idea of world state, or world government. He envisages the political constitution of a decentred world society to be a multilevel governance system. At the supranational level, there is a reformed United Nations that is centrally concerned with the maintenance of peace and the enforcement of human rights. At the transnational level, the great global actors tackle major global issues such as those of the world economy and ecology. The mechanisms through which to discuss and pursue those policies are permanent international conferences and the creation of 'international regimes'. Habermas is clearly envisaging the interaction of transnational civil society actors with international political actors. These political actors are not necessarily, or exclusively, nation-states. Rather, Habermas advocates for the diverse regions of the world the formation of continental regimes, similar in form to the European Union, which would have the capacity to act as unified actors in international relations. He concedes that such a system would depend for its legitimacy upon the support generated from constitutional, democratic nation-states (Habermas, 2004: 132–5, 177).

The normative integration of this decentred world society of global citizens is brought about by the shared revulsion of grave violations of human rights, crimes against humanity, and wars of aggression. Such violations, he asserts, stir the conscience of human beings everywhere and are the focal point for the tentative formation of a global public sphere which, in due course, will bestow legitimacy on global political responses to these violations and atrocities (Habermas 2004: 142).

Habermas's political writings bear the hallmark of this basic position. After a thorough review of Habermas's political interventions since the late 1980s, Perry Anderson offered the following summary statement (which, he asserted, also apply to the political writings of Norberto Bobbio):

> The response by the two philosophers [sc. Habermas and Bobbio, RA] to successive wars waged by the West after the collapse of the Soviet bloc . . . exhibits a consistent pattern. First, military action by Washington and its allies is justified on normative grounds, invoking either international law (the Gulf), human rights (Kosovo, Afghanistan), or liberation from tyranny (Iraq). Then, qualms are expressed over the actual way that violence is unleashed by the righteous party (Gulf, Kosovo, Afghanistan, Iraq), in a gesture of humanitarian punctilio. Finally, these in turn are casually minimized or forgotten in the name of the accomplished fact. (Anderson 2005: 30–1)

One similarity between Rawls and Habermas should be stressed. They share the view that the right of states to enjoy full sovereign rights within the international community depends on their institutionalising a particular kind of domestic political order. There is a difference, however, between Rawls and Habermas: for Rawls it is states (though only those that exhibit specific features), whereas for Habermas it is individuals that are given ontological priority in the respective theories. In distinguishing between 'well-ordered' and 'disordered' peoples, John Rawls accepts the idea that one can (and ought to) distinguish between states on the basis of their internal characteristics. This distinction carries legal and moral significance: for example, it is only 'well-ordered peoples' who possess the right of non-intervention; indeed, it is they, and they alone, who have the right to conduct wars because, *per definitionem*, only their wars can be 'just'. Rawls thus privileges in his theory of international politics a particular kind of state (namely, one with limited sovereignty, that is, 'peoples'). Habermas, on the other hand, sees humanity as a moral community of individuals each of which possesses inalienable human rights whose violation is a legitimate concern for the 'international community' and may justify 'humanitarian' military intervention. Yet, as we have seen, in Rawls's argument also, violations of human rights justify military intervention in 'outlaw states'.

In the next two chapters, we shall pursue a line of inquiry informed by the recognition of the diverse uses of the notion of 'human rights' in constituting legitimate polities. John Rawls and Jürgen Habermas argue as if it was incontestable of what kind of rights 'human rights' consist. The first section in the following chapter addresses this issue by presenting a summary account of statements in charters, conventions, and declarations since 1945 on the contents (or range) of human rights. This account is neither informed by philosophical reflection nor legal systematisation. Indeed, the intention is to allow for a cacophony of voices without attempting to ensure (through authoritative authorial intervention) that all members of the human rights choir will – in the end – sing from the same hymn sheet. Such marshalling of polyphony into monophonic harmony must come out of actual political contestation among the claimants of human rights – if such a result is desired in the first place. But there is another reason for being circumspect about the possibility (if not desirability) of finding a 'common denominator', a 'bottom line', for all and any human rights claims. It cannot be doubted that the language(s) of human rights are composed of ethical imperatives, telling, or even instructing, communities and individuals what they ought to desire. While the ethical values espoused in those pronouncements are varied and diverse, as an ethical invocation 'human rights' becomes 'an expression that carries the burden of a transformative vision of the world, in which the state (and the community of state and state-like global institutions) incrementally becomes ethical, government just, and power (in all its hiding places) accountable' (Baxi 2002: 8).

Yet, 'human rights' discourse is not confined to the field of political ethics. In Rawls's and Habermas's arguments we have already encountered an additional use of the language of 'human rights'. The standards and norms of human rights – of a 'particularistic' nature, as we shall see – are applied in order to ensure a particular form of 'global governance' by distinguishing between legitimate, 'bona fide' members of the community of states and 'outlaw' or 'rogue' states. However, 'human rights' is not only used to categorise (and thus ethically and politically to vilify) political communities, but also to justify (violent as well as non-violent) intervention in those states. 'Human rights' is thus not (just) the language in which 'the barbarism of power' is interrogated and through which voice is given to human suffering, making it visible and thus starting to ameliorate it (Baxi 2002: 2–5); it is also a tool through which power is exercised and augmented (rather than power being contained and controlled by it).

This ambivalence, or rather: this dialectic, of human rights being conducive to both containing and generating power is also evident when we notice the central role that human rights occupy in contemporary thinking about legitimate power or authority. On the one hand, human rights (above all, in liberal conceptualisations) are meant to rein in the power and coercive potential of state, organisation and other persons over the 'individual'. On the other hand, human rights are perceived to ground participatory rights of the people: the exercise of political authority and the making of binding laws are legitimate if mandated by the people on the basis of their democratic right to self-government and self-legislation. As we shall see, Habermas, for example, argues that the full realisation of human rights requires the institutionalisation of popular sovereignty and thus democratic governance, while constitutional democracy obtains its legitimation through human rights. Finally, as Baxi (2002) and Rajagopal (2003) show, 'human rights' has become the language spoken by 'insurrectionary' movements:

> Through myriad struggles and movements throughout the world, 'human rights' become an arena of transformative political practice that disorients, destabilizes, and at times even helps destroy deeply unjust concentrations of political, social, economic and technological power. Movements for decolonization and self-determination, elimination of apartheid, 'women's

rights are human rights', ecological integrity and the right sexual orientation provide archetypal illustrations of the potential for transformative
practice. (Baxi 2002: 10)

It is this diversity of uses to which 'human rights' are put that would
suggest an attempt to consolidate human rights in an 'essential'
(philosophically and legally grounded) 'core' would be rather doomed
to failure.

Yet, in the next two chapters we shall discuss how human rights and
democracy cohere; and how and to what effect both human rights and
democracy have become 'globalised'. 'Globalisation of human rights'
consists, as we shall see, 'in those practices of governance by the
dominant states that selectively target the enforcement of certain sets
of rights or sets of interpretation of rights upon "subaltern" state
members of the world system' (Baxi 2002: 95–6). 'Globalisation of
democracy' means the attempt by the dominant Western states to
spread the institutions of liberal-representative democracy together
with the institutions of market capitalism. In Chapter 4, we shall
reflect upon the effect of this twin process of globalisation on a key
institution of classical democratic thinking, sovereignty.

Notes

1 The following abbreviations will be used for references to Kant's most
  frequently cited writings:
  CPR = *Critique of Practical Reason* (= Kant [1788] 1996); CJ = *Critique of
  the Power of Judgement* (= Kant [1790] 2000); MM = *The Metaphysics of
  Morals* (= Kant [1797] 1996); PP = *Toward Perpetual Peace* (= Kant
  [1795] 1996); TP = *On the common saying: That may be correct in theory,
  but it is of no use in practice* (= Kant [1793] 1996); IUH = *Idea for a
  Universal History* (= Kant [1784] 1970); and Gemeinspruch = *Über den
  Gemeinspruch: 'Das mag in der Theorie richtig sein, taugt aber nicht für
  die Praxis'* (= Kant 1793). In the round brackets, the first page number
  refers to the English edition of Kant's texts; the reference in square
  brackets is to the German edition of Kant's *Gesammelte Schriften*
  (1910–), with the first figure referencing the volume, the second the
  page number.
2 The following abbreviations are used for Cicero's texts:
  Republic = *The Republic* [*De Re Publica*] (= Cicero 51 BC/1998); On
  Duties = *On Duties* [*De officiis*] (= Cicero 44 BC/1991); and De Finibus =
  De Finibus Bonorum et Malorum (= Cicero 45 BC/1914).
3 For a Professor of law, Teson has quite an interesting take on textual
  analysis:

> While offering a modern reconstruction of Kant's thesis rather than a meticulously faithful account of what Kant meant, the interpretation of Kant suggested in this Article is accurate . . . To be sure, this Article departs from Kant on a few important points, but the main thrust of his account remains intact. (Teson 1992: 55)

Which are the 'few important points' where Teson departs from Kant's position? First – and in the context of our present discussion of the least significance – is Teson's insistence that a modern reconstruction of Kant's political theory must make room for 'positive' socio-economic rights – alongside the more traditional 'negative' civil and political rights. This is an argument that I shall present in the next chapter and with which I do not take issue: but, as we saw when presenting Kant's position on citizenship, it is not in line with Kant's own thinking (Teson 1992: 65). Secondly – and this point now bears upon the current discussion – Teson claims that when Kant speaks of 'free states' he means 'republics', and 'republics' are best understood as 'liberal democracies': 'A liberal democracy is one in which individual rights are honored and rulers are appointed by the people' (Teson 1992: 61, fn. 39). Whether this is indeed an appropriate definition of 'liberal democracy' shall not concern us here – in a way, this book is an attempt to offer an historical-conceptual understanding of this regime type. Yet, clearly, if we remember Kant's definition of 'republic', 'liberal democracy' would appear to be a problematic 'translation'. Predictably, Teson's next step is to claim that Kant's world federation is an 'alliance of liberal democracies' (Teson 1992: 89). For Teson, it is quite clear that this alliance has a right to use force:

> [F]orce will sometimes have to be used against nonliberal regimes as a last resort in self-defense or in defense of human rights. Liberal democracies must seek peace and use all possible alternatives to preserve it. In extreme circumstances, however, violence may be the only means to uphold the law and to defend the liberal alliance against outlaw dictators that remain nonmembers. Such, I believe, is the proper place of war in the Kantian theory. (Teson 1992: 90)

This would be, for Teson, a 'just war' (Teson 1992: 91). There is also the burden carried by liberal democracies that, as defenders of human rights and punishers of human rights violations anywhere, they may have to intervene in other countries (Teson 1992: 91). Teson accepts that, unfortunately, this is not Kant's position: 'However, Kant seems to disagree' (Teson 1992: 90). Indeed, he does. However, Teson appears to think, why should such a disagreement hinder him to call his own theory 'Kantian'? We shall discuss the political implications of Teson's argument (and for that matter, Rawls's and Habermas's as well) in Chapter 4.

2

The Languages of Human Rights and the Liberal Dialect

'Moral' cosmopolitanism as the idea of 'humanity' as a moral community finds one of its most pronounced expressions in the notion of universal human rights. As we have seen in the previous chapter, the recourse to human rights is of central importance in arguments in support of cosmopolitanism, and global justice in particular, and in justifications of military intervention in the internal affairs of other states. We shall return to the use to which 'human rights' are put to justify 'humanitarian intervention', and its implication for the idea of 'sovereignty', in Chapter 4. For the moment, however, we should remain aware of the fact that the human rights discourse contains multiple, complex and contested claims as to the array of rights that should count as 'human rights'. A similarly diverse range of claims obtains with regard to defining the extent to which they are interdependent, the duties or responsibilities that attach to these rights, and the 'bearer' of those rights: whether it is 'the individual', a 'group', or both. In 'The Many Voices of the Human Rights Discourse', below, we shall present these controversies by reviewing declarations, conventions, and charters of human rights that, together, constitute the political discourse on human rights. In the next section, 'Human Rights as the New Standard of Civilisation', we address, by reference to liberal thought, the issue of whether there is a 'core' of 'human rights' which may rightly be seen as being 'universal'. In the context of that discussion, we develop Habermas's argument about the complementarities of human rights and democracy (or popular sovereignty).

The Many Voices of the Human Rights Discourse

After the Second World War, the human rights discourse truly became global.[1] We can find several references to human rights in the Charter of the United Nations of 1945 – although no 'declaration of human rights' was incorporated into the Charter, with the Great Powers objecting to such incorporation for fear their national (and colonial) interests might be detrimentally affected. The Preamble reaffirmed 'faith in fundamental human rights, in the dignity and worth of the human person, in the equal rights of men and women and of nations large or small'. Article 1 defined one of the main purposes of the United Nations as that of achieving 'international co-operation in solving international problems of an economic, social, cultural, or humanitarian character, and in promoting and encouraging respect for human rights and for fundamental freedoms for all without distinction as to race, sex, language, or religion' (see also Article 13, 1.b; Article 55 (c)). The Economic and Social Council was given the power to 'make recommendations for the purpose of promoting respect for, and observance of, human rights and fundamental freedoms for all' (Article 62.2). It was requested that a commission for the promotion of human rights be set up (Article 68) – the 'Commission on Human Rights' as well as its 'Subcommission on the Prevention of Discrimination and the Protection of Minorities' are based on that provision.

The connection between the pursuit of peace and security, on the one hand, and the promotion of human rights, on the other, which is implicit in the Preamble to the Charter of the United Nations, is made explicit in the Constitution of the United Nations Educational, Scientific and Cultural Organization (UNESCO) of the same year. Drafted after years of global warfare, the UNESCO Constitution (like the UN Charter) explicitly refers to the experience of war in order then to state the purpose of the Organization. UNESCO was to make a contribution to 'peace and security by promoting collaboration among the nations through education, science and culture in order to further universal respect for justice, for the rule of law and for human rights and fundamental freedoms which are affirmed for the peoples of the world, without distinction of race, sex, language or religion, by the Charter of the United Nations' (Article 1). By endorsing 'the democratic principles of the dignity, equality and mutual respect of men' and by rejecting 'the doctrine of the inequality of men and races', war will (allegedly) be eradicated and peace will be founded (Preamble).

This perspective also grounds the Universal Declaration of Human Rights of 1948. The Preamble states that 'recognition of the inherent dignity and of the equal and inalienable rights of all members of the human family is the foundation of freedom, justice and peace in the world', whereas 'disregard and contempt for human rights have resulted in barbarous acts which have outraged the conscience of mankind'. This founding document of the contemporary human rights discourse and global human rights regime is of interest for a number of reasons. First, human rights and fundamental freedoms are not grounded in any metaphysical principles, but they find their justification in historical experience and memory of the genocides and the atrocities that had been committed before and during the Second World War. Secondly, the explicit universalism of the Declaration is noteworthy. '*All* members of the human family' possess the same rights: 'All human beings are born free and equal in dignity and rights' (Article 1). No one may be deprived of any of the rights and freedoms set forth in the Declaration; no distinction of any kind – such as based on 'race, colour, sex, language, religion, political or other opinion, national or social origin, property, birth or other status' – must be allowed. Clearly, then, the human person as such, and therefore all human beings, possess the same rights (Article 2). Furthermore, 'no distinction shall be made on the basis of the political, jurisdictional or international status of the country or territory to which a person belongs, whether it be independent, trust, non-self-governing or under any other limitation of sovereignty' (Article 2). Whereas the Charter of the United Nations looked, as it were, backwards to the totalitarianism of the inter-war period and 'the scourge of war' (Preamble), the Universal Declaration is cognizant of this past, but also situates the challenge of human rights in the concrete reality of imperialism and colonialism past and present. This concern is reiterated in the claim of Article 28 that everyone is entitled to an international order in which the rights and freedoms set forth can be fully realised.

The third noteworthy feature of the Declaration is the claim that the rights and freedoms that are set out are indivisible: 'Everyone is entitled to *all* the rights and freedoms set forth in this Declaration' (Art. 2). These rights cluster into three groups. There are the civil rights of the individual with regard to the right to life, liberty, and security of the person, all of them embedded in the rule of law, and the proprietorial rights in civil society (Articles 3–17). The political rights (Articles 18–21) proclaim the rights of the person within a political community and *vis-à-vis* the state and political authority. The associational rights complement the right to political participation:

> Everyone has the right to take part in the government of his country, directly or through freely chosen representatives . . . The will of the people shall be the basis of the authority of government; this will shall be expressed in periodic and genuine elections which shall be by universal and equal suffrage and shall be held by secret vote or by equivalent free voting procedures. (Article 21)

The social, economic and cultural rights (Articles 22–27) – such as the right to social security, to work and free choice of employment, to equal pay, to rest and leisure, to adequate standards of healthcare and well-being more generally, to education, or to participation in the cultural life of the community – form the third cluster. We see, therefore, that already in the Universal Declaration of 1948, social, economic, and cultural rights together with civil and political rights were enumerated. These rights are interdependent and indivisible. At least from the point of view of the stated intention, it is clear that it would be wrong to suggest that civil and political rights together constitute the 'first generation' of human rights, which would later on be complemented by the 'second generation' of social, economic, and cultural rights. It would also contradict the intention of the Declaration to suggest that civil and political rights have a higher dignity than social, economic, and cultural rights, and that the enactment of the latter rights is optional. But it is significant, and important to recognise, that the Universal Declaration takes the individual person as its starting point and proclaims his or her rights and entitlements *vis-à-vis* the state, economic organisations, or the community. It is the individual as a rights bearer who is positioned centre-stage. That Article 29 stipulates that 'everyone has duties to the community in which alone the free and full development of his personality is possible', must not distract from the person-centred perspective of the Declaration.

Another noteworthy feature is the emphasis on human rights as being inalienable. This means, on the one hand, that these rights may not be derogated or annulled, but it also means, on the other hand, that these rights are outside of the realm of politics. Grounded as they are in the idea of human dignity, they are removed from political deliberation (once they have been declared and legally entrenched in treaties and covenants), save with regard to discussion as to the best, most appropriate, or most adequate policy through which to implement them. Human rights would, therefore, appear to have a higher dignity than citizenship rights. Manifestly, there is a semblance between human rights and citizenship rights though.

The British sociologist, T. H. Marshall (1963: 74) distinguished three types of citizenship rights: civil; political; and social citizenship rights. According to Marshall's history of citizenship rights in (western) Europe, civil citizenship rights are instrumental in securing 'liberty of the person, freedom of speech, thought and faith, the right to own property and to conclude valid contracts and the right to justice'. These civil rights can be defended through the system of formal law courts. The state in which civil rights prevail is a constitutional state. The struggle over the establishment of civil rights was waged in the late eighteenth and the first half of the nineteenth century between the privileged aristocracy and the rising bourgeoisie. The axis of this socio-political conflict was freedom versus privilege. The challengers to the established order were united by a common belief: liberalism and a common goal, that is, the establishment of the constitutional state. But the liberal-bourgeois movements of the nineteenth century also mobilised against the established order for political citizenship rights: 'the right to participate in the exercise of political power, as a member of a body invested with political authority or as an elector of the members of such a body'. The state in which such political rights can be exercised is a constitutional parliamentary system. To the extent that the winning of rights of political participation was restricted to the bourgeoisie, the working class, too, became involved in this political struggle, but not just against the old privileged class, but against the newly enfranchised middle class as well. In the struggle of the working-class movements, however, the socio-political struggle that had centred on the issue of freedom versus privilege was complemented, and somewhat marginalised, by another type of conflict, that is, the struggle of the working-class movement for social justice and economic security against private property, economic power, and concomitant political power of aristocracy and bourgeoisie alike. The challengers to the established order demanded not only civil and political liberties; the labour movement now also demanded rights to resources. The struggle was over the establishment of social rights: 'the whole range from the right to a modicum of economic welfare and security to the right to share to the full in the social heritage and to live the life of a civilized being according to the standards prevailing in the society'. The constitutional state with its parliamentary system should become a democratic welfare state. This, at least, was the aim of the social democratic labour movement (Offe 1985).

If we follow Marshall's analytical distinctions (rather than his problematic claim that there is an historical sequence to the extension of citizenship rights, with civil rights being followed by political rights, and these, in turn, being followed by social rights), then one may be tempted to overlook the difference between citizenship rights and human rights. Citizenship rights are rights of citizens: rights that citizens give themselves as a result of political struggle or social conflict or as political circumstances allow, and from which they may exclude non-citizens. They issue out of the exercise of political authority (which may or may not be democratically constituted and controlled). Certain categories of human beings possess these rights because they are citizens. Human rights, on the other hand, are rights that individuals possess because they are human beings with intrinsic dignity and worth. In particular, three 'political' rights in the Universal Declaration show the tension between 'universal' human rights and 'particularistic' citizenship rights. Article 13 gives 'everyone the right to freedom of movement and residence within the borders of each state' as well as the right 'to leave any country, including his own, and to return to his country'. Article 14 gives everyone the right 'to seek and to enjoy in other countries asylum from persecution'. Article 15 stipulates that 'everyone has the right to a nationality'. Furthermore, 'no one shall be arbitrarily deprived of his nationality nor denied the right to change his nationality'. Human rights, so it would appear, 'trump' citizenship rights and severely limit the exercise of sovereign political authority. We shall return to this issue in the second section of this chapter and encounter Habermas's counter-argument of the co-originality of human rights and democracy. But it is worth emphasising that 'democratic rights' are conceived as a sub-category of 'human rights', receiving their grounding and dignity, but also their limits, from 'human rights'.

Table 2.1 lists the most important human rights treaties which have come into force during the last six decades and shows the percentage of the member states of the United Nations that have ratified them.

The International Covenant on Civil and Political Rights and the International Covenant on Economic, Social and Cultural Rights, were adopted and opened for signature, ratification, and accession in 1966 and eventually entered into force in 1976. They specify the rights proclaimed in the Universal Declaration. In the context of the current discussion, it is worth emphasising two aspects of these covenants. First, the obligations of individuals are stressed more forcefully than in the Universal Declaration, with the (identical) preambles stating 'that the individual, having duties to other individuals and to the community to which he belongs, is under a responsibility to strive for the promotion and observance of the rights' recognised in the respective covenant. The second aspect is of even greater importance. The Charter of the United Nations had already stated that the development of friendly relations among nations must be based 'on respect for the principles of equal rights and self-determination of peoples' (Article 1.2). Both of the covenants of 1966 highlight the right to self-determination in their first article – and thus tie this right unambiguously to the 'human rights and fundamental freedoms' discourse. The right of the individual to self-determination was intricately linked to the right of collective self-determination: 'All peoples have the right of self-determination. By virtue of that right they freely determine their political status and freely pursue their economic, social and cultural development' (Article 1.2). Indeed, continuing the theme of anti-colonialism, which had already informed the Universal Declaration, it was stipulated that all States Parties to the covenants, 'including those having responsibility for the administration of Non-Self-Governing and Trust Territories, shall promote the realization of the right of self-determination, and shall respect that right' (Article 1.3). Evidently, 'human rights' were no longer perceived to pertain just to individuals, but to collectives as well: to peoples and nations.

Table 2.1 **Participation of States in Human Rights Treaties**

Treaty	Entry into force	Members of the UN who have ratified (%)
Convention on the Prevention and Punishment of the Crime of Genocide	1951	70
International Covenant on the Elimination of All Forms of Racial Discrimination	1969	88
International Covenant on Civil and Political Rights	1976	78
International Covenant on Economic, Social, and Cultural Rights	1976	77
Convention on the Elimination of All Forms of Discrimination against Women	1981	91
Convention against Torture and Other Forms of Cruel, Inhuman, and Degrading Treatment	1987	70
Convention on the Rights of the Child	1990	99

Source: Goldsmith and Posner (2005: 108) (who use as their source United Nations, Office of the High Commissioner for Human Rights, data available at www.unhchr.ch/pdf/report.pdf (as of 7 July 2003)

Yet, in particular, with regard to the right of self-determination, it is important to identify precisely to whom this right belongs. Within the context of decolonisation, we can perceive this right to pertain to states which had been incorporated into imperial or colonial structures and which endeavoured to overthrow the imperial power and its alien rule. But what is to be done about 'stateless nations', 'internal' nationalities and their demand for self-determination? We may think, for example, of countries such as the United Kingdom (with the constituent nations of England, Scotland, Wales – and the even more complex case of Northern Ireland), Spain (and the Catalan question), Belgium (Wallonia), or Canada (Quebec). But we may also think, for example, of the Kurds and their demands for self-determination with which they confront the governmental authority of Turkey, Iraq, Iran, and Syria. In these cases, the question of separatism and secession is being raised, and with it the issue of territorial integrity. While it is relatively unproblematic to define what an individual (as a bearer of 'human rights') is – even if the definition of a 'human being' is deeply problematic as the debates on the right of abortion have demonstrated – whether a group qualifies as a 'people' (with the attendant right to self-determination) is much more difficult to determine. The international recognition of a group as a people with a right to self-determination may bring about the fragmentation of established states as a result of secession or civil war and a likely destabilisation of the regional state system. As a result, bestowing the status of a people on a group may actually be conducive to a worsening of the human rights situation of individuals. One could think, for example, of the 'former' Yugoslavia.

Arguably, the right to self-determination by indigenous peoples poses yet another challenge to the governmental authority of established states. The Draft Declaration on the Rights of Indigenous Peoples of 1993 asserts their right to self-determination (Article 3). It also confirms their right 'to maintain and strengthen their distinct political, economic, social and cultural characteristics, as well as their legal systems, while retaining their right to participate fully, if they so choose, in the political, economic, social and cultural life of a State' (Article 4). Indigenous peoples 'have the right to autonomy or self-government in matters relating to their internal and local affairs, including culture, religion, education, information, media, health, housing, employment, social welfare, economic activities, land and resource management, environment and entry by non-members, as well as ways and means for financing these autonomous functions'

(Article 31). Furthermore, they have 'the collective right to determine their own citizenship in accordance with their customs and traditions. Indigenous citizenship does not impair the right of indigenous individuals to obtain citizenship of the State in which they live' (Article 32). They have the right 'to promote, develop and maintain their institutional structures and their distinctive juridical customs, traditions, procedures and practices, in accordance with internationally recognized human rights standards' (Article 33). Clearly, one reason why this declaration has not yet been passed is the perception by the 'white settler societies' that their sovereignty and territorial integrity, as they perceive it, would be damaged by accepting the validity of such rights claims. We shall return to this issue in the first section of Chapter 5.

The 'human right' to self-determination of peoples thus shows paradigmatically that human rights claims may clash; but it also highlights concern about the possibility of reconciling (potentially conflicting) normative ideals (such as internal stability or peace) with human rights norms and the potential cost attached to rights enforcement. With regard to title to territory, the principle of 'territorial integrity' (in legal terminology, *uti possidetis*) clashes with the other principle of self-determination. The General Assembly's 1960 Declaration on the Granting of Independence to Colonial Countries and Peoples asserted that '[a]ny attempt aimed at the partial or total disruption of the national unity and territorial integrity of a country is incompatible with the purposes and principles of the Charter of the United Nations' (GA Resolution 1514 (XV), 14 December 1960, Article 6; see also: GA Resolutions 2625 (XXV), 24 October 1079, Preamble). The Vienna Declaration of 1993 reiterated the by then widely shared understanding that 'the denial of the right of self-determination [is] a violation of human rights'. But it also asserted in the same paragraph that this right 'shall not be construed as authorizing or encouraging any action which would dismember or impair, totally or in part, the territorial integrity or political unity of sovereign and independent States conducting themselves in compliance with the principle of equal rights and self-determination of peoples and thus possessed of a Government representing the whole people belonging to the territory without distinction of any kind' (Vienna Declaration 1993: para. 2). In the light of this position, the issue of self-determination is treated as a problem of the protection of the right of minorities (that is, non-discrimination and full and free participation in all aspects of society) within a state (paras 19, 20, 25–32).

This position is close in spirit to the view expressed in Article 27 of the CCPR that 'ethnic, religious or linguistic minorities . . . shall not be denied the right, in community with the other members of their group, to enjoy their own culture, to profess and practise their own religion, or to use their own language'. Arguably, then, the right of self-determination is not (of necessity to be conceived as) a right of secessionist self-determination (Franck 1995; Musgrave 1997: Chapters 4–6).

In 1986, the Preamble to the Declaration on the Right on Development proclaimed the right to development as yet one more inalienable human right. The Declaration defined development as 'a comprehensive economic, social, cultural and political process, which aims at the constant improvement of the well-being of the entire population and of all individuals on the basis of their active, free and meaningful participation in development and in the fair distribution of benefits resulting therefrom'. Which are the obstacles to the exercise of the right to development? According to the Declaration, it is 'the massive and flagrant violations of the human rights of peoples and individuals affected by situations such as those resulting from colonialism, neo-colonialism, apartheid, all forms of racism and racial discrimination, foreign domination and occupation, aggression and threats against national sovereignty, national unity and territorial integrity and threats to war'. Once these violations have been overcome, circumstances more propitious to the development of a great part of humankind could be established (Preamble and Article 5). States are duty-bound 'to promote a new international economic order based on sovereign equality, interdependence, mutual interest and co-operation among all States, as well as to encourage the observance and realization of human rights' (Article 3).

With the incorporation of the right of peoples to self-determination and the right to development into the human rights discourse, one has politically (and analytically) moved away from a narrow conceptualisation of human rights as those inalienable rights that protect the individual human being against threats, encroachments or impositions emanating from the actions of other individuals, the state, and the community. If we look at declarations on human rights from outside the United Nations system, this observation is confirmed. In its Preamble, the African (Banjul) Charter on Human and Peoples' Rights (adopted in 1981 by the Organization of African Unity, now the African Union) forcefully brings together the themes that have been highlighted in the current discussion. It is proclaimed that it is henceforth essential 'to pay a particular attention to the right to development and the civil and political rights cannot be dissociated from economic, social and cultural rights in their conception as well as universality and that the satisfaction of economic, social and cultural rights is a guarantee for the enjoyment of civil and political rights'. As we saw, the Universal Declaration grounded the human rights that it enumerated on the experience and memory of 'barbarous acts which have outraged the conscience of mankind' – that is, the totalitarianism of the inter-war period and the Nazi atrocities in particular (Preamble). The 'historical', or 'political' experience of African countries was different and led to a different kind of grounding and focus for the OAU's Declaration: they remained conscious, as the Preamble stated, 'of their duty to achieve the total liberation of Africa, the peoples of which are still struggling for their dignity and genuine independence'. They are, therefore, duty-bound 'to eliminate colonialism, neo-colonialism, apartheid, zionism and to dismantle aggressive foreign military bases and all forms of discrimination, particularly those based on race, ethnic group, color, sex, language, religion or political opinion'. This historical experience then translates into specific claims and the formulation of rightful entitlements: 'Nothing shall justify the domination of a people by another' (Article 19). The right to self-determination bestows on colonised or oppressed peoples the right 'to free themselves from the bonds of domination by resorting to any means recognized by the international community' (Article 20.2). The 'liberation struggle against foreign domination' is not just directed against colonial states, but also aims at eliminating 'all forms of foreign economic exploitation particularly that practised by international monopolies so as to enable their peoples to fully benefit from the advantages derived from their national resources' (Article 21).

The right to self-determination and to development also figures prominently in the 'Bangkok Declaration' issued by Asian states in 1991 as the result of a meeting in the context of preparations for the UN World Conference on Human Rights (which was held in Vienna in 1993). Among the signatories of this declaration were China, India, Iran, Iraq, Japan, Pakistan, the Philippines, the Republic of Korea, Vietnam, and the Palestine Liberation Movement. The human rights regime and discourse was firmly placed within the framework of the unequal distribution of power in the international system. The Declaration demanded that 'the principles of respect for national sovereignty and territorial integrity as well as non-interference in the internal affairs of States, and the non-use of human rights as an instrument of political pressure' be acknowledged, and that any attempts be discouraged which aim 'to use human rights as a conditionality for extending development assistance'. The denial of self-determination was considered to constitute 'a grave violation of human rights'. This denial could take the form of apartheid, colonialism, foreign aggression and occupation as well as the illegal settlements in occupied territories. Explicit reference is made to 'the legitimate struggle of the Palestine people to restore their national and inalienable rights to self-determination'.

The Declaration further asserts that 'poverty is one of the major obstacles hindering the full enjoyment of human rights' (Article 19). As we shall see Chapter 3, the World Bank, too, would link human rights and poverty or, respectively, the level of socio-economic development. However, for the World Bank lack of development is ultimately caused by the malfunctioning of national economies – a malfunctioning that can be rectified by 'structural adjustment programmes' that bring the economies in line with global capitalism through policies of market liberalisation and privatisation. The Bangkok Declaration, on the other hand, identifies obstacles to development as being embedded in the structure of global inequalities and hence at the international macroeconomic level as reflected in the widening gap between the North and the South, the rich and the poor (Article 18). In pursuit of its economic, social, and cultural development, each state must be free in its decision about how to utilise its resources (Article 4, 5, and 6) – a position, as we shall see, quite at odds with that taken by the international financial institutions such as the World Bank or IMF. Yet, in effect, both the World Bank and the signatories of the Bangkok Declaration suggest that the right to development may reasonably be afforded precedence over other human rights.

The Bangkok Declaration claims that the universalism of human rights must be understood in the context of the particularism of local traditions: 'While human rights are universal in nature, they must be considered in the context of a dynamic and evolving process of international norm-setting, bearing in mind the significance of national and regional particularities and various historical, cultural and religious backgrounds' (Article 8). This claim arises out of the view that 'Asian values' give human rights a unique cultural complexion. In the light of this claim, but also in recognition of the fact that the Bangkok Declaration was issued by states whose human rights record has frequently been critically scrutinised and assessed, it is instructive to have a look at the Asian Human Rights Charter which was published as 'A Peoples' Charter' under the title 'Our Common Humanity' in 1998. This Charter was not formulated by states, but by a large network of non-governmental organisations in Asia.

The Charter maintains that 'human rights are violated by the state, civil society and business corporations' (Article 15.2a). Colonialism and other developments, such as the marketisation and globalisation of the economy, have significantly changed the nature of Asian political societies. For instances, 'the traditional systems of account-ability and public participation in affairs of state as well as the relationship of citizens to the government were altered fundamentally. Citizens became subject, while the government became more pervasive and powerful. Colonial laws and authoritarian habits and style of government persisted after independence.' The consequence was that the state 'has become the source of corruption and the oppression of the people' (Article 5.1). The Charter posits that in recent decades, Asians have suffered from various forms of conflict and violence that arose from 'ultra-nationalism, perverted ideologies, ethnic differences, and fundamentalism of all religions' (Article 1.4). It declares that 'wars, ethnic conflicts, cultural and religious oppression, corruption of politics, environmental pollution, disappearances, torture, state or private terrorism, violence against women' – all these acts of mass violence continue to be a scourge to humanity (Article 3.3). These acts can be committed because 'both the state and civil society have in many countries become heavily militarized in which scores are settled by force and citizens have no protection against the intimidation and terror of state or private armies' (Article 4.1). It cannot be doubted, then, that 'violence emanates from both the state and sections of civil society' (Article 1.4). In addition to these forms of violence, the marketisation and globalisation of economies add to the experience of insecurity and threaten many valued aspects of life because of 'the dehumanizing effects of technology, the material orientation of the market, and the destruction of the community' (Article 1.2). In their endeavour to reduce the costs of production and to create an envir-onment congenial to international investment, many Asian states and business corporations, 'often in collusion with foreign corporations and international financial institutions', violate workers' rights and take away their livelihood (Articles 12.1 and 12.2; also Article 2.8).

Engaging squarely with the idea of Asian 'particularity', the Charter postulates that 'authoritarianism has in many states been raised to the level of national ideology, with the deprivation of the rights and freedoms of their citizens, which are denounced as foreign ideas inappropriate to the religious and cultural traditions of Asia. Instead there is the exhortation of spurious theories of "Asian Values" which are a thin disguise for their authoritarianism' (Article 1.5). In a passage, well worth quoting at length, the Charter states that:

> the plurality of cultural identities in Asia is not contrary to the universality of human rights but rather as so many cultural manifestations of human dignity enriching universal norms. At the same time we Asian peoples must eliminate those features in our cultures which are contrary to the universal principles of human rights. We must transcend the traditional concepts of the family based on patriarchal traditions so as to retrieve in each of our cultural traditions, the diversity of family norms which guarantee women's human rights. We must be bold in reinterpreting our religious beliefs which support gender inequality. We must eliminate discriminations based on caste, ethnic origins, occupation, place of origin and others, while enhancing in our respective cultures all values related to mutual tolerance and mutual support. We must stop practices which sacrifice the individual to the collectivity or to the powerful, and thus renew our communal and national solidarity. (Article 6.2)

Clearly, what is being suggested is that there is a need for an 'intra-civilisational' (or, more modestly, 'intra-cultural') dialogue in order to gain an understanding of what is to count as 'Asian values'. Such a debate must be embedded in, and contribute to, the formation and development of a humane, open, tolerant, pluralistic, and accountable political system 'in which people are free to express their views and to seek to persuade others and in which the rights of minorities are respected' (Article 5.2). In such a system, a proper balance between the interests of the individual and the community must be achieved: 'Democratic and accountable governments are the key to the promotion and protection of rights' (Article 2.7). The idea of state sovereignty cannot be used to avoid moving towards a rights-promoting and rights-protecting system: 'The claim of state sovereignty is justified only when a state fully protects the rights of its citizens' (Article 2.5). Such a domestic transformation must go hand-in-hand with the radical transformation and democratisation of the world order 'as a necessary condition for the global enjoyment of human rights' (Article 2.6).

The most recent pronouncement on human rights in Asia has been the Charter of Human Rights for Asian Nations, approved in November 2005 by the Association of Asian Parliaments for Peace. In the Preamble, 'the right to self-determination, national independence, territorial integrity and national sovereignty' are held to be sacred and integral and to constitute the foundation for the protection and promotion of human rights. The 'interdependence and indivisibility of economic, social, cultural and political rights' is stressed as is the inherent interrelationship between 'development, democracy, universal enjoyment of all human rights, and social justice.' However, the Preamble already emphasises 'that the enjoyment of rights and freedoms also implies obligations or duties and the exclusive insistence on rights can result in conflict, division, and endless dispute and the neglect of responsibilities can lead to lawlessness and chaos'. In line with these sentiments, the Charter then qualifies the following rights: the enjoyment of freedom of thought, conscience, and religion (Article 11), of freedom of opinion and expression (Article 12), of freedom of assembly and association (Article 13), and freedom of movement (Article 14). It states that the enjoyment of these freedoms are subject to limitations in the interests of national security, territorial integrity and public safety, the protection of public order, health and morals and the protection of the rights and freedoms of others. This is a qualification that one also finds in other human rights charters, such as the Universal Declaration (Article 29), the ICPR (Articles 19, 21 and 22), or the European Convention for the Protection of Human Rights (Article 10, para. 2). However, the European Convention makes the application of both the rule and its exceptions subject to review by the European Commission on Human Rights and the European Court of Human Rights.

While the Charter refers to 'the virtues of the history and values of Asian civilizations' (Preamble), Asian cultural values are explicitly mentioned in the context of regard to the responsibilities of the individual:

'Every individual shall also have the duty:
   a. to preserve the harmonious development of the family and to work for the cohesion and respect of the family; to respect one's parents at all times, to care for them in case of need; to nurture and care for his/her child or children until adulthood;
   b. to serve one's national community by placing one's physical and intellectual abilities at its service;
   c. to preserve and strengthen social and national solidarity as well as national independence and the territorial integrity of one's country;
   d. to work to the best of one's abilities and competence, and to pay taxes imposed by law in the interest of the society;
   e. to preserve and strengthen positive Asian values in one's relation with

other members of the society, in the spirit of tolerance, dialogue and consultation and in general, to contribute to the promotion of the moral well-being of society.' (Article 26.3)

The emphasis on rights as well as on duties should not be misconstrued as a manifestation of an 'Asian' (authoritarian) communitarianism or unique 'Asian values'. In his Encyclical of 1963, *Pacem in Terris*, Pope John XXIII developed a Catholic vision of human rights. In their reflections on the jubilee of the Universal Declaration of Human Rights, published under the title 'Human Rights and the Catholic Church', the Catholic Bishops' Conference of England and Wales summarised this 'charter of rights' as follows. Human rights include:

the right to life; the right to bodily integrity and to the means necessary for the proper development of life, particularly food, clothing, shelter, medical care, rest, and the necessary social services; the right to be looked after in the event of ill-health, disability, widowhood, old age, unemployment; the right to a good name; freedom to investigate the truth, and freedom of speech and publication; freedom to pursue a choice of career; the right to be accurately informed about public events; the right to share in the benefits of culture; the right to receive a good general education; the right to raise children, which belongs primarily to the parents; the right not only to be given the opportunity to work but also to enjoy the exercise of personal initiative in that work; the right to a just wage; the right to the private ownership of property including that of productive goods; the right to meet together with others and to form associations; the right to freedom of movement; and the right to take part in public life, and to make a contribution to the common welfare. (Catholic Bishops' Conference 1998: para. 4)

In his Encyclical, Pope John XXIII provided a philosophical foundation for the human rights discourse based on 'natural law theory'. As the Bishops' Conference points out, in this context 'natural law' 'refers both to the use of human reason to work out the conditions necessary for individuals to live harmoniously together in community, and also the moral sense that guides people in their conduct towards one another' (Catholic Bishops' Conference 1998: para. 8). It is due to this natural law tradition that Pope John can balance rights with duties:

The natural rights of which We have so far been speaking are inextricably bound up with as many duties, all applying to one and the same person . . . Once this is admitted, it follows that in human society one man's natural right gives rise to a corresponding duty in other men; the duty, that is, of recognizing and respecting that right. Every basic human right draws its authoritative force from the natural law, which confers it and attaches to it respective duty. Hence, to claim one's rights and ignore one's duties, or only half fulfill them, is like building a house with one hand and tearing it down with the other. (*Pacem in Terris*: paras 28 and 30)

Thus, for example, the right to live involves the duty to preserve one's life. The inviolability of the right to life involves a duty to make a positive choice, a choice for life:

A genuine culture of life, just as it guarantees to the unborn the right to come into the world, in the same way protects the newly born, especially girls, from the crime of infanticide . . . To choose life involves [the duty of] rejecting every form of violence: the violence of poverty and hunger . . . the violence of armed conflict; the violence of criminal trafficking in drugs and arms; the violence of mindless damage to the natural environment. (Pope John Paul II 1999: para. 4)

Underlying this notion of duty is, manifestly, the key tenet of Catholic moral theology that it is the destiny and duty of each human being to become more fully human.

The Catholic grounding of human rights is ultimately embedded in the natural law tradition as well as in the doctrines of creation and of the Incarnation: natural law and scriptural revelation provide the philosophical foundation for the Catholic human rights discourse. The Universal Islamic Declaration of Human Rights of 1981, too, emphasises that 'God, and God alone, is the Law Giver and the Source of all human rights. Due to their divine origin, no ruler, government, assembly or authority can curtail or violate in any way the human rights conferred by God, nor can they be surrendered' (Foreword). For Muslims, the Charter asserts, 'our duties and obligations have priority over our rights, and . . . each one of us is under bounden duty to spread the teachings of Islam by word, deed, and indeed in all gentle ways, and to make them effective not only in our individual lives but also in the society around us' (Preamble). Rights (which carry corresponding duties), so the Charter stipulates, must be exercised within the limits set by the law, that is, the *Shari'ah*, 'the totality of ordinances derived from the Qur'an and the Sunnah and other laws that are deduced from these two sources by methods considered valid in Islamic jurisprudence' (Explanatory Notes).

The human rights discourse, as it manifests itself in declarations and proclamations by governments, inter-governmental and non-governmental organisations (as, for example, in the Asian Charter issued by NGOs), thus encompasses a wide range of rights, freedoms, and duties. Many of these themes, issues, and perspectives are bundled together in the Vienna Declaration and Programme of Action, which was adopted by the UN World Conference on Human Rights in 1993. The universality (or universalism) of human rights – and of conceptions of human rights in all their manifold diversity – are most clearly expressed in this document. There is the reference to the dignity and worth inherent in the human person from which all human rights are said to derive (Preamble). It reasserts that all human rights are universal, indivisible, interdependent, and interrelated. At the same time, the document notes the tension between universalism and particularism:

> The international community must treat human rights globally in a fair and equal manner, on the same footing, and with the same emphasis. While the significance of national and regional particularities and various historical, cultural and religious backgrounds must be borne in mind, it is the duty of States, regardless of their political, economic and cultural systems, to promote and protect all human rights and fundamental freedoms. (I. 5)

The Declaration thus emphasises the need for a culturally sensitive universalism, indeed, in several other paragraphs it does so as well (paras 1, 32, and 37). The tension between 'universalism' and 'particularism' (or 'relativism'), that had been highlighted in the 'Asian values' argument, while not solved, was thus nevertheless acknowledged (Cerna 1994/1955; Engle 1999/2000: 320–3; Otto 1997/1998: 10–11).

The Declaration refers to the right of peoples to self-determination and to development just as it also refers to civil, political, and economic rights. The human rights of women, of children – and the 'girl child' in particular – of the disabled, of refugees, asylum seekers, and migrant workers are especially enlisted; and so are the human rights of religious, ethnic, and national minorities as well as those of indigenous people (I. 18–27; II. 19–65). Dismay is expressed at the massive violations of human rights especially in the form of genocide, 'ethnic cleansing', and systematic rape of women in war situations (I. 28). The Declaration condemns the gross and systematic violations of human rights that occur in the form of:

> torture and cruel, inhuman and degrading treatment or punishment, summary and arbitrary executions, disappearances, arbitrary detentions, all forms of racism, racial discrimination and apartheid, foreign occupation and alien domination, xenophobia, poverty, hunger and other denials

of economic, social and cultural rights, religious intolerance, terrorism, discrimination against women and lack of the rule of law. (I. 30)

Such is the catalogue of sufferings and injustices, of human rights violations and of human rights claims, that well-nigh the whole field of domestic and international public policy has come under the purview of the Declaration.

Human Rights as the New Standard of Civilisation

In the previous overview, an attempt has been made to present the complex array of human rights and corresponding duties that makes up the human rights discourse. However, no attempt is made to distinguish between the charters, conventions, treaties, or (policy) pronouncements based on their respective dignity in international law. Highlighting the plurality of voices and positions in this discourse is more important than ranking or censoring rights claims by assigning them differential status in international law. It has become clear that human rights are being justified in a number of ways: philosophical and theological justifications complement or substitute those justifications that are grounded in historical experiences of cruelty, injustices and injuries, historical memory, and political interpretations. It has also become evident in the overview that an almost infinite number of political, social, economic, and cultural claims – made by, or on behalf of, individuals, groups, or states – can be, and have been, presented as grounded in human rights or fundamental freedoms entitlements. An equally infinite number of actions (and omissions to act) can be, and have been, condemned as human rights violations. The language of politics, so it would appear, is now spoken in one of the dialects of human rights.

We have encountered the controversy over the universality of human rights and the request for a culturally sensitive interpretation and application of human rights standards particularly in the context of the 'Asian values' debate. And the same controversy over 'culture' can be traced in the encounter of indigenous peoples with the former colonial powers and their successors in the white settler societies. We saw in connection with the Asian NGO Charter that the 'Asian values' debate is as much a debate between 'East' and 'West' as it is within and across Asian societies (Bell 2000; Davis 1998; Pollis 1996; Thompson 2001; Teson 1985 for a strong 'anti-relativist' argument). This has been a debate on whether there are substantive human rights standards that ought not to vary among different cultures (as the 'universalists' claim) or whether such standards necessarily reflect national idiosyncrasies (as the 'relativists' claim). The debate about the priority of certain rights over others, their respective precedence, has been related to this debate, but is not identical with it. As discussed in the next section, it is problematic to attempt, from within a liberal tradition, to rank human rights or fundamental liberties – such that (allegedly, 'first generation') civil and political rights, for example, are given precedence over (allegedly, 'second generation') social, economic, or cultural rights. Yet, in a sense, the Asian values debate has brought the 'liberal West' and the 'authoritarian East' together in their respective questioning of the indivisibility of human rights. From the position of the spokespersons of certain Asian states, the bundle of social, economic, and cultural rights had priority over civil and political rights. One prominent line of argument defended the idea of a trade-off between civil and political rights, on the one hand, and socio-economic rights, on the other. This argument held that, once political order and stability had been achieved in a state, one major precondition for economic growth had been put in place – this growth, in turn, being seen as the material precondition for the enjoyment of human rights. Kausikan suggested that poverty, insecurity, and in-stability bred human rights abuses:

> Good government may well require, among other things, detention with-out trial to deal with military rebels or religious and other extremists; curbs on press freedom to avoid fanning racial tensions or exacerbating social divisions; and draconian laws to break the power of entrenched interests in order to, for example, establish land reforms. Those are the realities of exercising authority in heterogeneous, unevenly modernized, and imperfectly integrated societies with large rural populations and shallow Western-style civic traditions. (Kausikan 1993: 38)

We shall return to this argument in Chapter 3.

This argument, however, leads directly to another aspect of the perceived all-encompassing comprehensivenesses of human rights. Arguably, there are certain forms of violence that are not 'visible' to human-rights discourse. This is an argument put forward forcefully by Rajagopal (2003). According to Rajagopal (2003: 195), human-rights discourse 'approves certain forms of violence and disapproves certain other forms'. He argues that, for example, violence committed in the name of development remains 'invisible':

> For example, the mass deportation of 1.5 million people from Phnom Penh by the Khmer Rouge in 1975 is argued to be a crime against humanity,

while the massive evictions/deportation of 33 million development refugees from their homes due to development projects such as dams, by the
Indian Government, is simply seen as the 'social cost' (if at all) of
development. (Rajagopal 2003: 195)

Rajagopal analyses the human rights discourse, as it was appropriated
and developed by elite groups in the 'Third World', as being deeply
implicated in the process of state formation, that is, the formation of
the post-colonial state, and also the bureaucratic 'etatisation' of the
political communities and social life. For him, 'development', insti-
gated not just by the 'West' but pursued by indigenous classes in the
'Third World' as part of the nationalist project, while legitimising the
role of the state also caused serious human rights violations among the
deprived sections of those countries. In a sense, there has been a high
degree of complicity between elites in the 'West' and the state elites in
the 'Third World' regarding the end of development, with disagreement focusing on the predominance of the market (West) or the state
(Third World) in this process. While the developed countries deny that
the right to development is a proper 'right', but see it rather as a goal
or a claim, for the political and economic elites in developing countries
in means 'the right to expand their economies rapidly, irrespective of
environmental or other costs' (Rajagopal 2003: 220). We can notice
here a similarity with the position taken by the Asian NGOs in their
Charter, as mentioned above. This particular argument is part of
Rajagopal's more general thesis that it is by no means the case that the
human rights discourse provides those people suffering oppression
and marginalisation in the Third World with an adequate language
of resistance or the appropriate political strategy of resistance. Or
perhaps one should rather say: it has been politically very difficult to
force Third World governments to adhere to the statement in the
Vienna Declaration (1993: Part I, para. 10): 'While development
facilitates the enjoyment of all human rights, the lack of development
may not be invoked to justify the abridgement of internationally
recognized human rights.' Indeed, for Rajagopal it is the social movements in the Third World that are the carriers of an alternative form of
resistance and protest, an alternative way of questioning the violence
of the post-colonial developmental state that is *not grounded in a
western human-rights ideology* (Rajagopal 2003: 254, italics in the
original). Their struggles demonstrate, so Rajagopal asserts, 'how
individuals and communities can achieve their autonomy and self-
realisation by participating in shaping their own destiny without being

constrained by theoretical boundaries' marked by the human rights and development discourses (Rajagopal 2003: 253). We shall see in Chapter 3 that such 'movement politics' is not the same as the activities of 'civil society'.

There is certainly sufficient ground for being weary of 'totalising' or 'essentialist' accounts of 'culture' or 'civilisation' (in the singular) and good reason for interrogating any claims put forward by states, governments, groups, or individuals authoritatively to 'represent' and 'interpret' such a culture. There is also good reason to appreciate that the pursuit of human rights must be cognisant of cultural and religious traditions: '[D]ifferent cultural and civilizational traditions have diverse notions of what it means to be human and for humans to have rights' (Baxi 1998: 153). Baxi correctly points out that without a notion of human suffering there can be no understanding of human rights. Such notions of human suffering are not wholly legible, so he claims, outside cultural scripts: 'Since suffering, whether defined as individual pain or as social suffering is egregious, different religions and cultural traditions enact divergent hierarchies of "justifications" of experience and imposition of suffering, providing at times and denying at others, language to pain and suffering' (Baxi 1998: 153). We may, therefore, not arrive at a universally shared hierarchy of suffering or evil. Nevertheless, we may, so he claims, share in a universal aspiration to bring new civility to power among states and human societies and 'to place the prerogative of the construction of this evil beyond the hands of those who have the power to inflict it' (Baxi 1998: 154). According to Baxi, such sharing must emerge from cross-, or inter-, or trans-cultural understanding – an idea of inter-cultural dialogue that we have encountered in Chapter 1 in connection with our discussion of cosmopolitanism.

We may also look at the question of 'universality' pragmatically. One way of doing so is by reference to Reservations, Understandings and Declarations (RUDs). RUDs are very common to international human rights treaties (Goodman 2002; Neumayer 2006).[2] Article 2, paragraph 1(a) of the Vienna Convention on the Law of Treaties defined 'reservations' as follows: 'a unilateral statement, however phrased or named, made by a state, when signing, ratifying, accepting, approving or acceding to a treaty, whereby it purports to exclude or to modify the legal effect of certain provisions of the treaty in their application to that State.' Eric Neumayer (2006) analysed RUDs for a number of human rights covenants: the International Covenant on Civil and Political Rights (ICCPR); the International Covenant on

Economic, Social and Cultural Rights (ICESCR); the International Convention on the Elimination of All Forms of Racial Discrimination (ICERD); the Convention against Torture and Other Cruel, Inhuman or Degrading Treatment or Punishment (CAT); the Convention on the Elimination of All Forms of Discrimination Against Women (CEDAW); and the Convention on the Rights of the Child (CRC). On the basis of RUDs registered by 2001, Neumayer arrives at the following data for all six treaties together: (a) total number of RUDs: 635; (b) the number of countries which have registered RUDs: 243; (c) the number of States Parties: 925; and (d) an average share of States Parties with RUDs: about 26 per cent. This means that about a quarter of the states which signed the treaties also registered qualifications. There is a degree of ambiguity as to what counts as a RUD: while Neumayer, for example, lists for the ICCPR 175 RUDs submitted by forty-three states (on the basis of data up to 2001), Goldsmith and Posner (2005: 129) list fifty-three states with a total of 202 RUDs (on the basis of data up to 2004). It is noteworthy, but outside the scope of the current discussion, that most RUDs are registered by Western 'liberal democracies', and not 'authoritarian' states. Goldsmith and Posner offer the following explanation for this fact: since there is no self-enforcement or external enforcement mechanism attached to the treaty, the costs of ratifying the ICCPR are low. Liberal democracies can agree to ratification because 'their practices already conform to the treaty. And when, at the margins, they do not, the incongruence can easily be resolved by RUDs' (Goldsmith and Posner 2005: 127). Authoritarian states can join the treaty because 'they suffer little cost from their non-compliance, and liberal democracies do so because, after RUDs, they can comply simply by following their prior domestic practices' (Goldsmith and Posner 2005: 128). It is well known, for example, that the United States – to the extent that they join international human rights conventions at all – use RUDs extensively in order to ensure that, wherever there may arise any doubt, the American Constitution has precedence over any human rights agreements (Buergenthal 1995: 290–8). In the light of the ubiquity and volume of RUDs, Baxi (1998: 149–50) argues that '[t]he "fine print" of reservations usually cancels the "capital font" of universality'.

If it is, indeed, the case that for 'liberal democracies' human rights treaties confirm their practices (and allow for qualified reservations where this is not fully so), and that for authoritarian states non-compliance is, mostly, cost free – then we may ask why there are such treaties at all? Goldsmith and Posner argue that the treaties clarify the human rights standards of the liberal states, laying down, in effect, the 'standard of civilisation' of the current age: 'Although the liberal states' use of RUDs muddies the standard a bit, there is a clear core of agreement that less liberal states can use as a guide. States know that when they comply with this guide or code, they are more likely to receive benefits (however small) and to avoid diplomatic, military, and economic pressure (even if minor)' (Goldsmith and Posner 2005: 130).

The thesis that human rights are the new 'standard of civilisation' (SOC) evidently qualifies any argument concerning universality of (non-coerced) shared values (Donnelly 1998). In the past, so the argument goes, a distinction could be made between 'Christian' and 'non-Christian' states, or between 'civilised' and 'non-civilised' ('barbarian') ones – a distinction that bestowed (selective) international legitimacy upon states and informed processes of inclusion and exclusion from membership in the community of nations. In the present age, it is the observance of human rights that legitimises states. Fidler (2001: 141) argues that the nineteenth-century 'standard of civilisation' was an attempt to solve a practical problem as to how to enable states to trade and interact and how best 'to protect Western citizens' life, liberty, and property in non-Western regions . . . The SOC solved the practical problem by requiring that non-Western countries treat Western citizens according to Western legal standards, which meant protections for life, dignity, property, and freedom of commerce, travel, and religion.' 'Capitulations' that established 'extraterritorial jurisdiction' by exempting Western nationals from the criminal and civil jurisdiction in a non-Western country on the basis that the non-Western nation did not have civilised political and legal systems were the main tool for the imposition of SOC (Fidler 2001: 143). However, '[t]he standard did not require that non-Western countries have specific forms of government or treat their own nationals in the same way that Western nationals had been treated. The standard did not require non-Western countries to be fully Western' (Fidler 2001: 145).

The new SOC, however, does not have such a limited design. Fidler (2000: 409) speaks of the 'standard of liberal, globalised civilisation' for which he enumerates six principles:

(1) respect for basic civil and political human rights; (2) respect for the importance of civil society in domestic and international politics; (3) commitment to democratic governance; (4) commitment to the 'rule of law' domestically and internationally; (5) commitment to free market

economics domestically and free trade and investment internationally; and (6) commitment to developing and applying science and technology to political, legal, economic, and social challenges. The imprint of liberalism is apparent because liberalism focuses on the freedom of the individual, democracy, the 'rule of law', market economics, economic interdependence between nations, and the power of reason to improve human welfare through scientific advance.

We shall see in Chapter 3 how the idea of Western liberal-capitalist 'modernity', if not 'civilisation', does indeed underpin the promotion of 'democratic governance'. In Chapter 4, we shall discuss how attempts to enforce human rights standards and the norms of Western democracy result in re-definitions of sovereignty that justify violent interventions.

Human Rights and Democracy: Liberal Perspectives

Is it possible to whittle down, as it were, the comprehensive list of human rights that we find in the Vienna Declaration? Is there a 'core' set of human rights? Perhaps there is agreement on 'basic' human rights that one must never derogate? Article 4 of the International Convention on Civil and Political Rights provides for the suspension of human rights in cases of emergency:

> In time of public emergency which threatens the life of the nation and the existence of which is officially proclaimed, the States Parties to the present Covenant may take measures derogating from their obligations under the present Covenant to the extent strictly required by the exigencies of the situation, provided that such measures are not inconsistent with their obligations under international law and do not involve discrimination solely on the ground of race, colour, sex, language, religion or social origin.

The article then details those articles where no derogation may be made: Articles 6 (genocide); 7 (torture); 8 (slavery); 11 (no imprisonment on the ground of inability to fulfil a contractual obligation); 15 (which contains the principle of *'nullum crimen, nulla poena sine lege'*); 16 (the right to be recognised everywhere as a person before the law); and 18 (freedom of thought, conscience, and religion). Pursuing such a strategy of identifying a hard core of rights that may not be derogated – based on Article 4 of the ICCPR – would, manifestly, amount to turning an 'emergency' into the 'rule'. Bilahari Kausikan, then the director of the East Asian and Pacific Bureau of the Ministry of Foreign Affairs of Singapore, suggested that there was a core of international law that would not admit of derogation on any grounds, and this core consisted of genocide, murder, torture, and slavery (Kausikan 1993). While there may, indeed, be a consensus on condemning these acts, this list is of little help given the huge range of human rights claims that it would simply disregard (Teson 1985: 871–5).

If we approach this question from a liberal (or 'Western') perspective, then we may indeed discern attempts to identify a 'liberal' core of human rights. One such attempt may build upon a liberal conceptualisation of liberty, the other on a particular conceptualisation of liberal democracy.

First, there is the argument on human rights and liberty. We begin with Michael Ignatieff's discussion of human rights. He makes a number of assumptions that are ultimately derived from liberalism. He suggests that, first, there is likely to be continued disagreement among people from different cultures about what is good, but likely to be a higher degree of agreement about what is insufferably, unarguably wrong. Secondly, such agreement may centre on the belief that human rights are above all about protecting the essential exercise of human agency, that is, 'the capacity of each individual to achieve rational intentions without let or hindrance . . . When individuals have agency, they define for themselves what they wish to live and die for' (Ignatieff 2001: 57). Human rights, thus, lay down 'the irreducible minimum beyond which group and collective claims must not go in constraining the lives of individuals' (Ignatieff 2001: 69). Thirdly, human rights thus define the universal interests of the powerless, 'namely, that power be exercised over them in ways that respect their autonomy as agents' (Ignatieff 2001: 68). While human rights adjudicate in cases where the individual finds themself confronted by external constraints and impositions, rights claims themselves may clash and create conflicts since there is no unarguable order of moral priority in rights claims. It follows for Ignatieff that '[w]e cannot speak of rights as trumps' (Ignatieff 2001: 20). Indeed, '[a]t best, rights create a common framework, a common set of reference points that can assist parties in conflict to deliberate together' (Ignatieff 2001: 20). Human rights entail the fundamental moral commitment to deliberation (Ignatieff 2001: 94).

In its understanding of the rational individual as a bearer of rights that protect him or her against external encroachments on his or her agency, Ignatieff's starting point is undoubtedly 'Western' and 'liberal'. Ignatieff's position is also decidedly 'liberal' in that he sees human rights as 'a systematic agenda of "negative liberty", a tool kit against oppression' (Ignatieff 2001: 57). As a 'thin' theory of the human good, this 'liberal individualism':

> defines and proscribes the 'negative', that is, those restraints and injustices that make any human life, however conceived, impossible; at the same time, it does not prescribe the 'positive' range of good lives that human beings can lead. Human rights is morally universal because it says that all human beings need certain specific freedoms 'from'; it does not go on to define what their freedom 'to' should consist in. (Ignatieff 2001: 75)

Yet this argument does not assist us in delimiting the scope of human rights. The reason lies in Ignatieff's neglect in developing a theory of human agency. Arguably, such a theory must be built around the interdependency of the civil, political, economic, and cultural rights of the individual as a member of collectivities.

Ignatieff's starting point is not wholly dissimilar from Friedrich Hayek's reformulation of classical liberalism. Hayek suggests that liberty 'describes the absence of a particular obstacle – coercion by other men' (Hayek 1960: 19). Defining liberty as a particular kind of relationship among individuals, Hayek moves away from a Hobbesian understanding of freedom as 'the absence of external impediments' and the logical corollary that it is equivalent to effective power to do whatever we want. Whether a person is free or not, he argues:

> does not depend on the range of choice but on whether he can expect to shape his course of action in accordance with his present intentions, or whether somebody else has the power so to manipulate the conditions as to make him act according to that person's will rather than his own. Freedom thus presupposes that the individual has some assured private sphere, that there is some set of circumstances in his environment with which others cannot interfere. (Hayek 1960: 13)

To be in a state of liberty means that it is up to us to decide what use we shall make of the circumstances in which we find ourselves. This freedom is premised on the existence of the rule of law. Hayek contends that 'when we obey laws, in the sense of general abstract rules laid down irrespective of their application to us, we are not subject to another man's will and are therefore free' (Hayek 1960: 153). More specifically, Hayek lists as the essential conditions of freedom that human beings are subject only to the same laws as all their fellow citizens, that they are immune from arbitrary confinement, that they are free to choose their work, and that they are able to own and acquire property. Once an individual enjoys these conditions, no other individual or group of individuals can coerce him or her to do their bidding (Hayek 1960: 20).

Hayek accepts that the notion of equality before the law leads to the demand that all individuals should also have the same share in making the law, and he concedes that this is the point where traditional liberalism and the democratic movement meet. Yet he claims that their main concerns are nevertheless different: 'Liberalism . . . is concerned mainly with limiting the coercive powers of all government, whether democratic or not, whereas the dogmatic democrat knows only one limit to government – current majority opinion' (Hayek 1960: 103). Hence, for Hayek, the essential political problem is not who governs but what government is entitled to do. To put it differently, Hayek's concern lies primarily with the protection of the right to be left alone ('negative liberty') and the protection of the sphere within which individuals can act unobstructed by others, not with ensuring the right to be involved in defining and deciding public matters ('positive liberty'). Yet, how convincing is this conceptualisation of ('negative') liberty? Ignatieff (2001: 57) muddies the issue by arguing that '[h]uman rights matter because they help people to help themselves. They protect their agency' – only then to go on to define 'agency' (by which he means 'more or less what Isaiah Berlin meant by "negative liberty"') as 'the capacity of each individual to achieve rational intentions without let or hindrance' (2001: 57). Arguably, 'the capacity to achieve rational intentions' is not just a matter of a person not being interfered with, but of possessing resources that can be deployed in the pursuit of those intentions, desires or interests.

In an important early statement that contributed to the theoretical turn in English liberalism, the political philosopher T. H. Green argued that true freedom was not merely the absence of restraint or compulsion but the maximum of power for all members of society alike to make the best of themselves. State interference in the form of legislation with the freedom of individuals to enter into mutually binding private contracts was seen as 'justified on the ground that it is the business of the state . . . to maintain the conditions without which a free exercise of the human faculties is impossible' (Green [1881] 1986: 202). Without absence of coercion and compulsion, there could be no freedom. But for true freedom to be achieved, the lack of compulsion had to be complemented by a positive capacity of self-determination that would enable individuals to be the author of their life plan. In this context, the state was not defined as a force potentially opposed to individual liberty, as it was in classical liberalism. Rather, the state was perceived as an instrument of freedom in that it provided each individual with certain conditions of life in which he or she could realise their powers and capabilities, and could strive towards their 'possible self' (Collini 1979; Freeden 1978: 53, 58 and *passim*; Nicholson 1990: 140–65; Vincent and Plant 1984: 59). Self-development of the individual thus remained the aim of liberalism, but it was now seen to depend upon the creation of enabling opportunities by a 'welfare' state. Vincent and Plant have succinctly summed up the thoughts of the 'British Idealists', who profoundly influenced this new liberalism. The Idealists assumed that:

> all citizens had capacities and powers, not necessarily of equal amounts or types, yet each should be given an equal footing and a means to develop what they possess. The aim was to achieve the fulfilment of the largest number through their citizenship. The state, by providing the basic services, was attempting to equalize opportunities through intervention. The rationale for this was liberty and citizenship based upon a modicum of economic welfare and a share in civilization. (Vincent and Plant 1984: 87)

However, this endorsement of equality of opportunity went hand-in-hand with the acceptance of diversity of reward. As against the Benthamite form of utilitarianism, which defined human beings as rational maximisers, the Idealists put forward a conceptualisation of human nature that stressed their desire to develop their capacities and powers. The state's task was to assist in this self-development. At the same time, however, this advocacy of an interventionist state was complemented by an endorsement of 'the operation of the market, with the inequalities to which that would lead and the ownership of private property and the right of accumulation. At the most, their welfare proposals were attempts to ensure that those who were disadvantaged would be able to act more effectively in the market' (Vincent and Plant 1984: 175).

Both liberal traditions share the view of human beings as bearers of rights. But they differ in their understanding of what these rights are. Do they contain only those (civil) rights that protect the individual against coercion by other individuals or by the state? Or do these rights also contain rights to resources and means of self-development? Such 'positive' rights would then comprise economic and social rights that provide individuals with legal claims to positive benefits from the state or another collective body. For example, both traditions would agree that there is a right to life, but they would debate whether this means the right not be killed ('negative' right) or the right to the means of life ('positive' right). They would agree that there is a right to property, but they would debate whether this is a right not to have legitimately acquired property interfered with or a right to the ownership of resources.

As we have already seen, Hayek defined freedom as the absence of intentional restraint and coercion. Only intentional action by a person or group of persons can result in the restriction of liberty. Liberty 'does not assure us of any opportunities'; it does not assure us of any possession of resources and powers; liberty is the freedom from coercion (Hayek 1960: 19). According to this view, the distribution of resources as a result of the operation of a free market, for example, cannot be seen as a limitation of liberty by those disadvantageously affected, because 'the outcomes of markets are an unintended and unforeseen result of individual decisions to buy and sell, taken on all sorts of different grounds' (Plant 1992: 115). To counter this argument, 'positive rights' liberals do not have to confront it head-on. They may ask: why should we attach (moral) importance to the idea of non-interference in the first place? Why is the liberty from coercion of overriding significance for our understanding of freedom? The answer is: because non-interference allows persons to do what they want to do; because it gives them space to be autonomous agents. However, does it make sense to speak of protection from interference in an action that one has no means of undertaking (Gould 1988: 198)? Should individuals not, therefore, be given the means that empower them to act based on this (alleged) autonomy? Does this right to free agency not require for its effective realisation a set of positive conditions and provisions? Is it not the case that the notion of agency, which is inherent in the idea of 'negative rights', involves the provision of resources that contribute, for example, to the physical integrity, survival, well-being, education, etc. of the agent? As Plant (1992: 117) argues, 'the right to freedom being secured by rights to these sorts of resources is not freedom to do any individual thing but rather a general set of conditions which will enable the individual to go on to the sorts of things s/he wants to do.' Plant states that, for free agency to be conceivable, negative rights to the freedom from coercion and interference have to be complemented by positive rights to resources which are necessary conditions for acting in a purposeful way at all:

> If we respect a person as a person because of this capacity of rational agency then we cannot both respect him in virtue of this capacity and be indifferent to the question of whether he has the means of exercising that

capacity. Hence the principle of respect for persons, which lies behind the negative idea of rights, combined with a limited argument in favour of positive liberty, would yield a set of positive rights to those resources which would satisfy his basic needs of agency. (Plant 1992: 129)

Inevitably, such a provision of positive rights involves some interference with the activities of individuals. But the exercise of civil and political rights is also premised on interference. These rights, insofar as they can be infringed, not only by the state, but by other people as well, need positive protection by the state to forestall their violation. Gould (1988: 196) argues that the right, for example, of property, as a civil right, would justify laws against the restraint of trade by monopolies, and thus would constitute an interference with the property rights of (and their exercise by) certain economic interests to protect the exercise of this right by other interests. And the right of free speech, too, may involve a curb on media monopolies.

'Positive' liberty as manifested in the right to resources is thus entrenched in the notions of agency and autonomy. These notions, in turn, give moral significance to 'negative liberty' as that right that is meant to assure a sphere of individual autonomy. And 'positive' liberty as manifested in the political right to be involved and participate in public affairs is entrenched in the concept of freedom under the rule of law. This is for the simple reason that legal norms that can be enforced by political sanctions are seen as legitimate only insofar as they guarantee the autonomy of the individuals living under them. This guarantee, in turn, is premised on a democratic procedure that installs the individual as lawmaker, acting and deliberating in public in accord with her or his fellow citizens. But the individual can act as deliberating lawmaker only if he or she is protected in their personal autonomy by 'negative liberties' that guarantee their dignity and inviolability as a person; individual self-determination is a necessary condition of political self-determination.

This argument regarding the interdependency of political and social rights – even in a theory of liberal (and moral) individualism such as the one espoused by Ignatieff – can be further expanded. The 'entry of the masses' into politics raised an important question for liberalism: how to square their status of economic dependency with the theoretical assumptions regarding personal autonomy (Ashford 1986: Chapter 2). One answer was to redefine freedom in a 'positive' way and to embrace a policy of social reform, ultimately issuing in the institutionalisation of social rights in the 'welfare' state:

Their [the masses'] private autonomy had to be secured through reliance on the status guarantees of a social-welfare state. This derivative private autonomy, however, could function as an equivalent of the original private autonomy based on control over private property only to the degree to which the citizens, as clients of the social-welfare state, came to enjoy status guarantees that they *themselves* bestowed on themselves in their capacities as citizens of a democratic state. This in turn appeared to become possible in proportion to the expansion of democratic control to the economic process in its entirety. (Habermas 1993: 434–5)

To the extent that the 'redistributive policies' of the 'welfare' state (in pursuit of the goal of ensuring 'agency') are premised on the availability of resources, 'welfare' rights presuppose a 'right of development'.

Habermas's distinction between 'private' and 'public' autonomy is pivotal for the systematic location of human rights within his political and legal theory. This argument leads us to a consideration of the relationship between human rights and democracy. Habermas does not accept that there is a choice to be made between a 'republican' embrace of 'public' autonomy in the form popular sovereignty and a 'liberal' understanding of (human) rights as the legitimate barriers against the 'tyranny of the majority' manifested in its (potential) encroaching upon inviolable spheres of individual freedom. Against the 'liberal' claim that there are inviolable pre-political liberties of private persons, the 'republicans' conceived of such rights as attaining legitimacy to that extent only that they express the ethical self-understanding and sovereign self-determination of the political community. Against this complementary one-sidedness, Habermas insists that 'the idea of human rights . . . must neither be merely imposed on the sovereign legislator as an external barrier nor be instrumentalized as a functional requisite for democratic self-determination' (Habermas 2002: 200). For Habermas, the central question that needs to be answered is: 'What rights must free and equal citizens mutually accord one another if they want to regulate their common life legitimately by means of positive law?' (Habermas 2002: 200; see also Habermas 1994).

Habermas offers an answer in his discourse theory that may be understood as a development of Kant's republicanism based on a theory of (intersubjective) communication. Jean Cohen and Andrew Arato (1992: 347–8) argue that the principle of discourse ethics postulates: '[A] norm of action has validity only if all those possibly affected by it (and by the side-effects of its application) would, as participants in a practical discourse, arrive at a (rationally motivated) agreement that such a norm should come into or remain in force'. This principle signals in which respect discourse ethics goes beyond Kant's position. Kant had proposed in the *Metaphysics of Morals* that there is one basic right: 'Any action is *right* if it can coexist with everyone's freedom in accordance with a universal law, or if on its maxim the freedom of choice of each can coexist with everyone's freedom in accordance with a universal law' (MM, 387 [6: 230]). In essence, Kant proposed that everyone should engage in a kind of thought experiment in order to determine what each could will without self-contradiction to be a universal law for all. For Kant, rational consent was basically the recognition of the reasonableness of the moral law. This is, in effect, a monological perspective: no actual discussion has to be held; it suffices to determine whether based on impartiality laws would gain the consent of reasonable men. Discourse ethics, on the other hand, privileges a dialogical attitude by grounding the validity of a norm on an agreement that issues out of a practical discourse in which all those affected by the norm must give 'good reason' for its validity.

The principle of discourse ethics contains a theory of political legitimacy as it proposes to consider as legitimate only those norms and institutions that would be validated by individuals who engage in a practical discourse. For such a practical dialogue to produce a rational consensus on the validity of a norm and its institutionalisation, procedures must be in place that give all those affected an equal chance to partake in the public deliberations and to initiate and continue communication unconstrained by economic or political force based on a mutual and reciprocal recognition of each by all as autonomous, rational subjects whose claims will be acknowledged if supported by valid arguments. As Seyla Benhabib argues, it follows from this principle that:

> [t]here are no *prima facie* rules limiting the agenda of conversation, nor the identity of the participants, as long as each excluded person or group can justifiably show that they are relevantly affected by the proposed norm under question. In certain circumstances this would mean that citizens of a democratic community would have to enter into a practical discourse with non-citizens who may be residing in their countries, at their borders, or in neighboring communities if there are matters which affect them all. Ecology and environmental issues in general are a perfect example of such instances when the boundaries of discourse keep expanding because the consequences of our actions expand and impact increasingly on people. (Benhabib 1994: 31)

From this perspective, discourse ethics is a theory of democratic legitimacy. However, it goes beyond a concern with legitimation by, first, raising the question of the composition of the democratic constituency, or the membership of the dialogic community, and, secondly, by insisting on problematising the boundary between 'public' and 'private' since all issues are seen as potentially open to public debate (Habermas 1996: Chapters 7–8). Only in and through unrestrained public deliberation will we discover what are our deepest disagreements. Only after public deliberation has been radically opened up in such a way that citizens feel free to introduce any and all moral arguments into the conversational field, will we be in a position 'to agree upon a mutually acceptable definition of the problem rather than reaching some compromise consensus' (Benhabib 1992: 98–9).

Deliberative politics is thus the mode of arriving at a common understanding of what are matters of public concern in a society 'in which a homogeneity of background convictions cannot be assumed and in which a presumptively shared class interest has given way to a confused pluralism of competing and equally legitimate forms of life' (Habermas 1993: 445). Such a practical discourse has a number of presuppositions. First, it is premised on mutual respect among the participants in the dialogue. The right of all human beings capable of speech and action to be participants in the moral conversation must be recognised. And so must their 'symmetrical rights to various speech acts, to initiate new topics, to ask for reflection about the presuppositions of the conversation, etc.' (Benhabib 1992: 29) As Gutmann and Thompson (1990: 76–86) have shown this amounts to a veritable 'political virtue'. Among other things, citizens must cultivate a disposition towards openness that allows for the possibility of change in their own moral position. In addition, they must also embrace an 'economy of moral disagreement' in that they seek that rationale that minimises rejection of the position they oppose; they must search for significant points of convergence between their own understandings and those of citizens whose positions they reject. Implicit in this argument is the further assumption that the capacity of individuals for autonomous judgment based on mutual respect will be enhanced through participation in practical discourses. Individual autonomy is thus achieved only in and through participation in public political discourse. There is a second presupposition. The formation and expression of an autonomous individual moral conscience is premised 'on a process of cultural modernisation that resulted in 'a communicative opening-up of the sacred core of traditions, norms and authority to processes of questioning and the replacement of a conventionally based normative consensus by one that is communicatively grounded' (Cohen and Arato 1992: 435). On one level, this simply means that individuals have to accept that the 'ought' cannot just be identified with the 'socially valid'. The 'ought' is thus opened up to critical questioning and hypothetical reasoning. On another level, it means the critique of any role-conformist attitudes and the sustained endeavour at reflexive role-distance, because such a critical self-reflexivity is the necessary precondition for embarking on an open-ended process of discursive will formation that involves a willingness to reverse perspectives and to reason from the other's (others') point of view. In short, discourse ethics presupposes 'modernity'. Finally, practical discourse assumes the institutionalisation of a distinct set of rights of the individual interlocutor. This prerequisite leads us into Habermas's concern with human rights. This discourse 'presupposes autonomous individuals with the capacity not only to be self-reflective regarding their own values but also to challenge any given norm from a principled standpoint' (Cohen and Arato 1992: 357). Discourse ethics, therefore, has a conception of the individual as a person whose autonomy, dignity, and uniqueness set external limits to any discourse. The protection of the autonomy of the individual moral conscience demands the institutionalisation of inviolable personality rights and 'negative liberties'. Whereas these rights and liberties ground discourse ethics, rights of communication such as free speech and expression as well as rights of assembly, association, and participation, are constitutive of discourse and thus implied by discourse ethics. The first set of rights identifies the subjects who have the right to have rights. The rights of communication and association point to the legitimate domain of formulating and defending rights and constitute that public space in which the rights securing personal autonomy and privacy can be reflexively justified.

Cohen and Arato (1992: 441) emphasise three complexes of rights: those securing the socialisation of the individual (protection of privacy, intimacy, and the inviolability of the person); those concerning cultural reproduction (freedoms of thought, press, speech, and communication); and those ensuring social integration (freedom of association and assembly). These clusters of rights ensure the possibility of the reproduction of identities, traditions, and solidarities, respectively, and form the basis of the societal institutions of reproduction, in particular, of those institutions that allow for public communication and publicity and collective action (voluntary associations).

Hence, discourse ethics is premised on a conceptualisation of human beings as bearers of rights. As such, our relations to each other must be governed by the norms of formal equality and reciprocity: 'If I have a right to X, then you have the duty not to hinder me from enjoying X and conversely . . . The moral categories that accompany such interactions are those of right, obligation and entitlement, and the corresponding moral feelings are those of respect, duty, worthiness and dignity' (Benhabib 1992: 159). However, Benhabib shows that this notion of the 'generalised other' as rights-bearer does not mean that we have to conceptualise 'the other' as an 'unencumbered self' (Sandel 1982). On the contrary, the significance of constitutive communities for the formation of one's self-identity should be accepted: 'The "I" becomes an "I" only among a "we", in a community of speech and action. Individuation does not preclude association; rather it is the kinds of associations which we inhabit that define the kinds of individuals we will become' (Benhabib 1992: 71). Thus, we enter into public discourse not as 'generalised others', but as 'concrete others' with a concrete history, identity and affective-emotional constitution. Our relation as 'concrete others' is governed by the norms of equity and complementary reciprocity:

> [E]ach is entitled to expect and to assume from the other forms of behavior through which the other feels recognized and confirmed as a concrete, individual being with specific needs, talents and capacities . . . The moral categories that accompany such interactions are those of responsibility, bonding and sharing. The corresponding moral feelings are those of love, care and sympathy and solidarity. (Benhabib 1992: 159)

The individuals who participate in public deliberation are thus best conceptualised as both bearers of rights and hence worthy of universal moral respect. They are 'concrete' persons immersed in ethical relations whose actions are not exclusively guided by the principles of justice, but also by an awareness of what is expected of them in virtue of the kind of social bonds that tie them to each other (Benhabib 1992: 10).

For Habermas, then, discourses are the place where a reasonable political will can develop. If this is so, 'then the presumption of legitimate outcomes, which the democratic procedure is supposed to justify, ultimately rests on an elaborate communicative arrangement: the forms of communication necessary for a reasonable will-formation of the political law-giver, the conditions that ensure legitimacy, must be legally institutionalized' (Habermas 2002: 201). The internal relation between democracy and the rule of law consists of two features:

> [O]n the one hand, citizens can make appropriate use of their private autonomy only if, on the basis of their equally protected private autonomy, they are sufficiently independent; on the other hand, they can realize equality in the enjoyment of their private autonomy only if they make appropriate use of their political autonomy as citizens. (Habermas 2002: 202)

The complementary relationship between public and private autonomy is not fixed once and for all. According to Habermas, the citizens themselves must 'debate and deliberate in public, and . . . have parliaments democratically decide, on the kind of rights they regard as necessary for the protection of both private liberties and public participation' (Habermas 1995: 851). There is a paradox: neither may human rights just be imposed on popular sovereignty as an external constraint, nor must popular sovereignty be able arbitrarily to dispose of human rights. For Habermas, the solution to this paradox is 'that human rights must be conceived in such a way that they are enabling rather than constraining conditions for democratic self-legislation' (Habermas 1995: 852).

We must beware, however, Habermas's conceptualisation of 'popular sovereignty'. Habermas argues that from the point of view of discourse ethics the success of deliberative politics does not depend on a collectively acting citizenry as in the classical republican tradition but on the institutionalisation of the corresponding procedures and conditions of communication. In line with this argument, Habermas analyses popular sovereignty as retreating into democratic procedures and the legal implementation of their demanding communicative presuppositions (Habermas 1996: 486–7, 505–6). According to Habermas, such a 'proceduralized popular sovereignty and a political system tied in to peripheral networks of the political public sphere go hand-in-hand with the image of a *decentred society*' (Habermas 1996: 298). This view was concisely formulated by Seyla Benhabib:

> [T]he procedural specifications of [the deliberative model of democracy, RA] privilege a *plurality of modes of association* in which all affected can have the right to articulate their point of view. These can range from political parties, to citizens' initiatives, to social movements, to voluntary associations, to consciousness-raising groups, and the like. It is through the interlocking net of these multiple forms of associations, networks and organisations that an anonymous 'public conversation' results. It is central to the model of deliberative democracy that it privileges such a public

sphere of mutually interlocking and overlapping networks and associations of deliberation, contestation and argumentation. The fiction of a general deliberative assembly in which the united people expressed their will belongs to the early history of democratic theory; today our guiding model has to be that of a medium of loosely associated, multiple foci of opinion-formation and dissemination which impact each other in free and spontaneous processes of communication. (Benhabib 1994: 35)

In Chapter 1 we encountered Habermas's notion of a decentred world society of global citizens. In the light of the present discussion, this decentred world society is best understood as made up of a plurality of modes of association at the global level. As we shall see in Chapter 5, this is the idea of cosmopolitan democracy, global civil society, and global governance. The truly 'anonymous' public conversation at the global level together with the stringent conditions for validity claims for 'moral norms' (as well as the multicultural composition of 'national' political communities of a multiplicity of ethico-political communities) privilege 'human rights' as the hard core of 'moral norms' which have found universal acceptance. However, I tried to suggest in the first part of this chapter, whether there is, indeed, an agreement on the universality of human rights – and of which rights specifically – is very much politically contested.

The reference to the 'multicultural' composition of modern societies brings a final consideration, now concerning 'cultural' rights, into our purview. The Western human rights discourse, as we have seen, is founded on the commitment to equal respect for persons and to recognition of their dignity – howsoever this belief in human dignity is grounded. This commitment does not extend to their beliefs only, but also to their culture which gives those beliefs 'significance' and 'meaning'. Slighting their culture, holding it up to ridicule, denying its value, hurts them, subjects them to contempt and thus offends their dignity (Raz 1994: 72). Bhikhu Parekh has summarised this argument succinctly:

> Since human beings are culturally embedded, respect for them entails respect for their ways of life. One's sense of personal identity is closely bound up with one's language, characteristic modes of thought, customs, collective memories, and so on, in a word with one's culture. To ignore the latter is to denude the individual of what constitutes him or her as a particular kind of person and matters most to him or her, and that is hardly a way of showing respect. (Parekh 1994: 103)

Whether there are any limits to 'cultural rights' or how they are best institutionalised are, of course, central questions in the debate on 'multiculturalism' – and we shall address some of the pertinent issues in this debate in Chapters 4 and 5. Suffice it to reiterate that even a liberal theory of human agency must accept the interdependency and indivisibility of human rights and the impossibility of an *a priori* ranking of these rights and thus, implicitly, a differentiation between a hard core of 'basic' rights (which is set apart from peripheral rights). This is the reason why Ignatieff is right when he argues that it would be wrong to think of human rights as being above politics, as 'a set of moral cards whose function is to bring political disputes to closure and conclusion' (Ignatieff 2001: 21).

In Chapter 3, we shall pursue one theme that has already been mentioned in this chapter: the globalisation of democracy based on an (allegedly) emerging norm of the entitlement to democratic governance grounded in the human rights discourse.

Notes

1 The bibliographical details of the constitutions, charters, conventions, covenants, declarations, and documents to which reference will be made in the first section of this chapter, are summarily given in this note. For ease of access, wherever possible I refer to a web site or web page:

African (Banjul) Charter on Human and Peoples' Rights: www.africa-union.org/official_documents/Treaties_%20Conventions_%20Protocols/Banjul%20Charter.pdf.
Asian Human Rights Charter: www.material.ahrchk.net/charter/mainfile.php/eng_charter/.
Bangkok Declaration: www.unhchr.ch/html/menu5/wcbangk.html.
Catholic Bishops' Conference: www.catholic-ew.org.uk/resource/hr01/.
Charter of the United Nations: www.un.org/aboutun/charter/index.html.
Constitution of the United Nations Educational, Scientific and Cultural Organization (UNESCO): www.portal.unesco.org/en/ev.php-URL_ID=15244&URL_DO=DO_TOPIC&URL_SECTION=201.html.
Declaration on the Right to Development: www.unhchr.ch/html/menu3/b/74.htm.
Draft Declaration on the Rights of Indigenous Peoples: www.unhchr.ch/huridocda/huridoca.nsf/(Symbol)/E.CN.4.SUB.2.RES.1994.45.En?OpenDocument.
European Convention for the Protection of Human Rights (including the Protocols): www.hri.org/docs/ECHR50.html.
International Covenant on Civil and Political Rights: www.unhchr.ch/html/menu3/b/a_cescr.htm.
International Covenant on Economic, Social and Cultural Rights: www.unhchr.ch/html/menu3/b/a_ccpr.htm.

Pacem in Terris: www.vatican.va/holy_father/john_xxiii/encyclicals/documents/hf_j-xxiii_enc_11041963_pacem_en.html.

Pope John Paul II: www.vatican.va/holy_father/john_paul_ii/messages/peace/documents/hf_jp-ii_mes_14121998_xxxii-world-day-for-peace_-en.html.

United Nations General Assembly Resolutions: www.un.org/documents/ga/res/15/ares15.htm (1960) and www.un.org/documents/ga/res/25/ares25.htm (1979).

Universal Declaration of Human Rights: www.un.org/Overview/rights.html.

Universal Islamic Declaration of Human Rights: www.alhewar.com/ISLAMDECL.html.

Vienna Declaration and Programme of Actions: www.unhchr.ch/huridocda/huridoca.nsf/(Symbol)/A.CONF.157.23.En?OpenDocument

2 The following web sites are useful sources for up-to date information:

United Nations Treaty Collection Homepage at: www.untreaty.un.org.
United Nations High Commissioner for Human Rights at: www.ohchr.org/english/law/index.htm.
Other useful web sites are: www.bayefsky.com/docs/php/are/reservations and www.liberty-human-rights.org.uk/resources/policy-papers/policy-papers-2002/pdf-documents-dec-2002.pdf. (the latter site detailing reservations registered by the UK governments).

3

The Globalisation of Democracy: The Right to Democratic Governance

The Entitlement to Democratic Governance in International Law and International Politics

In this chapter I wish to concentrate on one entitlement to which I have already referred in the previous discussion, the (emerging) right to democratic governance. In 'classical' international law, how a state was constituted internally was considered to be outside the purview of international law and to be irrelevant when it came to international recognition of a state. In one of the leading textbooks of international law at the turn of the last century, Lassa Oppenheim noted that '[t]he Law of Nations prescribes no rules as regards the kind of head a state may have. Every State is, naturally, independent regarding this point, possessing the faculty of adopting any Constitution it likes and of changing such Constitution according to its discretion' (Oppenheim 1905: 403 [§341]). In his 'General Theory of Law and State', the international law scholar, Hans Kelsen, answered the question as to under what circumstances a national legal order begins to be valid by stating that it 'begins to be valid as soon as it has become – on the whole – efficacious, and it ceases to be valid as soon as it loses this efficacy . . . The Government brought into power by a revolution or coup d'état is, according to international law, the legitimate government of the state, whose identity is not affected by these events' (Kelsen 1961: 220–1). This is an understanding of state legitimacy that was also expressed succinctly by Hersch Lauterpacht:

> It is a fundamental rule of international law that every independent state is entitled to be represented in the international sphere by a government which is habitually obeyed by the bulk of the population of that state and which exercises effective authority within its territory. To deny that right to a state is to question its independence. For this reason states are not normally concerned with the changes in the composition in the form of government which occur in other countries . . . This applies to changes

taking place both in conformity with and in violation of the constitutional laws of the state in question. (Lauterpacht 1947: 87)

As recently as 1986, the International Court of Justice ruled in the *Nicaragua* case that '[t]he Court cannot contemplate the creation of a new rule opening up a right of intervention by one state against another on the ground that the latter has opted for some particular ideology or political system' (*Military and Paramilitary Activities in and against Nicaragua (Nicaragua v. United States)*, ICJ Reports 1986, at para. 263).[1] The court concluded that, in the absence of a specific legal obligation, there was no commitment on the part of the state to hold free and fair elections (para. 261).

Yet, in a seminal article in 1992, Thomas Franck spoke of an emerging democratic entitlement norm, with democracy beginning to be seen 'as the *sine qua non* for validating governance':

> Increasingly, governments recognise that their legitimacy depends on meeting a normative expectation of the community of states. This recognition has led to the emergence of a community expectation: that those who seek the validation of their empowerment patently govern with the consent of the governed. Democracy, thus, is on the way of becoming a global entitlement, one that increasingly will be promoted and protected by collective international processes. (Franck 1992: 46)

Franck asked whether 'global society is ready for an era in which *only* democracy and the rule of law will be capable of validating governance' (Franck 1992: 49)? That this (alleged) emerging right to democratic governance must be seen in the context of the human rights discourse has been made quite explicit by the former Secretary-General of the United Nations, Boutros Boutros-Ghali. He stated in 1993 that 'democracy is the political framework in which human rights can best be safeguarded . . . a democracy is the political system which best allows for a free exercise of individual rights' (Boutros-Ghali as quoted in Cerna 1994/1995: 291).

These sentiments found reflection in the Vienna Declaration and Programme of Action of 1993. A particularly noteworthy feature of the Vienna Declaration is the exhortation of states and the international community to promote democracy, human rights, and fundamental freedoms:

> Democracy, development and respect for human rights and fundamental freedoms are interdependent and mutually reinforcing. Democracy is based on the freely expressed will of the people to determine their own political, economic, social and cultural systems and their full participation

in all aspects of their lives. In the context of the above, the promotion and protection of human rights and fundamental freedoms at the national and international levels should be universal and conducted without conditions attached. The international community should support the strengthening and promoting of democracy, development and respect for human rights and fundamental freedoms in the entire world. (I: 8)

Governments, the United Nations system as well as other multilateral organisations are urged to give priority to national and international action to promote democracy, development, and human rights – although non-governmental organisations (that is, 'civil society actors') are also recognised as important actors in this endeavour (while, at the same time, considered to be deserving of human rights protection themselves) (I: 38):

> Special emphasis should be given to measures to assist in the strengthening and building of institutions relating to human rights, strengthening of a pluralistic civil society and the protection of groups which have been rendered vulnerable. In this context, assistance provided upon the request of Governments for the conduct of free and fair elections, including assistance in the human rights aspects of elections and public information about elections, is of particular importance. Equally important is the assistance to be given to the strengthening of the rule of law, the promotion of freedom of expression and the administration of justice, and to the real and effective participation of the people in the decision-making process. (II: 68)

These values and principles that informed the Vienna Declaration were again confirmed in the United Nations Millennium Declaration, the resolution adopted by the General Assembly in September 2000: the sovereign equality of all states, respect for their territorial integrity and political independence, the right to self-determination of peoples and non-interference in the internal affairs of states, respect for human rights and fundamental freedoms (Article 4). At the same time, however, it was proclaimed that no effort will be spared 'to promote democracy and strengthen the rule of law, as well as respect for all internationally recognized human rights and fundamental freedoms, including the right to development' (Article 24). Manifestly, how to combine state sovereignty, on the one hand, and the enforcement of human rights (including the entitlement to democratic governance), on the other hand, is the main challenge.

Steven Wheatley (2002: 234) has succinctly summed up this emerging trend and its importance:

[W]hilst it might not yet be possible to identify a general obligation on states to introduce democratic government, the evolving internal aspect of the right of a people to self-determination, the increasing numbers of states party to universal and regional human rights instruments (which all contain provisions on free and fair elections and political participation), and recognition that a democratic system of government may not legitimately be replaced by an authoritarian one, indicates [sic] a progressive and irreversible movement to a world community of democratic states.

If a 'right to democratic governance' is indeed emerging, then the grounds for a state's legitimacy have shifted dramatically: '[I]nternational notions of legitimacy are no longer oblivious to the origins of governments, but have come to approximate quite closely those conceptions embodied in theories of popular sovereignty' (Fox 2000: 90). It is no longer sufficient for a state's legitimacy that its government is in effective control of its people and territory. It is no longer the case that, as long as there is a sufficiently high degree of effective control, what happens within a state's borders is protected from scrutiny by the principle of state sovereignty. Rather, for a state to be considered legitimate it has become necessary to demonstrate that it rules with the consent of the governed (Beutz 2003: 387–91; Fox 2003; Marks 2000: 38; McFaul 2004; Rich 2001). This is the position to which the claim of an entitlement to democratic governance amounts.

Before we discuss the significance of such a new democratic governance norm, however, we should review the documentary evidence for the claim of its emergence. In our review of human rights pronouncements in Chapter 2, we have already encountered references to political rights, and rights to political participation in particular. Not all of these references need to be rehearsed again in the current discussion. No doubt, of singular importance has been Article 21 of the Universal Declaration of Human Rights of 1948:

1. Everyone has the right to take part in the government of his country, directly or through freely chosen representatives.
2. Everyone has the right of equal access to the public service in his country.
3. The will of the people shall be the basis of the authority of government; this will shall be expressed in periodic and genuine elections which shall be by universal and equal suffrage and shall be held by secret vote or by equivalent free voting procedures.

Article 25 of the International Covenant on Civil and Political Rights of 1966/1976 reiterates the importance of the right and the opportunity of citizens to take part in the conduct of public affairs, either directly or through freely chosen representatives; to vote and be elected in fair and free elections; and to have access, without discrimination, to public services in their country. This right to participate in government is also enshrined in Article 23 of the American Convention on Human Rights and in Article 13 of the African (Banjul) Charter (which also speaks of 'the right of access to public property and services'). The importance of free elections at reasonable intervals by secret ballot on the basis of freedom of expression is also asserted in the First Protocol to the European Convention in Article 3. It should be noted, however, that the principle of popular sovereignty is expressly articulated only in the Universal Declaration (Article 21(3)).

In its Charter of 1948, the Organization of American States (OAS) expressed the conviction that 'representative democracy is an indispensable condition for the stability, peace and development of the region' (Preamble) and proclaimed as one of its essential purposes the promotion and consolidation of representative democracy – which had to be pursued, however, 'with due respect for the principle of nonintervention' (Article 2(b)). Clearly, from early on there was a realisation of outside interference in the domestic affairs of a state being justified with reference to promoting, consolidating, or upholding democracy. This 'classical' concern with 'non-intervention' into the domestic affairs of a state was buttressed in the Charter by the assertion in Article 1 that the purpose of the organisation was that of achieving peace and justice, the promotion of solidarity, strengthened collaboration, and the defence of the sovereignty, territorial integrity, and independence of each member state. International order, Article 3 maintained, 'consists essentially of respect for the personality, sovereignty, and independence of States'. In its Resolution 1080 of 1991 on 'Representative Democracy', the OAS reaffirms that 'the solidarity of the American states and the high aims which it pursues require the political organization of those states to be based on effective exercise of representative democracy' (Preamble). The OAS Inter-American Democratic Charter of 2001 confirmed as one of the purposes of the OAS the promotion and consolidation of representative democracy 'with due respect for the principle of nonintervention' (Preamble). It stated, in a language reminiscent of that used in human rights charters, that '[t]he peoples of the Americas have a right to democracy and their governments have an obligation to promote and defend it' (Article 1). Democracy is declared to be indispensable 'for the effective exercise of fundamental freedoms and human rights in their universality, indivisibility and interdependence' (Article 7). Representative democracy is defined as a system where respect for human rights and fundamental freedoms was secured and whose essential elements included:

> access to and the exercise of power in accordance with the rule of law, the holding of periodic, free, and fair elections based on secret balloting and universal suffrage as an expression of the sovereignty of the people, the pluralistic system of political parties and organizations, and the separation of powers and independence of the branches of government. (Article 3)

The Charter also contains a 'democracy clause' which established that any unconstitutional alteration or interruption of the democratic order in a member state would constitute 'an insurmountable obstacle to its government's participation' in the activities of the organisation (Article 19). In spirit, this clause is similar to the 'essential elements' clauses which we will encounter below in connection with the EU's treaty policies *vis-à-vis* third countries.

After the breakdown of state socialism in central and eastern Europe after 1989 and the collapse of the Soviet Union in 1991, the last decade of the twentieth century witnessed much diplomatic activity in the area of the promotion of democracy. One of the most detailed statements has been the Document of the Copenhagen Meeting of the Conference on the Human Dimension of the Conference on Security and Co-operation in Europe of June 1990. The participating states recognise that:

> pluralistic democracy and the rule of law are essential for ensuring respect for all human rights and fundamental freedoms, the development of human contacts and the resolution of other issues of a related humanitarian character. They therefore welcome the commitment expressed by all participating States to the ideals of democracy and political pluralism as well as their common determination to build democratic societies based on free elections and the rule of law. (Preamble)

On the basis of this general commitment, the Document sets out an extraordinarily comprehensive and detailed list of political and civil rights and their specific institutional manifestations. The participating states 'solemnly declare that among those elements of justice which are essential to the full expression of the inherent dignity and of the equal and inalienable rights of all human beings are the following':

- free elections . . .
- a form of government that is representative in character, in which the executive is accountable to the elected legislature or the electorate;
- the duty of the government and public authority to comply with the constitution and to act in a manner consistent with law;

- a clear separation between the State and political parties; in particular, political parties will not be merged with the State;
- the activity of the government and the administration as well as that of the judiciary will be exercised in accordance with the system established by law . . .
- military force and the police will be under the control of, and accountable to, the civil authorities;
- human rights and fundamental freedoms will be guaranteed by law and in accordance with their obligations under international law;
- legislation, adopted at the end of a public procedure, and regulations will be published, that being the condition for their applicability . . .
- all persons are equal before the law and are entitled without any discrimination to the equal protection of the law . . .
- everyone will have an effective means of redress against administrative decisions, so as to guarantee respect for fundamental rights and ensure legal integrity;
- . . .
- the independence of judges and the impartial operation of the public judicial service will be ensured . . . (I: 5(1–12))

After confirming that 'the will of the people, freely and fairly expressed through periodic and genuine elections, is the basis of the authority and legitimacy of all government' (I: 6), the Document then details a list of institutions and procedures that are to ensure that popular sovereignty is a reality. According to the Document, the participating states will:

- hold free elections . . .
- permit all seats in at least one chamber of the national legislature to be freely contested in a popular vote;
- guarantee universal and equal suffrage to adult citizens;
- ensure that votes cast are cast by secret ballot or by equivalent free voting procedure, and that they are counted and reported honestly with the official results made public;
- respect the right of citizens to seek political or public office, individually or as representatives of political parties or organizations, without discrimination;
- respect the right of individuals and groups to establish, in full freedom, their own political parties or other political organizations and provide such political parties and organizations with the necessary legal guarantees to enable them to compete with each other on a basis of equal treatment before the law and by the authorities;
- ensure that law and public policy work to permit political campaigning to be conducted in a fair and free atmosphere in which neither

administrative action, violence nor intimidation bars the parties and the candidates from freely presenting their views and qualification, or prevents the voters from learning and discussing them or from casting their vote free of fear of retribution;

- provide that no legal or administrative obstacle stands in the way of unimpeded access to the media on a non-discriminatory basis for all political groupings and individuals wishing to participate in the electoral process;
- ensure that candidates who obtain the necessary number of votes required by law are duly installed in office and are permitted to remain in office until their term expires or is otherwise brought to an end in a manner that is regulated by law in conformity with democratic parliamentary and constitutional procedures. (I: 7(1–9))

This procedural understanding of democracy is then complemented by the recognition of the importance of civil society groups to democratic politics (III: 26), and the protection of minorities in particular: the states 'recognize the important role of non-governmental organizations, including political parties, trade unions, human rights organizations and religious groups, in the promotion of tolerance, cultural diversity and the resolution of questions relating to national minorities' (IV: 30).

The CSCE 'Charter of Paris for a New Europe' of November 1990 reasserts the commitment to representative democracy but also addresses the question of the economic order of the 'new Europe'. In the section on 'Economic Liberty and Responsibility', the Charter asserts that:

[t]he free will of the individual, exercised in democracy and protected by the rule of law, forms the necessary basis for successful economic and social development. We will promote economic activity which respects and upholds human dignity.

Freedom and political pluralism are necessary elements in our common objective of developing market economies towards sustainable economic growth, prosperity, social justice, expanding employment and efficient use of economic resources. The success of the transition to market economy by countries making efforts to this effect is important and in the interest of us all. It will enable us to share a higher level of prosperity which is our common objective. We will co-operate to this end.

The 'increased integration, involving the acceptance of disciplines as well as benefits, into the international economic and financial system' together with the encouragement of free enterprise and trade, increased and diversified according to GATT rules, are considered to be an undisputed necessity (see the section entitled 'Economic Co-operation). Democracy, capitalism, and integration in the world economy and its disciplinary institutions are seen as an interdependent whole.

The Copenhagen Document gestured towards the duty of the participating states to promote and defend democracy through concerted international action. The states recognise, so it was asserted:

> their responsibility to defend and protect, in accordance with their laws, their international human rights obligations and their international commitments, the democratic order freely established through the will of the people against the activities of persons, groups or organizations that engage in or refuse to renounce terrorism or violence aimed at the overthrow of that order or of that of another participating State. (I: 6)

In 1991, the Document of the Moscow Meeting of the Conference on the Human Dimension of the Conference on Security and Co-operation in Europe – formulated under the vivid impression that the then recent attempted coup in Moscow had made – was much more explicit. The participating states 'categorically and irrevocably declare that the commitment undertaken in the field of the human dimension of the CSCE are matters of direct and legitimate concern to all participating States and do not belong exclusively to the internal affairs of the State concerned' (Preamble). The principle of non-intervention in the domestic affairs of a state does not apply when democracy is in peril: the constitution of a state is a matter of concern for all states and in international law. Indeed, the Document invites the participating states to withhold recognition from governments which have come to power as a result of the overthrow of a legitimately elected government by undemocratic means (II: 17.2): *de facto* and efficient control, it is implied, is no longer a sufficiently sound reason for granting international recognition to a government.

In 1999 the UN Commission on Human Rights passed a resolution on the 'Promotion of the Right to Democracy' and another one on 'Promoting and Consolidating Democracy' in 2000, the second of which being turned almost word by word into a resolution by the General Assembly, again under the title 'Promoting and Consolidating Democracy'. It is noteworthy that the title of the 1999 Resolution was controversially discussed, with Cuba's effort to delete the term 'right to democracy' being defeated by twenty-eight votes to twelve, with thirteen abstentions. In the text itself, the term 'right to democracy' is not repeated. The 2000 Resolution, in turn, does not use the expression 'right of democracy' at all. It is, however, significant that the resolution speaks explicitly of the right to vote in 'a free and fair process . . . open to multiple parties' (para. 1(d)(ii)). A functioning, 'genuine' democracy could no longer be argued to exist in a single-party system.

As the titles of these resolutions indicate, the promotion of democracy around the world had moved by now to centre-stage in diplomatic rhetoric. In the words of the United Nations Millennium Declaration: 'We will spare no effort to promote democracy and strengthen the rule of law, as well as respect for all internationally recognized human rights and fundamental freedoms, including the right to development' (V: 24). The Millennium Declaration commits all states '[t]o strive for the full protection and promotion in all our countries of civil, political, economic, social and cultural rights for all [and] [t]o strengthen the capacity of all our countries to implement the principles and practices of democracy and respect for human rights, including minority rights' (V: 25).

The resolution in 2000 of the General Assembly also contains quite a detailed definition of 'good governance', one of the buzz words in democracy promotion. 'Good governance' is said to refer to:

- improving the transparency of public institutions and policy-making procedures and enhancing the accountability of public officials;
- taking legal, administrative, and political measures against corruption, including by disclosing and investigating and punishing all those involved in acts of corruption and by criminalising payment of commissions and bribes to public officials;
- bringing government closer to the people by appropriate levels of devolution;
- promoting the widest possible public access to information about the activities of national and local authorities, as well as ensuring access by all to administrative remedies, without discrimination; and
- fostering high levels of competence, ethics, and professionalism within the civil service and its co-operation with the public, *inter alia*, by providing appropriate training for members of the civil service. (1(f))

Yet another statement on democracy, its promotion and consolidation was issued by the newly founded 'Community of Democracies' in its Warsaw Declaration of June 2000. 'Recognizing the universality of democratic values', the Declaration rehearses the definition, by now well established, of democracy as representative democracy and an understanding of democracy as an institutional and procedural arrangement. It emphasises in particular the need to reject ethnic and religious hatred, violence and other forms of extremism. The signatories commit themselves to the promotion of civil society, 'including women's organizations, non-governmental organizations, labor and business associations, and independent media in their exercise of their democratic rights'. They assert their willingness to 'collaborate on democracy-related issues in existing international and regional institutions, forming coalitions and caucuses to support resolutions and other international activities aimed at the promotion of democratic governance. This will help to create an external environment conducive to democratic development.' The Community of Democracies' 2005 Santiago Statement on 'Cooperating for Democracy' reaffirms the importance of developing links between governments and civil society groups (see its section 1: 'Democratic Governance and Civil Society').

Given the centrality of elections to the definition of the (emerging) right to democratic governance, it cannot be a surprise that the question of electoral assistance became a concern in international politics and diplomacy. The General Assembly of the United Nations passed several resolutions concerned with 'Enhancing the effectiveness of the principle of periodic and genuine elections' (A/Res/44/146; A/Res/45/150; A/Res/46/137). In 1991, pursuant to General Assembly resolution 46/137 of December 1991, the UN established the Electoral Assistance Unit (re-designated as the Electoral Assistance Division (EAD) in 1994).

The objectives of the United Nations electoral assistance are essentially two-fold:

1. to assist Member States in their efforts to hold credible and legitimate democratic elections in accordance with internationally recognised criteria established in universal and regional human rights instruments; and
2. to contribute to building the recipient country's institutional capacity to organise democratic elections that are genuine and periodic and have the full confidence of the contending parties and the electorate. (*Cf.* web site of the UN Department of Political Affairs)

Aware of concerns over the violation of the international legal norm of non-intervention, the UN is at pains to assert that its 'activities in the field of electoral assistance are conducted in conformity with the basic principles of the sovereign equality of States and respect for their territorial integrity and political independence . . . Assistance activities are carried out only where requested by national authorities of member States and broadly supported by the people of the country concerned' (http://www.un.org/Depts/dpa/ead/ea_content/ea_context.htm).

In October 2005, a Declaration of Principles for International Election Observation was published. It was endorsed, *inter alia*, by the African Union, the Commonwealth Secretariat, the Council of Europe, the European Commission, the Inter-Parliamentary Union, the Organization of American States, the Organization for Security and Cooperation in Europe, and the United Nations Secretariat. In the Declaration, international election observation is defined as:

> the systematic, comprehensive and accurate gathering of information concerning the laws, processes and institutions related to the conduct of elections and other factors concerning the overall electoral environment; the impartial and professional analysis of such information; and the drawing of conclusions about the character of electoral processes based on the highest standards for accuracy of information and impartiality of analysis. International election observation should, when possible, offer recommendations for improving the integrity and effectiveness of electoral and related processes, while not interfering in and thus hindering such processes. International election observation missions are: organized efforts of intergovernmental and international nongovernmental organizations and associations to conduct international election observation. (Declaration Observation 2005: para. 4)

Respect for the sovereignty of the country holding the election and for the human rights of the people of the country require, so it is declared, that election observation is premised on an invitation by the state holding the election and on the observation of the national laws of the host country by the election observers (paras 9 and 12).

We shall now look briefly at how the European Union has started to translate the exhortation and expectation of the promotion of human rights and democracy into its policies. Neither a comprehensive overview nor an attempt to go beyond a summary statement on the position the EU takes with regard to promoting human rights and democratisation is intended.

The Convention for the Protection of Human Rights and Fundamental Freedoms by the Council of Europe in 1950 had introduced early on 'certain of the rights stated in the Universal Declaration' (Preamble) into the political consciousness and legal discourse in Europe. The Convention emphasised civil rights and the rule of law, but did not mention either political rights or group rights. However, in the First Protocol to the Convention of March 1952, Article 3 stated that 'the High Contracting Parties undertake to hold free elections at reasonable intervals by secret ballot, under conditions which will ensure the free expression of the opinion of the people in the choice of the legislature'. The Charter of Fundamental Rights of the European Union, proclaimed in Nice in 2000, in effect condenses the key rights of the International Covenants on Civil and Political Rights and on Economic, Social and Cultural Rights into a text that reflects the constitutive principles of liberal democracy, social market economy, and the welfare state whose confluence was a central result of western European history after 1945. The Treaty of Amsterdam – which came into force on 1 May 1999 – had already reaffirmed in its Article 6 that the European Union 'is founded on the principles of liberty, democracy, respect for human rights and fundamental freedoms and the rule of law, principles that are common to the Member States'. Article 49 proclaimed that the respect of these principles was also required by countries which apply for EU membership. Such a demand had been clearly expressed in the 'Copenhagen criteria' of 1993 based on which the European Union would make its decision on its enlargement through admission of the countries of central and eastern Europe. The membership criteria required that the candidate country would have had to achieve 'stability of institutions guaranteeing democracy, the rule of law, human rights and respect for and protection of minorities; the existence of a functioning market economy as well as the capacity to cope with competitive pressure and market forces within the Union; the ability to take on the obligations of membership including adherence to the aims of political, economic and monetary union'.

One important mechanism in the EU's attempt to promote human rights and pluralistic democracy is the 'essential elements' clauses which have been incorporated into all agreements of the EU with third countries since 1992. These clauses stipulate that recognition of, and respect for, human rights and fundamental freedoms as well as the democratic principles as laid down in the Universal Declaration on Human Rights inform the domestic and external policies of the parties to the agreement and thus constitute an 'essential element'.

The EU considers a violation of the 'democracy clause' as a 'material breach' of the treaty. According to Article 60 of the Vienna Convention on the Law of Treaties, 'a material breach of a bilateral treaty by one of the parties entitles the other to invoke the breach as a ground for terminating or suspending its operation in whole or in part'. The EU has thus reserved for itself the right to suspend or terminate treaties, such as bilateral aid agreements, in the event of the breakdown or overthrow of a democratically constituted government.

The Cotonou Agreement between the EU and the Group of African, Caribbean and Pacific States (ACP) in 2000 is a prime example of the EU's incorporation of human rights into its external policy. One key objective of the Agreement is the commitment 'to work together towards the achievement of . . . poverty eradication, sustainable development and the gradual integration of the ACP countries into the world economy' (Preamble). Mentioned explicitly as integral to achieving this objective are respect for all human rights and fundamental freedoms, including social rights, democracy based on the rule of law and transparent and accountable government (Preamble and Article 9). The development of a functioning democratic society and market economy as well as the emergence of an active and organised civil society are seen as essential preconditions for sustainable development (Articles 1 and 10). In the context of the current discussion, there are two significant statements in the Agreement. First, there is a mutual commitment to 'good governance':

> Good governance is the transparent and accountable management of human, natural, economic and financial resources for the purposes of equitable and sustainable development. It entails clear decision-making procedures at the level of public authorities, transparent and accountable institutions, the primacy of law in the management and distribution of resources and capacity building for elaborating and implementing measures aiming in particular at preventing and combating corruption. (Article 9.3)

Secondly, the Agreement explicitly brings non-state actors into the ACP–EU partnership – 'in order to encourage the integration of all sections of society, including the private sector and civil society organisations, into the mainstream of political, economic and social life' (Article 2). The Agreement recognises the complementary role of, and potential for contributions by, non-state actors to the development process. They should play a consultative role, be provided with financial resources so that they can support local development processes, be involved in the implementation of co-operation projects and programmes, and be provided with capacity-building support 'in order to reinforce the capabilities of these actors, particularly as regards organisation and representation, and the establishment of consultation mechanisms including channels of communication and dialogue, and to promote strategic alliances' (Article 4). The representatives of civil society organisations shall also be associated with the political dialogue to be institutionalised by the parties to the Agreement. The precondition for civil society organisations to be incorporated into the political process of implementing the objectives of the Agreement is their being organised and managed democratically and transparently (Art. 6).

The EU's policy of promoting human rights and democracy is also quite pronounced in the case of its policy towards the Middle East. One key pillar of this policy is the Euro-Mediterranean Partnership (EMP), also known as the Barcelona process. The Barcelona Declaration of November 1995 divides into three 'baskets' of issues: with regard to the development of a political and security partnership, the aim is to establish a common area of peace and stability; the creation of an area of shared prosperity is the objective of the development of an economic and financial partnership; and the development of human resources, the promotion of understanding between cultures and exchanges between civil societies is the objective of a partnership in social, cultural, and human affairs. Common respect for human rights and democracy; sustainable and balanced economic and social development, and the creation of a Euro-Mediterranean Free Trade Area by 2010 'with due observance of the obligations resulting from the WTO' and 'with due respect to the results achieved within the GATT negotiations'; and intercultural dialogue are the main goals in the three baskets, respectively. As in the Cotonou Agreement, the promotion of human rights and fundamental freedoms goes hand-in-hand with the promotion of a market economy (whose institutions, rules, and mechanism would have to become, in the medium term, compatible with those of the EU) and the incorporation of civil society groups into the process of political and economic transformation. These principles of the Barcelona Declaration – including the 'essential elements' clause – inform all of the Association Agreements that the EU and its Member States, on the one hand, and each of the Mediterranean partners, on the other hand, have been concluding since 1995.

The MEDA programme is the principal financial instrument of the EU to support the implementation of the Euro-Mediterranean Partnership. Most of its spending has gone into the EMP's second basket, economic and trade assistance. The objectives and rules for the implementation of Article 2 of the MEDA Programme make evident, however, the importance that the EU attaches to the incorporation of civil society groups. These objectives include:

- the participation of civil society and populations in the planning and implementation of development measures;
- strengthening democracy, respect for, and defence of, human rights, in particular through non-governmental organizations;
- the networking of universities and researchers, local communities, associations, political sciences foundations, trade unions and non-governmental organisations, the media, private business, and cultural institutions in the widest sense. (MEDA II Regulation – Annex II)

The reference to 'good governance' also stresses the importance of civil society groups: 'Good governance shall be promoted by supporting key institutions and key protagonists in civil society such as local authorities, rural and village groups, mutual-aid associations, trade unions, the media and organisations supporting business, and by assisting in the improvement of the capacity of the public administration to develop policies and manage their implementation' (section IV).

The ideas and principles, embedded as they are in the EU's perceived self-interest in peace, stability, prosperity, and free trade also underpin the EU's European Neighbourhood Policy, which was launched in March 2003 and offers a new framework for relations with the EU's new neighbours after its enlargement in 2004. According to the European Commission, 'democracy, pluralism, respect for human rights, civil liberties, the rule of law and core labour standards are essential prerequisites for political stability, as well as for peaceful and sustained social and economic development' (COM(2003) 104 final, p. 7). These are sentiments, or beliefs, now widely endorsed or, at least, pronounced, by the Western powers. In their statement on 'Partnership for Progress and a Common Future with the Region of the Broader Middle East and North Africa' of June 2004, the leaders of the G8 proclaimed that 'the values embodied in the Partnership we propose are universal. Human dignity, freedom, democracy, rule of law, economic opportunity, and social justice are universal aspirations' (para. 4). 'Our support for reform will involve government, business leaders and civil societies from the region as full partners in our common effort' (para. 5.7). 'State reform, good governance, and modernisation' are declared to be necessary ingredients for building democracy (para. 11.1). And economic reform is understood to mean the promotion of entrepreneurship, the expansion of trade and investment, an increased access to capital, support for financial reforms and the securing of property rights as well as the promotion of intra-regional trade (para. 11.3).

The Ideology of Democracy Promotion

On the basis of the documentary evidence just presented, we can now consider the significance of the policy of democracy (and human rights) promotion and the thesis that there is a right to democratic governance emerging in international law. To start with, 'democracy' is presented both as an 'ideal' and as a 'form of government'. The Universal Declaration on Democracy, adopted by the Council of the Inter-Parliamentary Union in September 1997, highlights these complementary aspects of democracy:

> As an ideal, democracy aims essentially to preserve and promote the dignity and fundamental rights of the individual, to achieve social justice, foster the economic and social development of the community, strengthen the cohesion of society and enhance national tranquillity, as well as to create a climate that is favourable for international peace. As a form of government, democracy is the best way of achieving these objectives . . . (para. 3)

As a 'form of government', democracy is understood to be built around the key institution of elections:

> The key element in the exercise of democracy is the holding of free and fair elections at regular intervals enabling the people's will to be expressed. These elections must be held on the basis of universal, equal and secret suffrage so that all voters can choose their representatives in conditions of equality, openness and transparency that stimulate political competition. To that end, civil and political rights are essential, and more particularly among them, the rights to vote and to be elected, the rights of freedom of expression and assembly, access to information and the right to organise political parties and carry out political activities. (IPU Declaration, para. 12)[2]

We have seen above that this institutional definition of democracy as 'representative democracy' based on elections and the institution of a parliament whose members have the requisite powers and means to express the will of the people by legislating, hold to account public officials, and ensure transparency of public life (paras 11, 14, and 15) prevails in all statements. It is an understanding of 'democracy' that is quite similar to Robert Dahl's conceptualisation of modern democracy as 'polyarchy'. For Dahl (1998: 85–6), the political institutions of modern representative democracy are:

1. elected officials who, as the representatives of the citizens, have control over government decisions about policy;

2. free, fair, and frequent elections of these officials;
3. freedom of expression so as to enable citizens to express themselves on matters of concern to them;
4. access to alternative sources of information so that citizens may gather information not emanating from public authorities;
5. associational autonomy which enables citizens to form independent associations and organisations, such as political parties or interest groups; and
6. citizenship which is non-discriminatory and inclusive to the extent that '[n]o adult permanently residing in the country and subject to its laws can be denied the rights that are available to others and are necessary to the five political institutions just listed'. (Dahl 1998: 86)

It needs emphasising, however, that this 'institutional', or 'procedural', understanding of democracy is not devoid of substantive commitments: there is clearly a discernible notion of 'right' or 'just' outcomes of democratic procedures.

There is, first, the ritualistic incantation of the pursuit and protection of human rights and fundamental freedoms. As has been argued in Chapter 2, there is, however, by no means a universal consensus of what should count as human rights or, to be more precise, what should count as 'basic' human rights, and what the idea of an 'interdependence' of human rights means 'in practice'. This disagreement is political and not the result of an as yet incomplete shared understanding of the 'proper' meaning of human rights. Human rights claims are contested political claims.

Yet, arguably there is a more profound 'substantive' connotation that can be teased out of 'human rights'. Earlier in this chapter, we have already come across the statement in the Vienna Declaration of 1993 (Part I, para. 8) that '[d]emocracy, development and respect for human rights and fundamental freedoms are interdependent and mutually reinforcing'. Clearly, however, if there are indeed interdependencies, these are very fraught ones. The relationship between democracy and human rights is problematic – as we discussed in the context of a presentation of Habermas's discourse ethics and model of deliberative democracy in Chapter 2. Democracy aims to empower the people so that their will shall be the basis of the authority of the government. In itself, democracy does not qualify, or constrain, the sovereign authority of the people. Human rights, on the other hand, aim to empower individuals – even if they may do so indirectly by bestowing rights on the collectives of which individuals are members. As a result of the empowering of individuals, human rights aim to limit the power of the people and their government: 'Beyond *who* ought to rule – which is indeed given a democratic answer – human rights are concerned with *how* the people (or any other group) rules, and *what* they do so in ruling' (Donnelly 1999: 619). To a significant degree, so Donnelly (1999: 620) suggests, human rights are 'profoundly anti-democratic'. It is the constitution of democracy as 'liberal' democracy that attempts to marry collective empowerment and individual rights. In a liberal democracy:

> [t]he democratic logic of popular rule operates only within the constraints set by individual human rights. The liberal commitment to individual rights more than the democratic commitment to popular empowerment makes contemporary liberal democracies rights-protective. (Donnelly 1999: 621)

While Donnelly thus sees a compatibility of human rights with 'liberal' democracy, he also suggests that such a 'liberal' democracy must be embedded in a welfare state. Markets which foster efficiency but not social equity or the enjoyment of individual rights for all have 'profound human rights defects' (Donnelly 1999: 630): 'Rather than ensure that every person is treated with concern and respect, markets systematically deprive some individuals in order to achieve the collective benefits of efficiency' (Donnelly 1999: 628). This argument leads to a position that we have already encountered in Chapter 2 in the discussion over 'negative' and 'positive' rights:

> Free markets are an economic analog to a political system of majority rule without minority rights. The welfare state, from this perspective, is a device to assure that a minority that is disadvantaged in, or deprived by, markets is treated with minimum economic concern and respect. Because this minority is shifting and indeterminate . . . these 'minority rights' are actually individual rights for all . . . Free markets, like pure democracy, sacrifice individuals and their rights to a 'higher' collective good. (Donnelly 1999: 630)

Donnelly's argument about the ambiguous interdependency of human rights, democracy, and development (understood as market-generated economic growth) can be pursued a step further. We have noted that, over the years, references to 'democracy' and 'human rights' have increasingly been embedded in a linguistic field that contained references to civil society, market economy, and good governance. In the context of the current discussion, a closer look at 'market economy' and 'good governance' brings to light another 'substantive' commitment that propels democracy promotion beyond a narrow concern with political institution building.

One can readily comprehend this 'substantive' concern when we read in the United States' National Security Strategy of September 2002 that the USA 'will actively work to bring the hope of democracy, development, free markets, and free trade to every corner of the world' (Foreword). In order to 'make the world not just safer but better', the United States will 'ignite a new era of global economic growth through free markets and free trade [and] expand the circle of development by opening societies and building the infrastructure of democracy' (chapter 1). One means for doing so is to tie development assistance to performance criteria as set out in a 'Millennium Challenge Account'. Money will be made available 'for projects in countries whose governments rule justly, invest in their people, and encourage freedom. Governments must fight corruption, respect human rights, embrace the rule of law, invest in health care and education, follow responsible economic policies, and enable entrepreneurship' (chapter 7). The Communique of the G8 leaders that they issued after their meeting in July 2005 in Scotland reiterates this position: aid is to be focused 'on low income countries which are committed to growth and poverty reduction, to democratic, accountable and transparent government, and to sound public financial management' (G8 Document 2005: para 30).

The concept of 'good governance' became a prominent feature of the discourse of international organisations in the 1990s. Both the World Bank and the International Monetary Fund used the concept to embed their neo-liberal reform agenda in a wider political framework. The structural adjustment programmes for the 'crisis-ridden' states in the 'developing', 'third' world of the 1970s and 1980s had been geared towards the 'rolling back' of the state, the curtailing of public spending and austerity measures, devaluation of currency, trade liberalisation and market-oriented policies through privatisation, and the creation of incentives for savings and investments more generally. Both the relative lack of success of those programmes and the growing indigenous resistance to these externally imposed policies and their politically and socially disruptive consequences led the World Bank and the IMF to rethink their strategy. The Bank suggested in 1989 that 'underlying the litany of Africa's development problems is a crisis of governance' (World Bank 1989: 60; see Williams 1996: 162–5). In a report in 1994, the World Bank identified three distinct aspects of governance, with only the last two being said to be relevant for the Bank's activities:

1. the form of political regime;
2. the process by which authority is exercised in the management of a country's economic and social resources for development; and
3. the capacity of governments to design, formulate, and implement policies and discharge functions. (World Bank 1994: xiv)

'Good governance' is thus epitomised 'by predictable, open, and enlightened policymaking (that is, a transparent process); a bureaucracy imbued with a professional ethos; an executive arm of government accountable for its actions; a strong civil society participating in public affairs: all behaving under the rule of law' (World Bank 1994: vii).

The objective of 'good governance' was defined as achieving private sector-led growth through creating an 'enabling environment for the private sector' by a state apparatus much reduced in size and 'equipped with a highly professional bureaucracy that is accountable for results' (World Bank 1994: 56). Civil service reform as much as reform of accounting and auditing practices in order to achieve financial accountability were seen to be necessary elements of improved governance. The creation of a legal framework for development that would encompass laws on property rights, companies (bankruptcy laws), banking, competition, foreign investment, and the establishment of regulatory bodies, was also seen as an essential element in a 'good governance' architecture. In its 1994 report, the World Bank was still relatively hesitant in referring to human rights as an element of 'good governance':

> Although human rights are in a larger sense indivisible, the World Bank, as an international financial institution, deals with those aspects of human rights relevant to its mandate. Except in situations where the violation of human rights has created conditions hostile to effective implementation of projects or has other adverse economic consequences, or where there are international obligations relevant to the Bank, such as those mandated by binding decisions of the UN Security Council, the World Bank does not take into account the political dimensions of human rights in its lending decisions. The World Bank's Articles of Agreement prohibit the institution from taking political considerations into account, interfering in the political affairs of any country, or being affected by the political form or orientation of a country. (World Bank 1994: 53)

Given that the Bank's governance agenda aimed at a complete transformation of 'Third World' states, its profession of political neutrality and concern for state sovereignty and the norm of non-interference were disingenuous. In its report on Development and Human Rights of 1998, the Bank now claimed that there was a linkage between governance, development and human rights:

> The World Bank helps its clients build better governance. This assistance in improving the efficiency and integrity of public sector institutions – from banking regulations . . . to the court system – has a singularly important impact on creating the structural environment in which citizens can pursue and continue to strengthen all areas of human rights. (World Bank 1998: 11)

The Bank's fundamental claim is that while it is accepted that sustainable development is impossible without human rights, 'the advancement of an interconnected set of human rights is impossible *without development*' (World Bank 1998: 2). The Bank's policies would, it was claimed, thus contribute to the promotion of human rights: 'By helping to fight corruption, improve transparency and accountability in governance, strengthen judicial systems, and modernize financial sectors, the Bank contributes to building environments in which people are better able to pursue a broader range of human rights' (World Bank 1998: 3).

As Antony Anghie (2005: 261–2) argued, 'by asserting that economic development depends on good governance, on the political system of a country, the Bank can justify formulating an entirely new set of initiatives that seeks explicitly to reform the political institutions of a recipient state, on the basis that such reform is necessary to active development, the central concern of the Bank.' Presenting neo-liberal policies as begetters of development – even as the only certain begetter – and tying human rights to (neo-liberal) economic development, as the Bank does, also supports the claim that the removal of profit-constraining regulations including those that support welfare needs or rights (for example, concerning health or education) does not amount to a violation of (economic, social, or cultural) 'human rights'. Rather, it is better understood as 'a necessary cost that a society must bear in order to produce a higher rate of investment, productivity, growth and profit' (Gathii 1999: 108–9). Since the enjoyment of human rights presupposes development, the individual person, in the medium term, will be better off.

The International Monetary Fund also produced statements in the 1990s on 'good governance' (Thirkell-White 2004a; 2004b). Michel Camdessus, then the IMF Managing Director, explained in an address to the United Nations Economic and Social Council in July 1997 that the IMF's approach to 'good governance' concentrated on those aspects 'that are most closely related to our surveillance over macro-economic policies – namely, the transparency of government accounts, the effectiveness of public resource management, and the stability and transparency of the economic and regulatory environment for private sector activity' (quoted in IMF 1997: iv). The report on 'Good Governance, the IMF's Role' suggests that 'promoting good governance in all its aspects, including ensuring the rule of law, improving the efficiency and accountability of the public sector, and tackling corruption [is] an essential element of a framework within which economies can prosper' (IMF 1997: v). Indeed, it is considered to be one of the major task of the IMF to impress on governments that poor governance can 'adversely affect private market confidence and, in turn, reduce private capital inflows and investment' (IMF 'Good Governance' 1997: 7).

The OECD Report on 'Participatory Development and Good Governance' of 1997 defines 'development' not exclusively in economic terms, but speaks about sustainable social and economic development, mentioning in particular poverty reduction, promoting gender equality, raising basic education and health standards, and reversing environmental degradation. To achieve these developmental goals, the emergence of more participatory, transparent and accountable societies is seen to be essential (OECD 1997: 3). This is a sentiment that was also expressed by the World Bank in its 'Development and Human Rights' report: 'People whose lives are affected – and possibly harmed – by development projects and policies must be able to participate in their design and implementation. This is critical not just for the obvious concern for equity and voice, but also for the bottom line: stakeholder participation leads to better projects and more dynamic development' (World Bank 1998: 26).

We should remain cognisant of the fact that the notion of 'participation' is connected to that of 'partnership'. This notion of 'partnership' is key to the Bank's Comprehensive Development Framework (CDF):

> Enabling the country to be in the driver's seat requires strong partnership among government, at all levels, including representative institutions, civil society, the private sector, donors, international agencies and other development actors. Such partnership should: (i) bring together, within a single framework, under government leadership, analytical and diagnostic work; (ii) align donor actions to the national strategy and promote selectivity to avoid duplication; (iii) reduce wasteful competition; (iv)

encourage common procedures and practices amongst all development partners; and (v) support the government's lead in managing aid coordination. (World Bank 2002, quoted in: Mercer 2003: 744–5)

'Partnership' is thus conceived as a dialogue on policy reforms that brings together government, donors, international financial institutions (such as the World Bank or IMF), and civil society organisations. However, it is also clear that such 'partnership' comes with a price: the 'recipient' countries must pursue the 'correct' policies. As the British Prime Minister, Tony Blair, said in 1999:

> Real development can only come through partnership. Not the rich dictating to the poor. Not the poor demanding from the rich. But matching rights and responsibilities together. The developed world has the responsibility to transfer resources, expertise and assistance to the developing world. The developing world has the right to expect this. But also a responsibility to ensure that resources are used productively for the benefit of the poor, not on misguided policies, white-elephant projects, or the cancer of corruption. (Tony Blair, quoted in: Mohan 2002: 146–7)

'Participation' and 'partnership' operates firmly within the parameters of neo-liberal policies. Not the definition of the kind of policies which should be pursued but how to pursue predetermined policies is at issue in these 'partnerships; or, as Mercer (2003: 748) put it: what is being sought are 'partnership' and 'participation' 'in the interests of achieving consensus on continued adjustment through democratic means'.

In the OECD report of 1997, 'democratisation' is seen as one aspect of 'participatory development'. Support for processes of democratisation in 'developing countries' should, therefore, include:

- helping build and strengthen pluralistic civil societies and independent professional media;
- helping improve the functioning of representative political institutions and supporting electoral processes in their various stages; and
- helping to secure the rights of women to education, land tenure and family planning services, and strengthening their decision-making in civil society and the political process. (OECD 1997: 6)

Without 'good governance', there can be no 'participatory development'. 'Good governance' comprises, for the OECD, 'the rule of law' inclusive of viable and effective legal, judicial, and law enforcement systems; public sector management based on transparency and accountability and aiming for improved accounting practices, improved budgeting and public expenditure management, and a reformed civil service; an anti-corruption strategy; and, finally, the reduction in 'excessive' military expenditure (OECD 1997: 6).

A noteworthy feature of the OECD report is the sustained and prominent attention paid to the idea (and the concept) of civil society and its role in processes of democratisation. Civil society is understood to denote 'a public space between the state and individual citizens (women and men) in which the latter can develop autonomous, organised and collective activities of the most varied nature' (OECD 1997: 7). Civil society is, thus, populated by a plurality of organisations, some of which may be best seen as 'self-interest' or 'self-help' organisations, pursuing the (particular or idiosyncratic) interests and concerns of their members, while others may best be seen as 'civic' or 'advocacy' organisations, pursuing (allegedly) broader objectives for the 'common good' (OECD 1997 Part II: 7). It is through these organisations that citizens are said to interact with the state and experience a degree of protection from any arbitrary acts by the state. At the same time, the state has the trust of the people and achieves real effectiveness to the degree that there is a thriving civil society. Indeed, an effective state and a vigorous civil society are mutually supportive: 'The state has a critical role with respect to civil society first of all in providing a functioning and accessible legal system and in ensuring the existence of a legally protected 'public sphere where civil society can develop with no undue interference. Without a vigorous civil society, the state is narrowly based and susceptible to capture by political and economic opportunists' (OECD 1997: 7). Civil society performs, it is suggested, a pivotal role in relation to democracy. As a result of its being composed by a variety of organisations, it serves the function of representing and maintaining a society's plurality, heterogeneity, and diversity. But it also serves an educational and advocacy function, 'as groups learn to articulate their aspirations, design their projects, negotiate and bargain, and form alliances' (OECD 1997: 7). Furthermore, civil society represents a countervailing force to government:

> A dense network of associations can play a role in monitoring the boundaries of the public sphere so as to prevent or challenge authoritarian rule . . . civil society provides channels for popular participation in the political process, acts as a mouthpiece for weak and marginalized groups, and builds bridges between various groups in society, a function which is relevant to conflict prevention and resolution. (OECD 1997 Part II: 8)

The UNDP policy document on 'Good governance and sustainable human development', published in 1997, also assigns a central role to civil society. Like the OECD document, this statement takes its starting point from a definition of development that emphasises eliminating poverty, creating jobs and sustaining livelihoods, protecting and regenerating the environment, and promoting the advancement of women. The UNDP document understands 'good governance' to ensure 'that political, social and economic priorities are based on broad consensus in society and that the voices of the poorest and the most vulnerable are heard in decision-making over the allocation of development resources' (UNDP 1997: I-4). Sustainable human development depends on the state, the private sector, and civil society playing their proper roles. The state must have institutionalised representative democracy so that it can both empower its citizens and offer protection. The private sector must create jobs that provide enough income to improve living standards. In order to achieve this goal, the state has to provide an enabling environment for private sector activities. However, '[s]trengthening the enabling environment for sustainable human development . . . depends not only on a state that governs well and a private sector that provides jobs that generate income. It also depends on civil society organisations that make political and social interaction easier and that mobilise society to participate in economic, social and political activities' (UNDP 1997: I-12). While the UNDP document explicitly assigns to civil society organisation most of the functions that are highlighted in the OECD report, there is one further function to which the OECD report does not specifically refer. Surveying reforms in public and private sector management (all of them familiar from the World Bank and IMF reports) which are considered to be necessary for achieving sustainable human development, the report highlights as 'crucial elements . . . macroeconomic policies, management of the external sector (trade, aid, investment and debt), market regulation and privatisation, social safety nets and resource management' (UNDP 1997: II-4). It is in the context of these reforms that the report speaks of civil society as 'the well-spring of the social capital – people working together for common purposes – that is essential for good governance. Civil society organisations can fill the vacuum left by the slimmed-downed state, and can advocate and monitor reforms that foster sustainable human development' (UNDP 1997: II-6).

In this development discourse, civil society is understood to be composed of, indeed, to be identical with, non-governmental organisations (NGOs). Community-based organisations or grassroots social movements do not figure in the 'partnership' dialogue. The idea of 'building' civil society amounts to a policy of funding NGOs by donor countries and donor institutions: civil society must be built 'top-down' rather than 'bottom-up'. Igoe (2003) has observed that for Africa there has been a massive shift of donor money away from the state towards the NGO sector. There has been a trend toward donor-funded service provision by NGOs which have taken on the function of the slimmed-down state. 'Indigenous' NGOs are started in order to obtain donor funding, and often their initiatives are exclusively donor driven. Such is their dependence on foreign donors that NGOs are forced to adjust their political, social, and civic agenda to suit those of their benefactors. For Makumbe (1998: 316), this situation amounts to a wholesale 'dependence of civil society on foreign funding'.

This situation can be observed in all developing countries. To give one example: in her case study on civil society in Tanzania, Mercer (2003: 754) observes that in the 1990s NGOs proliferated at a staggering speed. According to the government's official records the country had just over 800 NGOs in 1995, of which at least 75 per cent had been registered after 1990. Government figures show that five years later at least 2,900 NGOs had registered. According to estimates in Tanzania's anglophone press, the number of NGOs is closer to between 3,500 and 4,000. On the basis of her fieldwork, Mercer (2003: 754) asserts that many of these NGOs 'are either corrupt or have done little to alleviate poverty in the country'. In her estimation, 'Tanzanian NGOs are more likely to be concerned with the practicalities of service provision and income generation than with policy debates on debt and macroeconomics. Their dependence on donors is indicated by the types of work popular among NGOs, which mirrors the shifting priorities of the international donor community' (Mercer 2003: 754). As a matter of fact, 'donor and international NGO attention has concentrated on the small group of established, professionalised, elite-led, urban-based NGOs which are most likely to be successfully moulded in the donors' vision' (Mercer 2003: 755).

In an earlier review of the literature on 'civil society and democratization', Mercer (2002) notes that in these NGOs the urban middle classes are over-represented. Indeed, not infrequently, former civil servants, laid-off in the course of 'civil service reform', are the founders and act as the directors of NGOs. As Mohan (2002: 148) pointed out, over the last decade or so 'a tier of professional NGO-managers [has emerged] who use foreign aid and locally generated income as a means of achieving or consolidating their middle-class status'. In 1999, James Ohayo, a Kenyan financial analyst, described NGOs as follows:

> Against the backdrop of worsening poverty in Kenya, the NGO sector has recorded a dramatic increase in numbers, especially since the advent of political pluralism. By the mid-nineties, the formation of NGOs had become something of a fad among the professional upper-middle classes. The perception among ordinary folk was that this was a get-rich-quick gimmick dreamed up by the resourceful individuals to exploit gullible foreign donors. The sudden and visible change in the lifestyle of a number of founders and directors of NGOs during this period – and the fact that many such NGOs have proved inconsequential while their founders trot from one foreign mission to another, hat in hand, seeking donor funding to continue underwriting their opulent lifestyles – has not been lost upon Kenyans either. (quoted in Igoe 2003: 872).

Deriving their power from their gatekeeper position between local people and powerful outsiders – the donor countries and multilateral organisations – NGOs and their leaders are bound to become distant from their local constituencies (Hudock 1999; Weber 2002). The accountability and legitimacy of NGOs thus becomes an issue. Conflicts among and within NGOs over money and power thus characterise much of the dynamics of NGO politics (see, for example, Makumbe 1998; McIlwaine 1998; Mohan 2002). At the same time, the 'NGOisation' of civil society does, of course, mean that 'social movements', and thus non-institutionalised collective action, disappear from view. Rajagopal argues that, as a result of confining civil society to NGOs, one narrows one's view to those entities 'that do not command much legitimacy in the Third World' (Rajagopal 2003: 262). He argues that the taking account of social movement activities would allow us to transcend the narrow focus on creating and sustaining the institutions of 'electoral democracy'. For Rajagopal, the social movements are the true manifestation of 'actually existing democracy' in the Third World.

In our review of the use of the concept of 'good governance' we have noted that its definition entails a degree of ambivalence. We have also seen that 'good governance' is part of a discursive field that is populated by the words 'human rights', 'democracy', 'civil society', and 'development'. All these terms are, in turn, cross-referenced to 'market economy' and 'liberalisation' ('free market', 'free trade'). These conceptual, and political, linkages are still maintained in the current repackaging of 'good governance' and the shift from 'conditionality' to 'selectivity'. Whereas in the past donor institutions and countries attempted to induce good governance in a recipient country by providing aid that was attached to political conditionalities, nowadays – as President Bush's Millennium Challenge Account initiative made clear – 'good governance' has been defined as a prerequisite that a recipient country must meet before it qualifies for aid assistance (Nanda 2006).

Antony Anghie summed up well the significance of the 'good governance' discourse and the policies that it justifies:

> Good governance . . . provides the moral and intellectual foundation for the development of a set of doctrines, policies and principles, formulated and implemented by various international actors, to manage, specifically, the Third World state and Third World people. Attempts by Western states to promote 'good governance' in the Third World – and this involves far-reaching transformations, relating to promotion of democracy, free markets and the rule of law – are directed at reproducing in the Third World a set of principles and institutions which are seen as having been perfected in the West, and which the non-European world must adopt if it is to make progress and achieve stability. (Anghie 2005: 249; see also Gathii 1999/2000)

The (emerging) right to democratic governance does entail, therefore, considerably more than just a confirmation, and legal entrenchment, of the claim that 'the will of the people shall be the basis of the authority of government' – as Article 21 of the Universal Declaration of Human Rights of 1948 maintained. 'Representative democracy' and 'capitalism' go together. What Gills et al. (1993: 4) said about American foreign policy under Ronald Reagan of promoting 'low intensity democracy' also applies to the 'good governance' policies: '[T]he formal democratization is the political corollary of economic liberalization and internationalization'. Indeed, '[t]his "crusade" for democracy is the new ideological agenda of global capitalism' (Gills et al. 1993: 7).

The connection between 'democracy' and 'capitalism' in the period of 'democratisation' is worth pursuing. With regard to this question, generalised statements such as the following abound:

> Capitalism does not inevitably result in democracy – much less in human rights . . . But without capitalism, democracy appears to be impossible, and without democracy, human rights cannot be protected. Far more than an economic system, capitalism relies on certain presumptions about the rule of law, and capitalism creates modern citizens – both bourgeois and worker – who in the medium to long term demand human rights. (Howard-Hassmann 2005: 26)

We may usefully attempt to gain some clarification on this matter through a brief review of the literature on the questions of whether there are any 'prerequisites' of democratisation. How important are economic 'factors' and a particular kind of economic structure – namely capitalism – in the process of democratisation? If there are such 'structural' prerequisites, does this fact qualify the idea that democracy can be 'promoted' – as it were, by an act of pure political will?

Excursus: Prerequisites and Causes of Democratisation

The political concern with the 'promotion' of democracy which has gathered pace since the 1980s can usefully be placed within the wider context of the 'spread' of democracy. But can democracy be promoted from outside a state (or country) through international action and what does it require for such 'promotion' to be successful? A look at some influential analytical approaches in political science to explain democratisation allows us to pinpoint the assumptions that underpin the politics of democracy promotion.

One influential conceptualisation uses the simile of 'waves' for the (global) spread of democracy (Huntington 1991). In 'operationalising' democracy, Huntington emphasises the accountability of government to parliament and universal (adult) suffrage as two key institutional aspects of representative democratic government. He aims to identify the moment at which these two institutions have been established in the countries under investigation. This approach leads to the construction of time sequences, or 'waves' of democratisation. A first 'wave' of democratisation could be seen as 'coming in' around the time of the First World War in northern and western Europe with the parliamentarisation of constitutional monarchies, the formation of republics, and the extension of the franchise. In central and eastern Europe, the newly independent states following the collapse of the multinational empires (Austro-Hungary, the Ottoman Empire, and Russia) start experiencing democracy at a somewhat later time. The second 'wave' after 1945 saw the defeated states, such as Germany and Japan, be given democratic constitutions, while others, such as Italy and France, instituted new democratic regimes. The third 'wave' affects the countries in southern Europe and in Latin America in the 1970s and 1980s, with military dictatorships being replaced by elected civilian governments. This wave also brings the decline of authoritarian regimes in parts of east and south Asia starting in the mid-1980s, and sees the collapse of the communist regimes in eastern Europe after 1989 as well as the break-up of the Soviet Union together with the formation of fifteen post-Soviet republics in 1991. The 'wave' reaches South Africa and brings about the decline of one-party regimes in several parts of sub-Saharan Africa in the first half of the 1990s, too. Even in the Middle East there are signs of liberalisation in the 1990s. This is a story that sees democracy spreading around the world from its European heartland.

The question arises as to whether there are any 'prerequisites' of democracy or, more broadly, what 'causes' democratisation (as well as what accounts for the consolidation of newly established democratic regimes). Samuel Huntington's (1991) analysis of 'waves' of democratisation provides a prominent example of such an analytical research programme. To account for the 'third wave', for example, Huntington (1991: 45–6) lists five key factors: the legitimacy problems of authoritarian regimes as a result of poor economic performance or defeat in war; rising expectations regarding material consumption and education on the part of the middle class; the liberalisation of the Catholic Church following the Second Vatican Council of 1963–5 and its turning into a proponent for change; policy changes of international actors in support of democratisation and human rights; and, finally, the demonstration effect, facilitated by the global growth of communication networks. We shall return to the question of causes in our discussion below.

Huntington's is one way in which the simile of the 'wave' with reference to 'democracy' and its 'global' spread can be used – and the remainder of this chapter will concentrate on these issues. There is, however, another way of using the notion of the democratic 'wave' to pinpoint concern with the 'globalisation of democracy' – and we shall return to this alternative conceptualisation in Chapter 5. This alternative approach could commence, for example, with a reconceptualisation of the 'waves' of democratisation. Following Robert Dahl (1989), one could see the formation of democracy in the Greek polis in the first half of the fifth century BC as the first time that the idea that a substantial number of free, adult males should be entitled as citizens to participate directly in governing the polis was formulated and institutionalised. Underlying this notion of democracy was the assumption that, in order for democratic rule to uphold the common good, the citizen body had to be highly homogeneous as high levels of economic inequality, of religious, cultural or racial diversity would tend to produce political conflict and disagreements over the common good.

The second transformation occurred once the notion of democracy and its institutionalisation could no longer be contained within the city-state and had to be reconceptualised and redesigned for geographically larger territories. In this phase, two significant additions to the classical democratic tradition were made. First, out of recognition of the unavoidable heterogeneity of civil and political society there arose an awareness of the fragility of civic virtue and the dangers of political corruption. Institutions had to be designed that would prevent the concentration of power. In order to balance the interests of 'the one', 'the few', and 'the many' (in the Aristotelian sense), forms of mixed government were advocated in which these interests were represented and pursued, respectively, the monarchy, an aristocratic upper chamber, and a lower house of commons. This was the solution entailed in the British constitution. The American Federal Constitution, however, went beyond this model of a 'mixed constitution'. It acknowledged that society was composed of different alliances and groupings, all of them pursuing a plurality of legitimate interests. However, in order for republican virtue to survive the struggle of political factions and social forces, authority was to be dispersed and many power centres were to be created to prevent the wholesale capture of authority by any one particular interest.

The notion of representation was the second idea added to the classical ideal. For large-scale communities, direct democracy was considered impossible as the people could not meet as a legislative body and had, therefore, to choose representatives to do what they could not do themselves. Democratic government would thus be conceptualised as representative government circumscribed by constitutional constraint. Political contestation became institutionalised through the mechanisms for the representation of 'the people' and special 'interests'. Above all, the struggles over universal franchise, free speech, and freedom of assembly during the nineteenth and twentieth centuries broadened the institution of political participation which came to lose its elitist, aristocratic/patrician limitations.

The first 'wave', then, affected the small-scale city-state. The second 'wave' transformed politics in the large-scale communities which developed in the process of the formation of the modern state since about the Renaissance. The third 'wave', so an argument could be put forward, is now upon us. Democracy has to be freed from the shackles of the modern state and has to become global. In an era of ever increasing global interconnectedness of people, places, capital, goods and services, democratic self-government of the people has to be institutionalised on the global level. Creating structures for a 'cosmopolitan democracy' is the task we have to face should we wish to uphold the ideal of democratic self-government of the people in the twenty-first century. At issue is the design of democratic institutions and procedures for such a global democracy. To this topic, we shall return in Chapter 5.

A review of some key approaches to the question about the causes of 'democratisation' enables us to consider the issue as to whether one can meaningfully speak of democracy being 'promoted'. There is considerable disagreement in the literature about this question.

DEMOCRATISATION AND 'MODERN DYNAMIC PLURALIST SOCIETY'

In the literature on democratisation there has been considerable controversy over the connection between the formation of democratic regimes and capitalism.

Before we review some positions on this issue, a general point about capitalism, democracy, and human rights needs to be made. There is a monumental literature about the rise of capitalism in the 'West', and this is not the place to review the scholarly debate. Yet, however one tells this story, and whatever theoretical framework and explanatory hypotheses one wishes to put forward, there is no denying the fact that without sustained violence – what we nowadays would call 'human rights violations' – capitalism would not have developed in the form it did. Whether one would wish to speak – with Karl Marx – of 'primitive capitalist accumulation' or not, the origins and the development of capitalism were linked to the institution of slavery, colonialism, genocide, massive population transfers, and the deportation of unwanted subjects (and citizens). Extra-economic violence deployed 'at home' and 'abroad', was systematically implicated in the genesis of capitalist economic development. It was the violence intrinsic in the formation and institutionalisation of the capitalist market economy – from child labour, the suppression of strikes, unemployment, the ignoring of basic economic needs to environmental devastations – that fired the engine of popular struggle for social and economic rights. These 'civilisational' achievements have come under sustained attack (and are denied wherever possible) by capitalism and its political allies in the age of neo-liberal capitalist restructuring. This shows that the taming of capitalism remains an urgent task (see also Howard-Hassmann 2005).

Turning to the analytical question concerning a connection between capitalism and democratisation, we may discern a strong argument that, on the one hand, 'the inequalities in resources that market-capitalism churns out produces serious political inequalities among citizens' (Dahl 1998: 178). On the other hand, it is also suggested that there is a kind of 'elective affinity' between democracy and market-capitalism. Seymour Martin Lipset famously argued in the late 1950s that '[t]he more well-to-do a nation, the greater the chances that it will sustain democracy' (Lipset 1983: 31; see also for a recent statistical account Przeworski and Limongi 1997). For Lipset, there are two main reasons for this linkage. First, regime legitimacy is grounded in effectiveness: 'Prolonged effectiveness which lasts over a number of generations may give legitimacy to a political system; in the modern world, such effectiveness mainly means economic development' (Lipset 1959: 91). Secondly, capitalism diminishes class conflict (and not, as Marx would have it, radicalises it):

> For the lower strata, economic development, which means increased income, greater economic security and higher education, permits those in this status to develop longer time perspectives and more complex and gradualist views of politics. A belief in secular reformist gradualism can only be the ideology of a relatively well-to-do lower class. Increased wealth and education also serve democracy by increasing the extent to which the lower strata are exposed to cross pressures which will reduce the intensity of their commitment to given ideologies and make them less receptive to supporting extremist ones . . . Increased wealth is not only related causally to the development of democracy by changing the social conditions of the workers, but it also affects the political role of the middle class through changing the shape of the stratification structure so that shifts from an elongated pyramid with a large lower-class base, to a diamond with a growing middle class. A large middle class plays a mitigating role in moderating conflict since it is able to reward moderate and democratic parties and penalize extremist groups. (Lipset 1959: 78)

Lipset also asserted that 'all the various aspects of economic development – industrialization, urbanization, wealth, and education – are so closely interrelated as to form one major factor which has the political correlate of democracy' (Lipset 1983: 41). Such has been the influence of this position that Adrian Leftwich, when offering 'two cheers for democracy', could write in 1996 that 'the West should . . . support only those dedicated and determined elites which are seriously bent on promoting economic growth, *whether democratic or not*. For by helping them to raise the level of economic development it will help them also establish or consolidate the real internal conditions for lasting democracy' (Leftwich 1996: 329; italics in the original).

Robert Dahl has listed the interrelated characteristics of 'modern dynamic pluralist society' (MDP), as he calls it, which are congenial to the development and sustenance of democracy:

> a relatively high level of income and wealth per capita, long-run economic growth in per capita income and wealth, a high level of urbanization, a rapidly declining or relatively small agricultural population, great occupational diversity, extensive literacy, a comparatively large number of persons who have attended institutions of higher education, an economic order in which production is mainly carried on by relatively autonomous firms whose decisions are strongly oriented toward national and international markets, and relatively high levels of conventional indicators of well-being, such as physicians and hospital beds per thousand persons, life expectancy, infant mortality, percentage of families with various consumer durables, and so on. (Dahl 1989: 251)

Dahl is, of course, aware of the fact that there are cases where a democratic political system has been established prior to the formation of an MDP society, such as the United States or India. Furthermore, 'although democracy has existed only in countries with a market-capitalist economy, market-capitalism has existed in non-democratic countries' (Dahl 1998: 170). But the often adduced cases of South Korea and Taiwan show, so Dahl claims, that, 'in the long run', market-capitalism and economic growth may be downright unfavourable for non-democratic regimes. The key factor is that market-capitalism 'creates a large middling stratum of property owners who typically seek education, autonomy, personal freedom, property rights, the rule of law, and participation in government. The middle classes . . . are the natural allies of democratic ideas and institutions' (Dahl 1998: 168).

The cases of India and the United States show, then, that an MDP society is not strictly necessary for the development of democracy; the cases of South Korea and Taiwan show that an MDP society is not sufficient for democracy. Hence, Dahl – but also Lipset (1994) and others writing in their tradition – lists further factors that are favourable to democracy. 'External' conditions must be favourable: 'Democratic institutions are less likely to develop in a country subject to intervention by another country hostile to democratic government in that country' (Dahl 1998: 147). The influence of the Soviet Union in eastern Europe after the Second World War may serve as an example.

In addition to the formation of an MDP society, Dahl identifies three further 'internal' conditions that are favourable and essential for democracy. The means of violent coercion must be dispersed or neutralised, and the military and police forces must be under civilian control. A political culture and beliefs must prevail in society, and particularly among political activists, that support democratic ideas, values, and practices. Finally, '[d]emocratic political institutions are more likely to develop and endure in a country that is culturally fairly homogeneous and less likely in a country with sharply differentiated and conflicting subcultures' (Dahl 1998: 149–50).

This approach, however, is not exclusively based on socio-economic or socio-cultural 'structural' preconditions of democratisation. Political institution building, or the 'crafting' of institutions, is given due consideration. To give an example: 'federalism' and 'consociational-ism' are two different kinds of institutional arrangements that aim to cope with cultural heterogeneity (or, to stay closer to the terminology used by Dahl and others, cultural cleavages). As the case of Switzer-land, which is highly fragmented in both religion and language, shows, for federalism to provide an adequate institutional solution to cultural cleavages, the units within the federal system must be sufficiently autonomous to accommodate the different communities and possess adequate powers to meet their cultural needs. These communities should be already separated along territorial lines and should, therefore, also be fairly homogeneous culturally, so that cultural cleavages within the unit are relatively few. For a federal system not to dissolve as a result of secessionist movements, 'the citizens must have a national identity and common values sufficiently strong to sustain the federal union' (Dahl 1998: 155). This appears to be the case in Switzerland, yet seems to be precarious, for example, in Belgium and possibly even more so in Canada.

Power sharing between 'cultural' communities in the form of 'consociational' democracy is a further way of meeting demands for cultural recognition. According to Arend Lijphart (1977), con-sociational democracy has the following features: grand coalition governments which incorporate the leaders of the political parties that represent the main segments of the culturally divided society; a 'proportional representation' (PR) electoral system that ensures each cultural community a share of seats in parliament that is roughly proportional to the relative size of its vote; proportional employment and expenditure rules that apply throughout the public sector; and each community enjoys a high degree of autonomy in dealing with all those matters that are central to its culture and 'identity' or 'interest' backed up by constitutional vetoes for each cultural community. Manifestly, for a consociational democracy to be created, and to work successfully, very special conditions have to prevail. According to Dahl, these conditions include:

> High tolerance for compromise; trustworthy leaders who can negotiate solutions to conflicts that gain the assent of their followers; a consensus on basic goals and values that is broad enough to make agreements attainable; a national identity that discourages demands for outright separation; and a commitment to democratic procedures that excludes violent or revolutionary means. (Dahl 1998: 154)

As we shall see below, this emphasis on political institution building, political action and strategic elite interaction can also be found in an explanatory approach to democratisation that marginalises the importance of 'structures'.

DEMOCRATISATION, CLASS AND CAPITALIST DEVELOPMENT

'No bourgeoisie, no democracy' has been the result of Barrington Moore's classic study on *The Social Origins of Dictatorship and Democracy*. However, at the centre of Moore's argument is an analysis of class relations and political institutions. In his wide-ranging comparative historical analyses, Moore sets out to explain the changes of the political institutional order that accompanied the transition from agrarian to industrial societies. The societies under investigation face the same problem: the destruction of the traditional agrarian economy by commercialisation, that is, the production of agrarian goods for urban markets. These societies, however, solve the task of 'taming' the agrarian sector in different ways – by bourgeois revolutions in the cases of England (1640–60), France (1789–1815) and the United States (1860–5) that led – eventually – to the establishment of capitalist-democratic regimes; by unsuccessful or abortive bourgeois revolutions in the cases of Germany (1848) and Japan (1868) that led – eventually – to fascist dictatorships; and by peasant revolutions as in the cases of Russia (1917) and China (1927–49) that led – eventually – to communism. Not all societies, therefore, cover an essentially identical path during 'modernisation'. Economic modernisation ('commercialisation' of agriculture) leads to variations in political structures: how can these variations be explained? Moore asserts that an explanation of these alternative developmental routes must focus on the class structure as well as on the set of existing class coalitions in each society. Moore's hypothesis stipulates that '[t]he ways in which the landed upper classes and the peasants reacted to the challenge of commercial agriculture were decisive factors in determining the political outcome' (Moore 1966: xvii).

Moore concentrates on four major variables in order to account for variations in political structure: the relationship of the landed upper classes to the monarchy; the response of the landed upper classes to the requirements of production for the market and its consequence for the agrarian class structure; the relationship of the landed upper classes with the urban elite; and the role of revolutionary violence. In the last instance, the historically specific form of the integration of the agrarian and urban economies is the decisive factor in Moore's explanatory model. The greater the distance between the elites in the countryside and the cities, the more likely the uncontrolled and unbalanced growth of state power and the possibility of a crisis-ridden transition into the modern world with either a fascist or communist dictatorship. On the other hand, the closer the contact and co-operation between these elites, the more likely the development of a democratic political order. According to Moore, for democracy to triumph, it is necessary for the monopolistic power of arbitrary rulers to be broken. An alliance between aristocracy and bourgeoisie must check royal absolutism. However, this alliance must not be so strong as to permit a common front against the urban and rural working class because, ultimately, the bourgeoisie needs allies against the aristocracy which allow it to demand and institute democracy. In the case of the 'democratic' path to modernity, Moore thus highlights the importance of a plurality of class forces with the bourgeoisie in a dominant, yet not a monopolistic position. An important factor for this constellation to obtain was the use of revolutionary force in order to repress those rural interests which were opposed to commercialisation. In the facist route, on the other hand, landed interests retain the privileged political position in the state and their social dominance in society, whereas an economically strong bourgeoisie remains politically weak. Revolutionary violence is directed against the peasantry in order to protect the landed interests and against the urban working class in order to incorporate them into the authoritarian regime. Finally, in the communist route, a revolutionary elite, leading the peasantry and the working class, achieves state power since neither bourgeoisie nor the landed upper classes succeed with political or economic modernisation. Revolutionary violence 'in the countryside' is directed, initially, against the agrarian ruling class; but state violence is then used against the 'reactionary' peasantry such as the 'Kulaks'.

This line of inquiry has been followed by Rueschemeyer et al. (1992) in a study that examines the relation between the transformations of society that came with capitalist economic development and the long-term chances of democratic forms of rule. The authors identify three main explanatory factors: the balance of power among different classes and class coalitions; the structure, strength and autonomy of the state apparatus and its interrelations with civil society; and the impact of transnational power relations on both the balance of class power and on state–society relations (1992: 5). They see the chances of democracy as fundamentally shaped by the balance of class power and they, therefore, put forward two key assertions. First, 'capitalist development is associated with democracy because it transforms the class structure, strengthening the working and middle classes and weakening the landed upper class'; and secondly, 'democracy was a result of the contradictions of capitalist development and . . . it could be consolidated only if the interests of the capitalist classes were not directly threatened by it' (1992: 7, 10).

Consistent with Moore's argument, the authors show that the landed upper classes, which were dependent on labour-intensive and labour-repressive agrarian production, were the most consistently anti-democratic force (1992: 7–10, 270–3; see Ertman 1998, for a critical evaluation of this thesis). The most consistently pro-democratic force, so they claim contrary to Moore, was the working class, particularly in those constellations in which it was insulated from the hegemony of the dominant class and where it was not mobilised by a charismatic but authoritarian leader or a hegemonic party linked to the state apparatus:

> The organized working class appeared everywhere as a key actor in the development of full democracy . . . In most cases, organized workers played an important role in the development of restricted democracy as well. The Latin American . . . working class played a lesser role in the historical events there: the relative weakness of the working class certainly has contributed to the infrequence of full democracy in the region and to the instability of democracy where it did emerge . . . In all regions, however, pressure from the organized working class alone was insufficient to bring about the introduction of democracy; the working class needed allies . . . Democracy could only be established if (1) landlords were an insignificant force, or (2) they were not dependent on large supply of cheap labor, or (3) they did not control the state. (Rueschemeyer et al. 1992: 270)

The bourgeoisie – the capitalist class or 'big business' – would generally only support the installation of constitutional and representative government, but would oppose the political inclusion of the lower classes. The political position of the middle class, which the authors define in the Latin American context as composed of 'urban professionals, state employees and employees in the private sector, artisans and craftsmen, and small entrepreneurs, sometimes joined by small and medium farmers' (1992:185), is seen as ambivalent. Where the middle classes were confronted with intransigent dominant classes and had the option of allying with a sizeable working class, they embraced full democracy: 'However, if they started feeling threatened by popular pressures under a democratic regime, they turned to support the imposition of an authoritarian alternative' (1992: 8). Since the working class could nowhere push through democracy on its own but depended on finding allies, the position of the middle classes determined regime outcomes. Finally, the peasants and rural workers played a varied role in the development of democracy. Though they shared an interest in democracy with the urban working class, 'they acted much less frequently in support of it, in part, because they followed the lead of large landlords and in part because they had much greater difficulty organizing themselves' (1992: 272–3).

Rueschemeyer et al. (1992: 65–6) argue with regard to state structure that the more resources state elites control independently of socio-economic classes and civil society groups, and the more they constitute a hierarchically integrated and ideologically united state apparatus, the less likely it is that the subordinate classes of the population are strong enough to impose democratic rule on the system of domination. In this context, it is important to point out the authors' disagreement with positions such as Robert Dahl's. In Dahl's notion of a 'modern dynamic pluralist society', democracy is seen to be facilitated by social mobilisation and by the development of relatively autonomous groups which are arising in an ever more differentiated modern structure as a result of market-capitalism. For Rueschemeyer et al., however, the shift in the power of conflicting class interests as the correlate of social mobilisation and pluralisation is fundamentally important to democratisation. They insist that the density of autonomous organisations in civil society – which they define as 'the totality of social institutions and associations, both formal and informal, that are not strictly production-related nor governmental or familial in character' (1992: 49) – is important on three counts: '[A]s a way in which the empowerment of subordinate classes is realized, as a shield protecting these classes against the hegemonic influence of dominant classes, and . . . as a mode of balancing the power of state and civil society' (1992: 49).

Finally, transnational power structures have highly contingent effects. For example, if economic dependency in the periphery of the world system manifests itself in economic growth being dependent upon agrarian exports, then the power of the 'anti-democratic' landed upper classes is consolidated. If industrialisation is being attempted with imported capital-intensive technology, then the 'pro-democratic' working class is being kept small and weak. Geopolitical structures may both strengthen and weaken democracy. For example, there is a strong relation between warfare and democratisation: modern mass-mobilisation warfare involves the willing participation of the sub-ordinate classes, both in the field and at home in the factories. This has typically led states to making concessions to the subordinate classes. However, whether these concessions can be retained after the end of the military conflict is by no means certain. There is also Dahl's argument about the interests of foreign powers in trying to promote or prevent democratisation (1992: 69–73). Moreover, as the geopolitical and geo-economic restructuring of central and eastern Europe since 1989 demonstrates, the desire of former state socialist countries to join the European Union has not only resulted in determined efforts at democratisation, but has made foreign economic support and the marketisation of the economy dependent on the prior formation of a democratic polity: democracy preceded capitalism.

We should pause here and ask how these arguments relate to the discussion presented in the first part of this chapter. In the 'modernisation theory' of the 1950s and 1960s there was indeed a strong acceptance of the idea that economic development in the form of capitalism would eventually result in democracy in the 'Third World', a process mediated by the dynamics of the market and associational pluralism of civil society which, in turn, was perceived to be constituted either by non-ideological classes or status groups. With neither economic development nor democracy emerging as predicted, the neo-liberal 'structural adjustment programs' (SAPs) of the 1980s and 1990s were premised on the assumption that there was an inevitable, if politically deplorable, trade-off between growth and democracy. Indeed, there was a willingness to claim there to be a need for authoritarian regimes in order to achieve 'development' or make 'progress'. Rao (1984/1985: 75) argued that '[g]overnments must resort to strong measures and they must enforce them with an iron hand in order to marshal the surpluses needed for investment. If such measures were put to popular vote, they would surely be defeated'. Indeed, Deepak Lal (1983: 33) suggested that 'a courageous, ruthless and perhaps undemocratic government is required to ride roughshod over newly created interest groups'. 'Cruel choices', it was suggested, needed to be made:

> Fear of losing votes would . . . prevent democratic governments from embarking on long-term investment schemes, as the electorate was seen as unwilling to accept the required reduction in public services and restraints on wages and consumption . . . Democratic regimes . . . were regarded as inherently prone to populist, expansionist policies and preoccupied with issues of distribution rather than accumulation. In order to be re-elected, they would have to appease powerful interest groups like trade unions, urban consumers and domestic industrialist, and their hands would therefore be tied in terms of economic policies. (Abrahamsen 2000: 113–14)

As we have discussed above, this 'trade-off' argument has vanished in step with the coming to prominence of the 'good governance' discourse. 'Good governance' is seen to be conducive to, and congenial for, a capitalist market economy embedded in the global economy. It is now believed that there exists an 'elective affinity' between democracy (as defined in the 'good governance' discourse) and economic development. An informed public and an active parliament generate information and debate on policy alternatives while, at the same time, they scrutinise public expenditure and reign in corruption and rent seeking. Since democracy is based on the rule of law, it safeguards property and contractual rights which are an essential part of an environment that is conducive to investment and long-term economic commitments (Abrahamsen 2000: 114–15).

Reviewing this literature, one is confronted with a multiplicity of contradictory insights: capitalism precedes democracy; democracy precedes capitalism; democracy and capitalism go hand-in-hand; autocracies promote capitalism; capitalism thrives under autocracy; no bourgeoisie, no democracy; no working-class, no democracy. It would appear that context is all-important; generalisations are to be avoided.

DEMOCRATISATION AND ELITE TRANSACTIONS

To the extent that the 'structuralist' approach emphasises 'prerequisites', it tends to downplay the importance of concrete political actors, and the concrete choices they may make in historically specific situations are downplayed in their significance for regime change. However, it has been argued forcefully that such neglect seriously hampers our understanding of regime transition. As Karl (1990) has put it:

> Rather than engage in a futile search for new preconditions, it is important to clarify how the mode of regime transition (itself conditioned by the breakdown of authoritarian rule) sets the context within which strategic interactions (between elite groups, R.A.) can take place because these interactions, in turn, help to determine whether political democracy will emerge and survive.

In the process of democratisation, individual and collective actors must 'translate' economic and social forces into democratic political institutions. Political action is, therefore, a pivotal factor of democratisation. How do 'democrats' manage to achieve democracy without being killed by those political forces of the 'old regime' that have the control over weapons and other means of physical coercion? How can they achieve democracy without being starved to death by those economic actors who control the productive resources? Strategic political action is indispensable for their survival. There is, finally, then, the 'elitist' approach to democratisation to be considered.

To situate the analytical concern with elite interactions, we may turn to Alfred Stepan's (1986) discussion of ten alternative paths from authoritarian, non-democratic regimes to political democracy. In the first three paths, warfare and conquest play integral parts in redemocratisation. First, redemocratisation takes place 'when a functioning democracy that has been conquered in war restores democracy after the conqueror is defeated by external force' (1986: 66). Denmark, the Netherlands, Norway, and Belgium after the end of their occupation by Nazi Germany are the obvious cases. Secondly, redemocratisation after external liberation may entail deep, constitutional democratic reformulation. France and the foundation of the Fourth Republic after the Second World War or Greece after the 1944–9 Civil War are, despite different outcomes, the main examples for this path. Thirdly, as the cases of Germany and Japan after their defeat in 1945 demonstrate, democratisation may result from the defeat of an authoritarian regime by democratic powers who then install a working political democracy by dismantling the military and the institutions of the authoritarian state apparatus.

International war and external intervention may thus lead to democratisation. Yet, the termination of authoritarian regimes and the move towards redemocratisation can also be initiated by the elites of the authoritarian regime themselves. Again, Stepan distinguishes three paths in those transitions in which authoritarian powers make the move towards democracy. First, as in the case of Spain after the death of Franco in 1975, redemocratisation may be initiated by the civilian or civilianised political leadership; or, secondly, as in Brazil in 1974, individual leaders of the military government may be the prime mover for regime termination; and, finally, the 'military-as-institution' may want to return to democracy in order to protect its fundamental corporate interests. Greece in 1973 and Portugal in 1974 are prime examples for this path. In both cases, external threats – the risky intervention in Cyprus in the case of Greece, and the colonial wars in the case of Portugal – played a central role in the extrications of the military-as-institution.

Finally, rather than the transition to democracy being initiated by regime forces, the termination of the authoritarian regime may be caused by oppositional forces. First, in 'society-led regime termination', 'a transformation could be brought about by diffuse protests by grassroots organizations, massive but uncoordinated general strikes, and by general withdrawal of support for the government' (Stepan 1986: 78). The student uprising in Greece in 1973 and the general strike in Peru in 1977 make these two cases approximations of this type of regime transition. More recently, the German Democratic Republic and Czechoslovakia in the autumn of 1989, when the state socialist societies in central and eastern Europe collapsed, may serve as examples. Secondly, a grand oppositional pact may be constructed that brings together reform-minded members of the regime and members of oppositional groupings. Columbia and Venezuela in 1958, Spain after the Monclao Pact of 1977 are Stepan's examples, and we may add Poland and Hungary in 1989 as further examples of a transition to democracy through transaction. Thirdly, democratisation may be the result of an organised violent revolt co-ordinated by democratic reformist parties, as happened in Costa Rica in 1948 where a Social Democratic 'National Liberation Movement' defeated the regime, or in Bolivia in 1952 where the 'National Revolutionary Movement' (MNR) seized power. Finally, as the cases of Russia, China, Vietnam or Cuba show, there may be Marxist-led revolutionary wars which lead to regime change; however, as these cases also demonstrate, the transition did not lead to either a 'liberal' or a 'democratic' regime.

While the taking of any of these paths depends on strategic choices made by individual and collective actors, strategic elite interactions are of singular importance in three of them. In the transition, in which redemocratisation has been initiated by the civilian or civilianised political leadership, the military-as-institution remains a force of significant power: 'Thus the civilian leadership is most likely to persist in its democratizing initiative (and not to encounter a military reaction) if the democratic opposition tacitly collaborates with the government in creating a peaceful framework for the transition' (Stepan 1986: 73). As the case of Spain after Franco shows, the co-operation between the government and oppositional forces in the transition decreased the chances of a military reaction. Redemocratisation as a result of the extrication of the military from the political arena also depends on the creation of a political and legal framework, agreed upon by the power-holders and the opposition, since a re-entry of the military can only be prevented if its corporate interests are secured and its officers are not prosecuted for earlier crimes and wrongdoings. The case of the former Chilean dictator, General Pinochet, should be seen in this light, for example.

Yet, the path that leads towards redemocratisation as a result of a party pact is, manifestly, the prime case for the importance of strategic elite interactions and elite settlements. Typically, in this case, several groupings of political actors can be discerned, depending on, first, whether they are committed to maintaining authoritarian rule, to political reform, or to a complete 'rupture' with the regime, and, secondly, with which degree of intensity they are prepared to fight for achieving their preference. Within the elite of the authoritarian regime, 'hardliners', who would be prepared to confront any opposition head-on and, if necessary, by coercive means, may be confronted by 'softliners', who would be prepared to negotiate with the opposition about political liberalisation or even a move towards democracy. Within the opposition, 'opportunistic' former supporters of the regime who may not have a serious commitment to democratisation but would hope to secure their position or gain something from it, will form one grouping. 'Radicals' within the regime opposition will demand major political and economic changes, and are not prepared to compromise with the old regime and opt, if necessary, for violent revolutionary 'rupture'. Finally, the 'moderates' will be in favour of democratisation yet consider it imperative to respect the position of the traditional political, military, and economic elites (Colomer 1991; Potter 1997: 15).

As comparative evidence from Latin America or from eastern Europe (in particular, from Poland and Hungary) suggests, for a negotiated transition to succeed, the regime 'hardliners' and the opposition 'radicals' should be neutralised by the 'softliners' and 'moderates', respectively or else be persuaded to follow a reformist course. Much depends on the agreement on the question as to 'who shall govern in the interim between the decision to liquidate an authoritarian regime and the moment in which a government can be formed that would be based on a free democratic election' (Linz 1990: 151). At stake, obviously, is the key question about the control of political resources in the transition period and the changes to regime structure and in the society prior to elections. Juan Linz asserts that there are three factors that have an impact on these transactions and the solution to the fundamental issue of establishing basic rules of the political process. There is the relative balance of power among the negotiating parties; but much depends also on the level of trust in the fairness of those participating in the institutionalisation of democracy. But there is also the 'pressure from below' that propels the negotiations onwards and constitutes one of their constraining conditions. However, Linz hastens to put the importance of 'the people' into perspective:

> It should never be forgotten that in transitions, average men and women, students, and workers are demonstrating in the streets, taking risks in organizing illegal groups, distributing propaganda, and in a few cases, such as in Romania and Nicaragua, assaulting the seats of power ... However, a leaderless and disorganized people filling the squares and demanding a change of regime may be unable to negotiate a transfer or sharing of power, or processes to achieve such a goal, and may be pushed to intransigent positions, and, thus, their efforts will end if not in revolutions, then in repression. (Linz 1990: 152)

Hence, for Linz (and Stepan, too) the emergence of 'structured opposition' in favour of democratisation is a necessary condition for bringing about democracy.

In general terms, an emphasis on the importance of strategic elite interactions for the development of democracy goes hand-in-hand with a critical assessment of popular mobilisation and 'mass participation' in the transition 'from authoritarianism to democracy'. Time and again, the role of 'mass actors' has been decried. 'No stable democracy', so Terry Karl argued (1990: 8), 'has resulted from regime transitions in which mass actors have gained control even momentarily over traditional ruling classes.' For Huntington, it was clear that 'democratic regimes that last have seldom, if ever, been instituted by mass popular action' (Huntington 1984: 212). And Adam Przeworski argued that 'complete docility and patience on the part of organized workers are needed for a democratic transformation to succeed'. He suggested that 'the democratic system was solidified in Belgium, Sweden, France, and Great Britain only after organized workers were badly defeated in mass strikes and became docile as a result' (quoted in Bermeo 1997: 306).

At one level, these assessments of the causal significance of the organised working class, the unorganised ('unstructured') masses or movements for democratisation are part of 'normal' scholarly debate. We saw, for example, that Barrington Moore or Rueschemeyer et al. would, for different reasons, disagree with Linz, Stepan, or Przeworski. And there are, of course, possibilities for achieving some kind of mediation of these conflicting positions. Ruth Berins Collier (1999), for example, suggested that – to sum up her argument in a very compressed manner – the working class was the pivotal actor in the democratisation of the first and second waves, whereas elites played the significant part in the democratisation in South America in the third wave. Nancy Bermeo, in turn, wants to hold on to an essentially elite interactionist approach but also accommodate the role of the 'masses'. Not under all circumstances do radical popular organisations threaten democratic transitions. In the end, it boils down to elite perceptions. She identifies three scenarios:

- if pivotal elites forecast that the extremists will win, they will reject democracy because they see it as an intolerable threat (as happened in China in 1989);
- if pivotal elites forecast that the extremists will be defeated but moderate challengers will win, they may accept democracy as a means of escape from a politically insecure and volatile situation (as happened in Peru in 1977 or Greece in 1975); or
- if pivotal elites forecast extremists' defeat and their own victory, they may accept democracy because they see democracy as a form of legitimation (as happened in Portugal 1974 or Spain in 1976). (Bermeo 1997: 317, table 3)

Yet, arguably the 'fear of the masses' and their exorcism from the history of (successful) democratisation is ultimately embedded in the elite theories that underpin these actor-centred analyses. One particularly influential 'elitist' understanding of democracy was offered by

Joseph Schumpeter in 1942 in his book *Capitalism, Socialism, and Democracy*. For Schumpter, democracy was not 'government by the people', but 'government approved by the people'; democracy was the rule of the politician:

> [T]he role of the people is to produce a government, or else an intermediate body which in turn will produce a national executive or government. And we define: the democratic method is that institutional arrangement for arriving at political decisions in which individuals acquire the power to decide by means of a competitive struggle for the people's vote. (Schumpeter [1942] 1976: 269)

Democracy is thus an arrangement for the establishment of political leadership. The citizens' role in a democracy is limited to the act of voting. Furthermore, once politicians have been elected, the voters should withdraw from politics. However, '[t]hey must not withdraw confidence too easily between elections and they must understand that, once they have elected an individual, political action is his business and not theirs' (Schumpeter [1942] 1976: 295). This emphasis on voting as the defining characteristic of a 'democratic' regime is also present in Huntington's definition of democracy as that system in which 'its most powerful collective decision makers are selected through fair, honest, and periodic elections in which candidates freely compete for votes' (Huntington 1991: 7). Yet, for elections to be fair and honest and for competition for votes to be free and meaningful certain other rights beyond the political right to vote have to be entrenched: for example, the right to assembly or freedom of speech – in short, arguably the Schumpeterian definition of democracy ('electoral democracy') comprises the institutions and freedoms contained in Robert Dahl's model of 'polyarchy'.

In the 'classical' democratic tradition, the direct participation of citizens in all aspects of public affairs was considered to be imperative for the person to achieve the full development of 'his' individual capacities. Whereas such direct involvement of an active citizenry in public life was seen to enhance freedom, for democratic elitists such direct popular democracy is impossible and undesirable: democracy needs competent leadership, not the irrationality of the masses; in complex societies democracy presupposes organisation, and organisation implies oligarchy – democracy and oligarchy are not starkly contrasting types of political rule (as Aristotle had suggested), but two sides of the same coin. It is within this Weberian and Schumpeterian tradition that contemporary democratic elitism considers elite competition for electoral support as a key element of a democratic system. In elections, the passive and disorganised mass of voters becomes the arbiter of the political conflict. Elections enable the masses to remove from power an elite group which is unresponsive to their wishes. Furthermore, the multiplicity of sectional elites, their relative autonomy from each other based on their respective control of resources, and the relative autonomy of some other elites from the elites of the state and government restrict elite power (Etzioni-Halevy 1993). It is this model of Schumpeterian 'elite' democracy that underpins the democracy promotion with its strong emphasis on elections that we discussed in the first half of this chapter.

The political contestation between hardliners and softliners of an authoritarian regime may lead to political liberalisation and thus create an opening for 'democratisation'. This may lead to a breakthrough to democracy as the old regime collapses and a democratic regime based on a new constitution and national elections takes its place. This breakthrough must then be consolidated in the post-transition period. According to democratic elite theorists, just as the transition from an authoritarian regime to a democratic one is engineered through elite transactions, so the consolidation of democracies requires rational and reasonable elite behaviour. Dahl's optimal path to stable polyarchy was characterised by the rise of political competition that preceded the expansion of political participation. The culture of democracy first took root among a small elite and only later diffused to the larger population as it became gradually incorporated into electoral politics (Dahl 1971: 33–6). Political institution building – the 'crafting' of institutions – is essential in order to ensure continuing elite co-operation. Jack Goldstone and Jay Ulfelder, two leading academic members of the CIA-convened 'State Failure Task Force', argue that their research shows that:

> what 'works' in establishing a stable democracy is moving toward a political system with completely open and fully competitive parties that maintains strong checks on executive authority . . . Whatever constitutional provisions, electoral systems, or other institutions are adopted for a given country, they must encourage political parties to seek support from varied social groups to gain power and must reward the ability to compromise. (Goldstone and Ulfelder 2004: 17)

According to them, it is crucial not to define 'democracy' mainly in terms of elections and majority rule. It should rather be defined 'as a system of institutions that places limits on authority': 'Rules that limit the power of popular majorities based on communal identities or regional groupings thus appear to be a critical part of building stability into democratic systems' (Goldstone and Ulfelder 2004: 18).

The literature on democratisation initially analysed the 'transition to democracy' in a rather teleological manner, leading from 'opening' via 'breakthrough' to 'consolidation' (Carothers 2002: 7). However, it has become clear over the last decade or so that many new regimes of the 'third wave' 'are not themselves democratic, or any longer "in transition" to democracy' (Diamond 2002: 23; see also McFaul 2002). They occupy a 'grey zone' between fully-fledged democracy and outright dictatorship:

> [T]hey suffer from serious democratic deficits, often poor representation of citizens' interests, low levels of political participation beyond voting, frequent abuse of the law by government officials, elections of uncertain legitimacy, very low levels of public confidence in state institutions, and persistently poor institutional performance by the state. (Carothers 2002: 9–10)

Carothers distinguishes between those regimes characterised by 'feckless pluralism' and 'dominant-power' systems. Regimes whose political life is characterised by 'feckless pluralism' do have a significant amount of freedom which includes regularly held elections and alternations between political groupings representing different interests or ideologies. However, political participation is limited to voting and, generally, members of the political elite are widely perceived as corrupt, self-interested or plain ineffective. A weak state is unable to address the country's problems efficiently (Carothers 2002: 10–11). In a dominant-power system, too, the population is disaffected from politics, and large-scale corruption and crony capitalism are ripe: 'Yet one political grouping – whether it is a movement, a party, an extended family, or a single leader – dominates the system in such a way that there appears to be little prospect of alternation of power in the foreseeable future' (Carothers 2002: 11–12).

These regimes in the 'grey zone' pose a conceptual challenge: how can they be best 'categorised' – possibly for the purpose of comparison? As we have noted above, for a regime to be properly called an 'electoral democracy', elections have to be (and have to be perceived to be) free, fair, and genuine. Manifestly, elections held in the regimes of the 'grey zone' have none of these features. Still, elections are being held, and such regimes have been defined as 'electoral authoritarian' (Diamond 2002) or 'competitive authoritarian' (Levitsky and Way

2002). Levitsky and Way describe the features of competitive authoritarianism in the following way:

> [F]ormal democratic institutions are widely viewed as the principal means of obtaining and exercising political authority . . . [Yet] [a]lthough elections are regularly held and are generally free of massive fraud, incumbents routinely abuse state resources, deny the opposition adequate media coverage, harass opposition candidates and their supporters, and in some cases manipulate electoral results. Journalists, opposition politicians, and other government critics may be spied on, threatened, harassed, or arrested. Members of the opposition may be jailed, exiled, or – less frequently – even assaulted or murdered . . . [Indeed,] [r]ather than openly violating democratic rules . . . incumbents are more likely to use bribery, co-optation, and more subtle forms of persecution, such as the use of tax authorities, compliant judiciaries, and other state agencies to 'legally' harass, persecute, or extort cooperative behavior from critics. (Levitsky and Way 2002: 52–3)

There are, then, several paths leading out of authoritarianism. One of them leads towards democracy – in whatever qualified form: as, for example, 'illiberal' democracy, 'electoral' democracy, 'tutelary' democracy, 'protective' democracy, or 'restrictive' democracy (see Collier and Levitsky 1997). Another may lead to 'qualified' authoritarianism. While either way of categorising a regime – as either not fully 'democratic' or not fully 'authoritarian' – allows holding fast to the notion of democracy as a telos, the longevity (and in many cases, the relative stability) of such 'hybrid' regimes suggest that they should be seen as regime types in their own right. Their formation deserves an explanation that goes beyond the notion of a 'stalled' transition to democracy.

Clearly, in the post-Cold War era, the liberal democratic model became hegemonic as a result of international influences such as 'demonstration effects, conditionality (as in the case of European Union membership), direct state-to-state pressure (in the form of sanctions, behind-the-scenes diplomacy, and even direct military intervention), and the activities of emerging transnational actors and institutions' (Levitsky and Way 2002: 62). With the collapse of the Soviet Union, alternative sources of military and economic aid subsided and put a premium on being on good terms with Western governments and the Western-dominated global institutions such as the World Bank, the IMF, or GATT/WTO. State weakness as a result of resource depletion (and the ensuing difficulty in maintaining patronage networks) and elite fragmentation undermined the capacity of many authoritarian regimes to ride out crises. Yet, a number of authoritarian regimes were in position to keep political concessions to a minimum:

> Some benefited from pockets of permissiveness in the international system, due in large part to economic or security issues that trumped democracy promotion on Western foreign policy agendas. Others benefited from state control over revenues from valuable commodities (such as oil), which undermined development of an autonomous civil society and gave rulers the means to co-opt potential opponents, and still others took advantage of quasi-traditional elite networks that facilitated the establishment of neopatrimonial regimes (as in Central Asia). (Levitsky and Way 2002: 62)

In a later article, Levitsky and Way present a set of hypotheses to explain the transformation of authoritarian regimes either in the direction of democracy or of competitive authoritarianism. They distinguish, and then cross-reference, two variables: Western leverage, that is, governments' vulnerability to external pressure exerted by Western states; and linkage to the West, that is, the density of a country's ties to the United States, the EU, and Western-led multi-lateral organisations. In their estimation, the impact of Western pressure on authoritarian regimes depends upon three factors. First, small states with underdeveloped economies are far more vulnerable than larger states with substantial military or economic power: states in sub-Saharan Africa are, in principle, subject to Western leverage to an extent that China and Russia are not. Secondly, geo-strategic or economic interests of Western states may limit their leverage: demands for political reform in much of the Middle East or East Asia will be counter-balanced by geo-political considerations. Thirdly, if author-itarian governments are in a position to avail themselves of political, economic, or military support from an alternative regional power, Western leverage is much reduced.

Levitsky and Way argue that leverage is most effective when it is combined with extensive linkage to the West. These linkages may exist in a number of areas: economic; geo-political (security and military alliances); social (such as tourism, migration, the existence of diaspo-ric communities, or elite education in the West); communication (for example, cross-border telecommunications or Western media pene-tration); and transnational civil society (such as links to international NGOs, churches, or party organisations). Linkage, so they claim, 'raises the cost of authoritarianism by (1) heightening the salience in the West of authoritarian government abuse; (2) increasing the probability of an international response; (3) creating domestic constituencies with a stake in adhering to democratic norms; and (4) strengthening democratic forces in relation to autocrats' (Levitsky and Way 2005: 23).

Cross-referencing these two 'variables', that is, 'linkage' and 'leverage', they postulate the following connections: 'Where linkage is extensive, international influences may be decisive, contributing to democratisation even in countries with highly unfavorable domestic conditions (Albania, Nicaragua, Romania). Where linkage is lower, international influences are weaker, and regime outcomes are more likely to be a product of domestic factors' (Levitsky and Way 2005: 33). Hence, in central Europe and the Americas, where linkage with the West is extensive, democratisation was widespread in the post-Cold War period. On the other hand, in those regions which have low or medium levels of linkage – such as East Asia, sub-Saharan Africa, and the former Soviet Union between 1990 and 1995 – we notice a different situation: 'Of the 25 competitive authoritarian regimes . . . only five (Benin, Ghana, Mali, Senegal, and Taiwan) democratised, and one of them, Taiwan, is a case of exceptionally high linkage to the United States. In these regions, not only were the prospects for democratization weaker, but the prospects for competitive authoritarian stability was greater' (Levitsky and Way 2005: 32).

To sum up, 'democratisation' is a highly complex process in which structural prerequisites and the actions of individual and collective actors are contingently interwoven, making predictions of a successful outcome of action strategies highly problematical. Under such circumstances, 'promotion' of democracy is in effect limited to offering 'ideological' support for democracy as a desirable regime type. 'Material' support may be offered in the hope but without any certainty that, in an unspecified way, outside intervention will promote, rather than prevent, the development of democratic institutions and attitudes.

Notes

1 For reasons of the reader's convenience, the bibliographical details of the reports, charters, documents, etc. to which reference is made in this section are summarily listed in this note:

African (Banjul) Charter: www.africa-union.org/official_documents/Treaties_%20Conventions_%20Protocols/Banjul%20Charter.pdf.
American Convention on Human Rights: www.oas.org/juridico/english/Treaties/b-32.htm.

Barcelona Declaration 1995: http://ec.europa.eu/comm/external_relations/euromed/bd.htm.

COM(2003) 104: http://ec.europa.eu/world/enp/pdf/com03_104_en.pdf.

Community of Democracies Warsaw 2000: www.demcoalition.org/pdf/warsaw_english.pdf.

Community of Democracies Santiago 2005: www.santiago2005.org/archivos_pdf/reunion%20f/003%20Declaraci%F3n%20Final%20ingles.pdf.

Copenhagen Criteria: www.auswaertiges-amt.de/diplo/en/Europa/Erweiterung/KopenhagenerKriterien.html.

Cotonou Agreement: http://ec.europa.eu/comm/development/body/cotonou/index_en.htm.

CSCE Copenhagen 1990: www.osce.org/documents/odihr/1990/06/13992_en.pdf.

CSCE Moscow 1991: www.osce.org/documents/odihr/1991/10/13995_en.pdf.

CSCE Paris Charter 1990: www.osce.org/documents/mcs/1990/11/4045_en.pdf.

Election Observation 2005: www.cartercenter.org/documents/2231.pdf.

European Convention (including Protocols): www.hri.org/docs/ECHR50.html.

EU Amsterdam Treaty 1999: www.eurotreaties.com/amsterdamtext.html.

EU European Neighbourhood: http://ec.europa.eu/world/enp/index_en.htm.

EU Nice Charter 2000: http://ue.eu.int/uedocs/cms_data/docs/2004/4/29/Charter%20of%20fundemental%20rights%20of%20the%20European%20Union.pdf.

G8 2004 Partnership: www.g7.utoronto.ca/summit/2004seaisland/partnership.html.

ICJ Reports: www.icj-cij.org/icjwww/icases/inus/inus_ijudgment/inus_i-judgment_19860627.pdf.

International Covenant on Civil and Political Rights: www.unhchr.ch/html/menu3/b/a_ccpr.htm.

MEDA II Regulations: http://ec.europa.eu/comm/external_relations/euromed/meda2_reg.htm

OAS Charter: www.oas.org/main/main.asp?sLang=E&sLink=http://www.oas.org/juridico/english/charter.html.

OAS Democratic Charter: www.oas.org/main/main.asp?sLang=E&sLink=http://www.oas.org/OASpage/eng/Documents/Democractic_Charter.htm.

OAS Res 1080: www.oas.org/main/main.asp?sLang=E&sLink=http://www.oas.org/juridico/english/regeneas.html.

UN Commission on Human Rights Resolution 1999: http://ap.ohchr.org/documents/E/CHR/resolutions/E-CN_4–RES-1999–57.doc.

UN Commission on Human Rights Resolution 2000: http://ap.ohchr.org/documents/E/CHR/resolutions/E-CN_4–RES-2000–47.doc.

UN Department of Political Affairs: www.un.org/Depts/dpa/ead/ea_content/ea_context.htm.

UN General Assembly Resolutions: UN GA Res A/Res/44/146: http://daccessdds.un.org/doc/RESOLUTION/GEN/NR0/549/05/IMG/NR054905.pdf?OpenElement.

UN GA Res A/Res/45/150: http://daccessdds.un.org/doc/RESOLUTION/GEN/NR0/565/39/IMG/NR056539.pdf?OpenElement.

UN GA A/Res/46/137: http://daccessdds.un.org/doc/RESOLUTION/GEN/NR0/582/25/IMG/NR058225.pdf?OpenElement.

UN Millennium Declaration: www.ohchr.org/english/law/millennium.htm.

Universal Declaration of Human Rights: www.un.org/Overview/rights.html.

Vienna Convention . . . Treaties: www.walter.gehr.net/wvkengl.html.

Vienna Declaration: www.unhchr.ch/huridocda/huridoca.nsf/(Symbol)/A.CONF.157.23.En?OpenDocument.

2 Once more, for reasons of the reader's convenience, the bibliographical details of the reports, charters, documents, etc. to which reference is made in this section are summarily listed in this note:

G8 Document 2005: www.g-8.org.

IMF Good Governance 1997: www.imf.org/external/pubs/ft/exrp/govern/govindex.htm.

IPU Declaration on Democracy: www.ipu.org/cnl-e/161–dem.htm.

National Security Strategy of the United States of America 2002: www.whitehouse/gov/nsc/nss.pdf.

OECD Participatory Development (1997): http://www.eldis.org/static/DOC4062.htm.

UNDP 1997: http://magnet.undp.org/policy/chapter1.htm; http://magnet.undp.org/policy/chapter2.htm; http://magnet.undp.org/policy/chapter3.htm.

UNGA Res 1966 (xviii), Dec. 1963: http://daccessdds.un.org/doc/RESOLUTION/GEN/NR0/186/41/IMG/NR018641.pdf?OpenElement.

Vienna Declaration: http://www.unhchr.ch/huridocda/huridoca.nsf/(Symbol)/A.CONF.157.23.En?OpenDocument.

4

Sovereignty and Democracy

In the first part of this chapter, I shall argue that the globalisation of liberal-representative democracy (together with its two pillars of capitalism and human rights) is premised upon a wholesale and sustained assault on the idea of 'sovereignty'. The cosmopolitan agenda of spreading liberal democracy, human rights, and free markets is being pursued based on the destruction, or at the very least, the undermining of the idea (and the legal institution) of 'sovereignty'. 'Sovereignty' is being denied to a wide range of states: 'rogues states' (or 'outlaw states'), 'failed states', non-democratic states, and states which violate human rights – they have all had their 'sovereignty' questioned over the last couple of decades and have become targets for outside intervention by violent or non-violent means. In the following discussion, I shall address the political discourse of 'sovereignty', the strategic and rhetorical use of the idea of 'sovereignty' that intends both to assert and to deny autonomy. In the first section of this chapter, 'sovereignty' as a category in international law takes centre-stage. We shall see how a denial of the 'sovereign equality' of states leads to a pronounced 'liberal anti-pluralism' that opens the door to a policy of intervention. The second section then provides a sustained argument (and a timely reminder) that the idea of 'democracy' has always been premised on the acceptance of the idea of 'sovereignty of the people'. 'Popular sovereignty', in turn, went hand-in-hand with 'state sovereignty'. The chapter ends with observations on the connection between liberalism, sovereignty and democracy and the exercise of democratic rule in the territorially consolidated nation-state.

Conceptual Distinctions

According to F. H. Hinsley (1986: 25–6):

> at the beginning, at any rate, the idea of sovereignty was the idea that there is a final and absolute political authority in the political community; and

everything that needs to be added to complete the definition is added if this statement is continued in the following words: 'and no final and absolute authority exists elsewhere'.

As we shall see in the second part of this chapter, it was the concern of Jean Bodin and Thomas Hobbes to establish some one final source of authority, and thus to identify the site of sovereignty. In a recent contribution to the literature on sovereignty, Stephen Krasner (1999) suggested an 'unbundling' of the concept of sovereignty and thus to comprehend Bodin's and Hobbes's conceptualisation as just one of several meanings of 'sovereignty'. In Krasner's terminology, the 'classical' conceptualisation is best understood as referring to domestic authority structures (see Goldsmith 1999/2000). In his classic text *International Law*, to which reference has already been made in Chapter 3, Lassa Oppenheim understood the core of sovereignty to include the authority of a nation to (1) 'adopt any Constitution it likes'; (2) 'adopt any commercial policy it likes'; and (3) 'treat its subjects according to [its] discretion' (Oppenheim 1905: §124). It is these aspects of which 'domestic sovereignty' is comprised. It involves 'the specification of legitimate authority within a polity and the extent to which that authority can be effectively exercised' (Krasner 1999: 4). A concern with the source and site of sovereignty à la Jean Bodin and Thomas Hobbes is combined with a concern for the effective control of activities within a state's boundaries.

The determination of the domestic authority structures is an exclusively internal matter – or so the basic rule of 'Westphalian sovereignty' stipulates. 'Westphalian' sovereignty gives the state the right to exclude external actors from authority structures within its territory; it thus upholds the principle of non-intervention and grounds the norm of autonomy. If, and when, external actors influence or determine domestic authority structures, then 'Westphalian' sovereignty is being violated. This has been a fundamental norm of international law since at least the middle of the eighteenth century, when it was formulated by Emer de Vattel in his *Le droit des gens*. This being the case, in later publications Krasner changed the term 'Westphalian' sovereignty – which, after all, refers to the region where the peace treaties were concluded that brought to an end the Thirty Years' War in 1648 – to 'Westphalian/Vattelian' sovereignty. It is 'domestic sovereignty' as 'authority' that is affected by violations of 'Westphalian/Vattelian sovereignty' through the policies and initiatives discussed in the previous two chapters, such as the IMF's conditional lending, the insistence upon 'good governance', the promotion of democracy, or international human rights law and its (selective) enforcement – issues to which we shall turn presently.

A third meaning of sovereignty refers to the mutual recognition of juridical independent territorial entities that is the basis for accepting that a state has the authority to engage in international agreements. The 'sovereign equality' of states, which we saw enshrined in the UN Charter, has its basis in this 'international legal sovereignty'. Finally, Krasner identified a fourth aspect of sovereignty – a dimension which he dropped in later publications: 'interdependence sovereignty'. This term refers to public authorities' control of transborder movements. It addresses the capacity of a state 'to regulate the flow of information, ideas, goods, people, pollutants, or capital' across its borders (Krasner 1999: 4). This is, of course, one of the main issues thrown up by the debate on globalisation. A consideration of 'interdependence sovereignty' shows nicely why, for Krasner, these four aspects of sovereignty are separate but also interconnected. For example, a decline in 'interdependence sovereignty' manifestly undermines 'domestic sovereignty' understood as 'effective control'. It does not necessarily undermine the legitimacy of a particular kind of ruler–ruled relationship and the identification of 'ultimate' sovereignty underpinning the domestic authority structure. A state's international recognition ('international legal sovereignty') is not necessarily affected nor does a decline in 'interdependence sovereignty' mean that a state is no longer capable of excluding external actors (hence losing 'Westphalian sovereignty'). However, 'Westphalian sovereignty' is affected should a state decide to create, or participate in, international organisations in order to regain some regulatory control that it lost at the nation-state level.

Conceptual distinctions, which are informed by distinguishing between an 'authority' and a 'control' ('effectiveness') aspect of sovereignty, can also be found in other definitions of sovereignty. To give two examples: in an important discussion, Robert H. Jackson (1990) distinguished between 'negative' and 'positive' sovereignty. For Jackson, 'negative' sovereignty was a formal-legal condition under which states enjoyed rights of non-intervention and other international immunities. Upon this legal foundation, a society of independent and formally equal states fundamentally rests (Krasner's 'international legal sovereignty' and 'Westphalian/Vattelian sovereignty'). A state which possesses not only 'negative' sovereignty but also the capabilities and the wherewithal to provide political goods for its citizens, enjoys 'positive' sovereignty (an approximation to

Krasner's 'domestic sovereignty' as control): 'positive' sovereignty is 'the means which enables states to take advantage of their independence usually indicated by able and responsible rulers and productive and allegiant citizens' (Jackson 1990: 29).

Jackson argued that, due to a shift in international norms after the Second World War, many of the newly founded states in the era of decolonisation attained 'statehood' not as a result of any evidence of capacity to rule ('empirical statehood') but through 'juridical qualifications' ('juridical statehood'). These 'quasi-states' by definition are deficient and defective as apparatuses of power. Their 'sovereignty is derived not internally from empirical statehood but externally from the states-system whose members have evidently decided and are resolved that these jurisdictions shall not disappear. The quasi-state is upheld by an external covenant among sovereign states' (Jackson 1990: 168–9).

In his analysis, Jackson disregarded the involvement of European powers in demolishing many viable African polities in the course of the nineteenth century in pursuit of geo-political aggrandisement and economic profit. As Carolyn Warner has argued, 'through treaty violations, military conquest and occupations, and alliances with disaffected groups, Europeans chipped away at the integrity of African political systems' (Warner 1999: 254). After 1945, the same Western powers, which in the nineteenth century had destroyed 'real' states in Africa, now created 'quasi-states'. Still, Jackson's analytical distinctions allow us to suggest that the principle of 'negative' sovereignty was universalised after 1945, not that of 'positive' sovereignty. Structured around the principle of 'negative' sovereignty the interstate system since the second half of the twentieth century has been populated – to use Jackson's terminology – by both 'real' and 'quasi'-states. We can see that a 'sovereign' right to ultimate authority does not imply an ability to exercise it. The history of state formation can be analysed as the protracted efforts of rulers and their staff to translate 'juridical' sovereignty into 'empirical' sovereignty.

Jackson's conceptualisations have recently been taken up by Kjell Goldmann (2001: 62–5) who distinguishes between 'sovereignty' and the capacity of the state for effective action, or what he calls 'autonomy' defined in terms of 'action possibilities'. In his reading, the concept of 'sovereignty' refers to a legal right. 'Internal sovereignty' (Krasner's 'domestic sovereignty') is a constitutional concept that pertains to the ultimate source of legitimate authority inside a state. 'External sovereignty' is, in a sense, an international law concept

(Krasner's 'international legal sovereignty'). A state's 'external sovereignty' 'is a function of its recognition by other countries as being in legitimate possession of rights such as the right of non-interference by others in its internal affairs, and the right not to be submitted to international norms and decisions to which it has not consented [Krasner's 'Westphalian sovereignty', RA]' (Goldmann 2001: 63). State capacity is considered to be conceptually, and empirically, quite separate from either notion of 'sovereignty'. However, arguably for a democratic regime such a distinction would seem to be problematic. What could it possibly mean for a 'people' to possess 'sovereign' rights while being incapable of acting upon these rights and turning its collective will into an actuality? We have raised a similar question in our discussion of human agency in Chapter 2: what could it possibly mean to speak of the 'freedom' of agency that an individual possesses without at the same time allowing for the resources needed to exercise this agency? We shall return to this question of 'sovereignty' and 'agency' later in this chapter.

We may now use these conceptual distinctions to connect these considerations on sovereignty with the discussion in the previous two chapters on human rights and 'the emerging norm of democratic governance'. We have noted in Chapter 3 that a state's legitimacy (and based on it, its international recognition) used to be premised on its being in effective control of its people and territory. This is Krasner's 'domestic sovereignty' as control. The thesis of the 'emerging norm of democratic governance' pitches its argument at the level of 'domestic sovereignty as authority': if a state has effective 'control' but exercises its authority not in accordance with (certain) human rights standards or democratic and/or 'good' governance norms, then its 'international legal sovereignty' may not necessarily be challenged, but its 'Westphalian' sovereignty may become undermined as a result of external actors' trying to intervene to redesign domestic authority structures. At stake is a restructuring of the ruler-ruled relationships and identifying a new 'ultimate' sovereign – the people as a collectivity made up of (human) rights-bearing individuals. 'Domestic sovereignty as authority' is also the target of outside intervention in the case of so-called 'outlaw states' – as we shall see presently. If a state is perceived to have lost 'control' – and is hence defined as a 'failed state' – its 'domestic sovereignty' has 'collapsed', undermining its 'international legal sovereignty' and providing an opening for the violation of its 'Westphalian sovereignty' as well. The following discussion focuses upon the interplay between 'domestic' and

'Westphalian' sovereignty. At issue are the 'external' enforcement of the 'democratic governance' norm and the justifications of such enforcement through reference to the notion of 'sovereignty'. A good starting point is the sovereignty discourse that underlies American foreign policy.

The Politics of the Sovereignty Discourse

The sovereignty discourse informs American foreign policy in at least two respects. One is to do with the sovereign right to self-defence and the other with the ideology of democracy promotion.

'The National Security Strategy of the United States of America' (September 2002) speaks (in chapter V) of one particular type of state that poses one of the greatest security risks to the United States, namely, 'rogue states' – a terminology that we have already encountered in Chapter 1 in John Rawls's (and Fernando Teson's) concept of 'outlaw state'. These 'rogue states':

> brutalize their own people . . . display no regard for international law, threaten their neighbors, and callously violate international treaties to which they are party; are determined to acquire weapons of mass destruction . . . to be used as threats or offensively to achieve the aggressive designs of these regimes; sponsor terrorism around the globe; and reject basic human rights and hate the United States and everything for which it stands.

Against these 'foes' (as these states are called in the document's preface), it is right and legitimate to take pre-emptive and anticipatory actions – ideally by a 'coalition of the willing' under the leadership of the United States, but if necessary, also unilaterally. The purpose of these actions 'will always be to eliminate a specific threat to the United States or our allies and friends. The reasons for our actions will be clear, the force measured, and the cause just' (Security Strategy, chapter V: 16). The United States will only fight 'just wars', which will 'make the world not just safer but better' – even if this goal may only be achieved through the violation of international law (Security Strategy, chapter I: 1). Importantly, the United States will ensure that it will not be impaired by any international organisations in its pursuit of this objective (Security Strategy, chapter IX: 31).

In January 2006, George W. Bush proclaimed in his State of the Union Address that he remained committed to 'an historic, long-term goal – the end of tyranny in the world':

Dictatorships shelter terrorists, and feed resentment and radicalism, and seek weapons of mass destruction. Democracies replace resentment with hope, respect the rights of their citizens and their neighbors, and join the fight against terror. Every step toward freedom in the world makes our country safer – so we will act boldly in freedom's cause. (www.whitehouse.gov/stateoftheunion/2006/print/index.html)

Two arguments converge in this statement, both of which relate to international security. There is the view that although democracies often go to war, they do not fight each other: they are inherently inclined to conduct peaceful foreign policies – at least, this is the claim put forward (see Lipson 2003 as an up-to-date introduction to a huge scholarly literature on the 'democratic peace' thesis). Democratisation and the promotion of democracy are thus not only desirable on their own and required by considerations of justice, but also because they bring about a more peaceful, stable and secure international order. In the case of 'tyrannies', it is the other way around. Bush expressed this view in his State of the Union Address: 'At the start of 2006, more than half the people of our world live in democratic nations. And we do not forget the other half – in places like Syria and Burma, Zimbabwe, North Korea, and Iran – because the demands of justice, and the peace of this world, require their freedom as well.'

This position ties in with the debate on 'failed' or 'collapsed' states. 'Rogue' states possess sufficient capacity to 'terrorise' their people within and other states without; to acquire, and deploy, nuclear, biological, and chemical weapons; and to arm and support 'terrorists' around the globe. 'Failing' states, on the other hand, pose a different kind of threat. Such states are beset by many problems:

In such states, infrastructure deteriorates; corruption is widespread; borders are unregulated; gross domestic product is declining or stagnant; crime is rampant; and the national currency is not widely accepted. Armed groups operate within the state's boundaries but outside the control of government. The writ of the central government . . . may not extend to the whole country; in some cases, it may not extend beyond the capital. Authority may be exercised by local entities in other parts of the country, or by no one at all. (Krasner 2004b: 91–2)

In Krasner's terminology, 'failed' states are defined by an absence of 'domestic sovereignty' – both as 'authority' and 'control'. It is because of their weakness, rather than their 'strength' as in the case of 'rogue' states, that 'failed' states constitute an economic and security risk for other states. Even states with limited means and decaying institutions can procure biological or chemical weapons; and they, too, may harbour terrorists and provide them with territory in which they can operate freely. They open up space for drug trafficking and trafficking in persons and are thus a nodal point in the network of transnational criminality. And their 'gross violations of human rights present unpleasant political choices for democratic leaders in powerful states', as they have to respond to domestic public opinion (Krasner 2004b: 95). It is for these reasons – or, at least, because of an acceptance of the validity of this kind of analysis – that powerful states have an interest in disregarding the norm of non-intervention ('Westphalian sovereignty') and pursue a policy of regime change, that is, a policy to change the domestic authority structure in weaker states by imposition (Krasner 2004a: 1078).

This policy can be justified on the basis of the sovereign right to 'self-defence'. And so can the doctrine of pre-emptive strike:

> We cannot let our enemies strike first . . . We must adapt the concept of imminent threat to the capabilities and objectives of today's adversaries . . . The greater the threat, the greater the risk of inaction – and the more compelling the case for taking anticipatory action to defend ourselves, even if uncertainty remains as to the time and place of the enemy's attack . . . the United States will, if necessary, act preemptively. (National Security Strategy 2002: chapter V)

For some, or possibly many, analysts of international politics, these distinctions among states in international politics out of which then ensues a policy of military intervention, possibly, if need be, beyond the bounds of international law, may carry a whiff of traditional 'power politics'. There is, however, a second, interrelated, kind of argument that also utilises the idea of sovereignty in pursuit of intervention which proffers arguments in favour of military 'humanitarian' interventions on the basis of 'the responsibility to protect'. For some, such arguments may appear to be more in tune with the development of international law and international ethics and, therefore, to be more broadly acceptable.

According to the report of the International Commission on Intervention and State Sovereignty of December 2001, 'sovereignty', 'classically', comprises a number of ideas. First, there is the assumption of the sovereign equality of states as enshrined in Article 2.1 of the UN Charter. Secondly, there is idea that sovereignty signifies – as 'territorial sovereignty' – the capacity of a state to make authoritative decisions with regard to the people and resources within its territory and the right to exercise exclusive and total jurisdiction within its territorial borders without outside interference or intervention. Thirdly, it is assumed that a state has the sovereign right to self-defence – as expressed in Article 51 of the UN Charter (ICISS 2001: 2.7–2.10). It is the central claim of the Report that '[t]he defence of state sovereignty . . . does not include any claim of the unlimited power of the state to do what it wants to its own people'. Indeed, sovereignty, so it is argued, implies a dual responsibility: 'externally – to respect the sovereignty of other states, and internally, to respect the dignity and basic rights of all the people within the state' (ICISS 2001: 1.35). The principle of sovereign equality, the norm of non-intervention and the sovereign right of self-defence must be subordinated in the last instance to the idea of sovereignty as 'responsibility to protect':

> Sovereign states have a responsibility to protect their own citizens from avoidable catastrophe – from mass murder and rape, from starvation – but that when they are unable or unwilling to do so, that responsibility must be borne by the broader community of states. (ICISS 2001: Foreword, viii)

According to the Report, thinking of sovereignty as responsibility has a threefold significance:

> First, it implies that the state authorities are responsible for the functions of protecting the safety and lives of citizens and promotion of their welfare. Secondly, it suggests that the national political authorities are responsible to the citizens internally and to the international community through the UN. And thirdly, it means that the agents of state are responsible for their actions; that is to say, they are accountable for their acts of commission and omission. The case for thinking of sovereignty in these terms is strengthened by the ever-increasing impact of international human rights norms, and the increasing impact in international discourse of the concept of human security. (ICISS 2001: 2.15)

The Commission defines human security broadly as the physical safety of people, their economic and social well-being, respect for their dignity and worth as human beings, and the protection of their human rights and fundamental freedoms (ICISS 2001: 2.21). Based on their reading of 'state practice, [UN] Security Council precedent, established norms, emerging guiding principles, and evolving customary international law, the Commission believes that the [UN] Charter's strong bias against military intervention is not to be regarded as absolute when decisive action is required on human protection grounds' (ICISS 2001: 16). There is, therefore, no absolute legal right of a state to be left alone: '[T]here must be limited exceptions to the non-intervention rule for certain kinds of emergencies' (ICISS 2001: 31). Who decides on the exception? According to the Commission, this decision is best taken by the UN Security Council. But should the Security Council fail 'to discharge its responsibility in conscience-shocking situations crying out for action, then it is unrealistic to expect that concerned states will rule out other means and forms of action to meet the gravity and urgency of these situations' (ICISS 2001: 55).

In a more recent report for the United Nations, published in 2004 under the title 'A More Secure World: Our Shared Responsibility', this idea of sovereignty as responsibility was adopted and its corollary, the acceptance of a potential breach of the norm of non-intervention, cogently summarised:

> In signing the Charter of the United Nations, States not only benefit from the privileges of sovereignty but also accept its responsibilities. Whatever perceptions may have prevailed when the Westphalian system first gave rise to the notion of State sovereignty, today it clearly carries with it the obligation of a State to protect the welfare of its own peoples and meet its obligations to the wider international community. But history teaches us all too clearly that it cannot be assumed that every State will always be able, or willing, to meet its responsibilities to protect its own people and avoid harming its neighbours. And in those circumstances, the principles of collective security mean that some portion of those responsibilities should be taken up by the international community, acting in accordance with the Charter of the United Nations and the Universal Declaration of Human Rights, to help build the necessary capacity or supply the necessary protection, as the case may be. (More Secure World 2004: para. 29)

The authors of the 2004 report for the United Nations are adamant that we are witnessing the emergence of the 'norm of a collective international responsibility to protect' (para. 202) – after the 'entitlement to democratic governance', this is yet another (so it is alleged) 'emerging' norm. This norm is emerging, it is claimed, as a result of the successive humanitarian disasters in Somalia, Bosnia and Herzegovina, Rwanda, Kosovo, and Darfur (Sudan). These disasters:

> have concentrated attention not on the immunities of sovereign Governments but their responsibilities, both to their people and to the wider international community. There is a growing recognition that the issue is not the 'right to intervene' of any State, but the 'responsibility to protect' of *every* State when it comes to people suffering from avoidable catastrophe. (More Secure World 2004: para. 201)

It cannot be argued, the authors claim, that the principle of non-intervention in internal affairs could be used 'to protect genocidal acts or other atrocities, such as large-scale ethnic cleansing, which can properly be considered a threat to international security and as such provoke action by the Security Council' (More Secure World 2004: para. 200). The authors suggest that because of this threat to international security military intervention can be justified under Chapter VII of the UN Charter.[1]

These views are reflected in a growing body of international law scholarship, much of it published by scholars located at law schools in the United States. Michael Reisman has forcefully argued that international law still protects sovereignty, but 'it is the people's sovereignty rather than the sovereign's sovereignty' (Reisman 2000: 243). In modern international law, he claims, an indigenous force can violate sovereignty as effectively and ruthlessly as an outside force; and it can be liberated as much by an indigenous as by an outside force (Reisman 2000: 250). On the basis of this claim, Reisman is consistent when he suggests that:

> [t]he Chinese Government's massacre in Tiananmen Square to maintain an oligarchy against the wishes of the people was a violation of Chinese sovereignty. The Ceausescu dictatorship was a violation of Romanian sovereignty . . . Fidel Castro violates Cuban sovereignty by mock elections that insult the people whose fundamental human rights are being denied. (Reisman 2000: 250)

In their summary of the 'democratic entitlement' literature, Fox and Roth (2000: 11) point out that the claims made in favour of an 'emerging norm of democratic governance' would commit one to the view that:

> [t]he sovereignty affirmed by the international legal system belongs to the people, and can be cognizably asserted on the people's behalf only where the government conforms to the right to political participation; therefore, measures to implement democratic right, undertaken by foreign States collectively and/or individually, need not respect the sovereign prerogatives of governments that violate those rights. This is especially so where a 'free and fair election' has actually taken place, and those elected have been denied, or ousted from, office by force of arms.

If one accepts the force of this argument, then specifying the criteria which must be met for an intervention to be justified is one of the key issues. The criteria which the authors of the UN report, 'A More Secure World', put forward are, by and large, identical with those laid down by the ICISS (2001: xii):

(a) *Seriousness of threat* . . .
(b) *Proper purpose.* Is it clear that the primary purpose of the proposed military action is to halt or avert the threat in question . . .
(c) *Last resort.* Has every non-military option for meeting the threat in question been explored . . .
(d) *Proportional means.* Are the scale, duration and intensity of the proposed military action the minimum necessary to meet the threat in question?
(e) *Balance of consequences.* Is there a reasonable chance of the military action being successful in meeting the threat in question, with the consequences of the action not likely to be worse than the consequences of inaction? (A More Secure World 2004: para. 207)

The idea of sovereignty, rather than protecting a state from outside intervention, is now being interpreted in such a way that 'sovereignty as responsibility' in effect allows – indeed, morally justifies and necessitates – intervention under the 'right' circumstances. What the right circumstances are and who decides upon the action to be taken: these are matters of power politics. The 'international community' – which may exist as idea, ideal, or ideology, but certainly not as a unified actor – is composed of states which are highly unequal: '[T]he vast majority of the world's states are so poor that they cannot will the means to any major ends that they decide to pursue in common. The rich states, by contrast, who [sic] have the means, will not cede the power of decision over them to the majority of poor states' (Hirst 2001: 270). And leaving the final decision to the five permanent members of the UN Security Council does not mean that once they have spoken, the 'international community' has spoken nor that this bickering 'Holy Alliance' is not guided, in the last instance, by power politics.

For many of those states which teeter on the brink of collapse as a result of intrastate conflict based on ethnic mobilisation for self-determination, (substatal) autonomy, or independent statehood, none of these analytical dimensions of sovereignty any longer apply. The idea of trusteeship, so prominent in the era of the League of Nations, has recently been revived – the idea, and its actualisation, of the 'international administration of war-torn territories', with Kosovo or East Timor being two particularly prominent recent examples (Caplan 2002). As Fearon and Laitin (2004) rightly point out, contemporary 'neotrusteeship' is a form of 'postmodern imperialism'. In contrast with classical imperialism, when a single imperial or trust power asserted monopoly rights within a territory, 'in these new forms of rule subjects are governed by a complex hodgepodge of foreign powers, international and nongovernmental organisations (NGOs), and domestic institutions', on the basis of some kind of international legal mandate (Fearon and Laitin 2004: 7). And rather than exercise governance functions for a long time, 'the agents of neotrusteeship wish to exit as quickly as possible, after intervening to reconstruct or reconfigure states so as to reduce threats arising from either state collapse or rogue regimes empowered by weapons of mass destruction (WMD)' (Fearon and Laitin 2004: 7). Krasner (2005; 2004b) perceives 'shared sovereignty' arrangements as involving the creation of institutions for governing specific issue areas within a state. He refers, paradigmatically, to natural resource exploitation and the case of the Chad, in particular, where the Chad, Exxon-Mobil, the World Bank, and Cameroon developed a form of 'shared sovereignty' to allow oil from Chad's landlocked oilfields to be pumped through a pipeline running through Cameroon to reach the Atlantic coast.

A more broadly conceived approach is centred on the notion of 'earned sovereignty', as it has been formalised by Paul Williams et al. (2003). 'Earned sovereignty' is designed, as Williams and Pecci (2004: 354–5) assert, to provide for the managed devolution of sovereign authority and functions from a state to a substate entity: 'In some instances, the substate entity may acquire sovereign authority and functions sufficient to enable it to seek international recognition, while in others the substate entity may only acquire authority to operate within a stable system of heightened autonomy' (Williams and Pecci 2004: 355). One core element of 'earned sovereignty' is 'shared sovereignty':

> During an initial period of shared sovereignty, the state and sub-state entity may both exercise sovereign authority and functions over a defined territory. In some instances, international institutions may also exercise sovereign authority and functions in addition to or in lieu of the parent state. In rare instances, the international community may exercise shared sovereignty with an internationally recognized state. (Hooper and Williams 2002/2003: 360)

Institution building – that allows, so it is hoped, for the development of democracy and respect for human rights – is one of the main objectives of these shared sovereignty arrangements. These arrangements, while still embedded in (if not justified by) the 'sovereignty' discourse, do no longer allow for clear answers to the questions as to 'who is sovereign' and 'what is sovereignty'.

'Sovereignty as control' is still demanded of states lest they should be defined as 'failed' or 'collapsing' and thus bereft of the protection in international law. However, 'control' no longer provides the legal ground for claims to sovereign statehood unless such control is paired with liberal-democratic domestic authority structures. We have noted that the Bush administration in its National Security Strategy document and the International Commission on Intervention and State Sovereignty as well as the authors of the report on 'A More Secure World' concur that there is a right, even more, a duty, of intervention and the use of military force, if considered appropriate. If Security Council authorisation for the intervention can be obtained, then this is welcome. If not, then a multilateral 'coalition of the willing' (which would seek *ex post facto* UNSC authorisation) would be the second-best option; but there is also room in the argument to accommodate unilateral action by one state. Both the power-political universalism of the United States administration that aims 'to bring the hope of democracy, development, free markets, and free trade to every corner of the world' (Strategy 2002: preface) and the human rights cosmo-politanism of the two UN reports legitimate the use of force against 'rogue' or 'irresponsible' states.

Admittedly, the justifications for military intervention differ: the sovereign right to self-defence in the case of the United States administration; human security concerns and the adoption of the idea of 'sovereignty as responsibility' in the case of the Commission. There may be strong disagreement as to whether there are any emerging norms of humanitarian interventions (grounded, for example, in human rights conventions). Yet, there would appear to be a broadly shared view that emerging norms of democratic governance can be discerned and that the ideas of 'domestic sovereignty' and of 'West-phalian sovereignty' do only apply to those states that are constituted internally in accordance with those norms – states, in short, which exercise sovereignty 'responsibly'.

Krasner is quite sanguine about the violation of 'Westphalian sovereignty' as a result of interventions. For him, 'sovereignty' is a norm that, historically, has been more honoured in the breach than in the observance – the frequent breaches turning the idea of 'sover-eignty' into an 'organized hypocrisy' (as the subtitle of Krasner's book states). For him, the contemporary concern with human rights – and the attendant policy of humanitarian intervention – 'is but the latest example of a long-standing tension between autonomy and inter-national attempts to regulate relations between rulers and ruled'

(Krasner 1999: 126). He argues, for example, that every major peace treaty from Westphalia to Versailles contained provisions for the protection of minorities: the proliferation of international agreements in the post-Cold War era, which we have observed in a previous chapter, is thus not a new development. While minorities were initially defined in terms of religious affiliation (after all, the peace treaties that ended the Thirty Years' War needed to address the political fall-out of religious diversity and strife), later on ethnicity and linguistic identity became the marker for minority groups (Krasner 1999: 73–127).

Krasner's 'nothing-new-under-the-sun' position can draw support from John Owen's empirical analysis of foreign imposition of domestic institutions. He identified 198 cases of forcible domestic institutional promotion in the period between 1550 and 2000. He thus concentrates on those cases in which a state A directly applies violence 'to create, preserve, or alter the political institutions (as distinguished from the ruler or government) in state B' – while this state still possesses 'juridical sovereignty' (in Krasner's terminology, 'international legal sovereignty') (Owen 2002: 377). Most of these impositions occurred during three periods of ideological conflict among major powers: the Reformation and Counter-Reformation (roughly between 1580 and 1650), the French Revolution and its aftermath (1789 and 1849), and the ideological conflicts in the twentieth century (since the Russian Revolution of 1917 and the collapse of the Soviet Union in 1991). These interventions peaked during times of intensified hegemonic struggle and international insecurity: the Thirty Years' War, the French revolutionary and Napoleonic wars, and the beginning of the Cold War. Reviewing the historical data, Owen identifies the following ten patterns:

1. Institutional imposition has occurred in the modern states system in three clusters: 1600–48; 1790–1849; and 1918–today.
2. Monarchies, republics, fascist states, communist states, liberal democracies, and theocracies all promote domestic institutions.
3. In all periods a few states do a majority of the promoting (that is, a few states do it repeatedly).
4. Promoters strongly tend to be great powers.
5. Targets tend to be undergoing civil unrest.
6. Promotion correlates to scarcity of international security.
7. Promotion correlates to transnational ideological strife.
8. In the great majority of cases, the target is located near the promoting state; in the great majority of cases promoter and target share a border.

9. Many targets are of objective strategic value.
10. In the great majority of cases, the intervening state promotes its own institutions in the target. (Owen 2002: 398, table 4)

It bears repeating that Owen only looks at cases of *forcible* imposition or promotion. For the 1990s, his cases thus include Somalia, Haiti, Bosnia-Herzegovina, Sierra Leone, and Yugoslavia (Kosovo) as targets for the promoters, that is, the United States, Great Britain, France, Nigeria, Canada (and other NATO countries). For the first decade of the new millennium, Afghanistan or Iraq would qualify as cases. Hence, the non-violent democracy promotion, of which we treated in Chapter 3, remains outside the purview of Owen's analysis. If we do look at these cases, however, it is possible to discern yet another pattern in which 'sovereignty' plays a pivotal role.

In a brilliant and important study, Gerry Simpson analyses the contemporary international legal order and puts current transformations into a wider historical context. As in the case of Krasner and others, Simpson's analysis is organised around a series of conceptual distinctions. One concept is 'sovereign equality'. We have encountered the various dimensions of 'sovereign equality' in previous discussions. Emer de Vattel's statement in his *Le droit des gens* that 'nations treat with each other as bodies of men and not as Christians or Mohammedans' refers to the 'formal' equality that states possess:

> Since men are by nature equal, and their individual rights and obligations the same, as coming equal from nature, Nations, which are comprised of men and may be regarded as so many persons living together in a state of nature, are by nature equal and hold from nature obligations and some rights . . . A dwarf is as much a man as a giant is; a small republic is no less sovereign than the most powerful Kingdom. (de Vattel, §§ 18 and 19, quoted in Simpson 2004: 32)

Lassa Oppenheim summarised this view by stating that '[w]hatever inequality may exist between states as regards size, power, degree of civilisation, wealth or other qualities, they are nevertheless equals as international persons' (Oppenheim 1920: 15, quoted by Simpson 2004: 27). This is the 'sovereign equality' of which the UN Charter speaks in its Article 2(1). It is a 'juridical' equality in the sense of equality before the law. While states do not have the same rights, and are hence not equal in an absolute sense, all states nevertheless have 'the *legal* capacity to enjoy the rights they already possess in *judicial* settings' (Simpson 2004: 44). This 'sovereign equality' does not mean that states are free to do as they please in their external behaviour.

Rather, 'sovereign equality' is relative sovereignty in that it permits of co-existence and hence some measure of security for other states. However, 'sovereign equality' assumes that states are bound only by those legal norms to which they have explicitly given their consent and to whose creation they had an equal opportunity to contribute. Such 'legislative equality' is thus a second dimension of the concept of 'sovereign equality'.

The third aspect of 'sovereign equality' is 'existential equality', understood as 'the right [of a state] freely to choose and develop its political, social, economic and cultural systems' – as the General Assembly Resolution 1966 (XVIII) of December 1963 stated. This is a central aspect of the right to self-determination as the right to exist in a form of a state's own choosing. Together with this right, 'existential equality' includes, according to Simpson (2004: 53–4), 'a state's sphere of domestic jurisdiction (Article 2(7) of the UN Charter), its right to territorial integrity, its right to political independence and its right to participate in international institutions'. 'Existential sovereignty' thus defined is basically coterminous with conventional understandings of sovereignty and independence (Simpson 2004: 54).

According to Simpson (2004: 53), '[e]xistential equality . . . is the foundation of a pluralist conception of the legal order.' The recognition of sovereign statehood is independent of the internal characteristics of states, and so is membership in the international system: qualification for membership does not depend upon a particular regime type. As we can now see, for Simpson, ideas about emerging norms of democratic governance and the distinctions between democratic and non-democratic states, between bona fide members of the international community and 'outlaw states' or 'failed states', fundamentally undermines the *legal* conceptualisation of the global order as a community of 'sovereign equals'. Simpson does, of course, recognise – indeed, makes it a core concern of his analysis – that this idea of a 'pluralist' international order was both *de facto* and *de jure* a fiction. 'Legislative sovereignty' has always been heavily curtailed by the juridical dominance of the Great Powers acting in concert: indeed, it is one characteristic of 'Great Powers' that they realise their prerogatives through legal forms. We may think here of the 'Holy Alliance' in the nineteenth century, but also of the 'Holy Alliance' of the permanent members of the UN Security Council (which itself is a form of 'Holy Alliance'). Another example is the voting procedures in important financial organisations that favour Great Powers – not just *de facto* but (in our context, above all) *de jure*.

The prevailing distinctions between 'Christian' and 'heathen' nations; between 'civilised' and 'barbarian' nations; or between those nations of a conservative persuasion and those of a nationalist-liberal one (a distinction made by the Holy Alliance and its successors in the course of the nineteenth century) have also always violated the idea(l) of pluralism and undermined 'existential equality' as 'a doctrine of constraint' as a result of its insistence on territorial integrity, non-intervention, and autonomous domestic jurisdiction. Simpson thus places the current trend towards 'anti-pluralism' within a much longer tradition.

Simpson suggests that the present international order can best be understood as a struggle between two competing versions of liberalism. 'Classical' liberalism (or 'liberal pluralism') emphasises the virtues of tolerance, diversity, and openness together with agnosticism about moral truth. It is associated with the idea of existential equality. It is a liberalism of inclusion and universality. According to Simpson, after considerable debate, this liberalism came to inform the Charter of the United Nations (prominently in its Article 2(7)). Arraigned against this liberal pluralism is a 'liberal anti-pluralism' that is harking back to the 'standards of civilisation' arguments (which we encountered in Chapter 2) and that distinguishes between states based on their internal characteristics. It is a 'liberalism of certainty' which is endowed with a kind of moralistic fervour that results in a 'lack of tolerance for non-liberal regimes' (Simpson 2004: 78, and *passim*; Simpson 2001). This liberal anti-pluralism:

> lays emphasis on the rights of individuals themselves and the norms of democracy as defining qualities of a workable international order. To this extent, international human rights law with its intellectual roots in the enlightenment and its emphasis on popular sovereignty and civil rights is the engine of this new liberal anti-pluralism. (Simpson 2004: 81)

In this liberal anti-pluralism, '[t]he individual's democratic and human rights prevail over the state's claims to territorial integrity or political sovereignty' (Simpson 2004: 302–3). This 'liberalism of exclusion' underpinned the legal construction of the League of Nations and informed its debates on whether liberal standards within states or sovereign statehood should be the sole criterion of membership. While *de jure* the League of Nations was closer to an exclusive club of like-minded (liberal/democratic) states, *de facto*, as Simpson suggests, it came to embrace 'pluralism' as, for example, the cases of post-revolutionary Russia and the defeated Germany demonstrate.

Simpson summarises the current anti-pluralist conceptions of the present international order crisply:

> The pluralist conception is universalist and egalitarian in orientation. The salient norms are those of non-intervention, sovereign immunity and state equality. The anti-pluralist conception emphasises the existence of two spheres of order. In one, there is . . . a solidarist international society composed of a core of liberal states that share certain cultural attributes and ideological presuppositions and whose common values and interests support a deepening constitutionalism within that society. In the other sphere, are outlaws and outsiders subject to repressive international criminal law and denied the benefits of full sovereign equality. (Simpson 2004: 231)

'Outlaw states' and 'undemocratic states' are being treated differently by liberal anti-pluralism. 'Outlaw states', on the one hand, are 'incarcerated within a separate legal regime without rights and subject to continual surveillance and occasional disciplinary violence'. The criminalisation of states and their subjection to military intervention are two main means of taming, punishing, and changing them. In the case of 'undemocratic', or 'illiberal' states, on the other hand, the idea is 'to enmesh them in a system of transnational networks designed to ease them into a liberal-democratic order' (Simpson 2004: 313–14).

In the previous two sections of this chapter, we have focused on sovereignty understood as international legal sovereignty and as Westphalian/Vattelian sovereignty and the role these conceptualisations of sovereignty play in the globalisation of liberal democracy. 'Sovereignty' is being redefined and politically put under attack. It is against this background that we shall now turn to a more detailed discussion of the connection between 'domestic sovereignty', particularly in the form of 'popular sovereignty', and democracy.

'Domestic Sovereignty' as 'Popular Sovereignty'

THE SOVEREIGNTY OF THE STATE

In *The Rise and Decline of the State*, Martin van Creveld (1999) reminds his readers of the fundamental distinction between 'government' and 'the state'. On the one hand, the government, says van Creveld (1999: 415) 'is a person or group which makes peace, wages war, enacts laws, exercises justice, raises revenues, determines the currency, and looks after internal security on behalf of society as a whole, all the while attempting to provide a focus for people's loyalty and, perhaps, a modicum of welfare as well.' The state, on the other hand, should be understood as a corporation, hence as possessing a legal *persona* of its own:

> [I]t has rights and duties and may engage in various activities *as if* it were a real, flesh-and-blood, living individual. The points where the state differs from other corporations are, first, the fact that it authorizes them all but is itself authorized (recognized) solely by others of its kind; secondly, that certain functions (known collectively as the attributes of sovereignty) are reserved for it alone; and, thirdly, that it exercises those functions over a certain territory inside which its jurisdiction is both exclusive and all-embracing. (Creveld 1999: 1)

van Creveld is at pains to emphasise that the state is merely one of the forms the organisation of government has assumed.

This fundamental distinction between 'government' and 'the state' has long been forgotten in mainstream political and social science. The revival of historical macrosociology, however, has issued in a renewed interest in the concatenation of those circumstances that welded 'government' and 'the state' together (Axtmann 1993). The description and explanation of the transformation of the multiplicity of overlapping and divided authority structures of the medieval polity into the 'modern', territorially consolidated sovereign state has been a central concern in historical sociology. Arguably, it is the current discussion of 'globalisation', and, in particular, the (alleged) decline of the power and capacity of the modern state in the 'age of globalisation', that raises the question as to how 'government' and 'the state' may come apart again.

In retracing the history of this development, a number of themes have been pursued. In 'pre-modern' Europe, political authority was shared between a wide variety of secular and religious institutions and individuals – between kings, princes and the nobility, bishops, abbots and the papacy, guilds and cities, agrarian landlords, and 'bourgeois' merchants and artisans. The modern state project aimed at replacing these overlapping and often contentious jurisdictions through the institutions of a centralised state. The theory of sovereignty legitimised this endeavour. This theory claimed the supremacy of the government of any state over the people, resources, and, ultimately, over all other authorities within the territory it controlled. 'Sovereignty' meant that final authority within the political community lay with the state whose will legally, and rightfully, commanded without being commanded by others, and whose will was thus 'absolute' because it was not accountable to anyone but itself.

'Governing' by the 'sovereign' thus aimed to take on the form of the artful combination of space, people, and resources in territorialised containments, and the policing, monitoring, and disciplining of the population within these spaces became the foundation, and the manifestation, of state sovereignty. As a result of historical developments that spanned several centuries, the modern territorial state came into existence as a differentiated ensemble of governmental institutions, offices, and personnel that exercises the power of authoritative political rule-making within a continuous territory that has a clear, internationally recognised boundary. It thus possesses 'internal' sovereignty that is typically backed-up by organised forces of violence and that grounds the state's 'external' sovereignty *vis-à-vis* other states and its demands for non-interference in internal matters. Hence, 'sovereignty' has a spatial dimension in that it is premised on the occupation and possession of territory. This spatial dimension manifests itself most clearly in the drawing of territorial boundaries that separate the 'inside' from the 'outside'. This territorial exclusion is, in turn, the prerequisite for identifying the source of sovereignty within the bounded territory and for defining 'us' in contradistinction to 'them'.

Let us look more closely at the discourse on 'sovereignty' as a theory of political legitimacy. In the past, the claim of legitimacy of monarchical domination had been based on the notion that the rulers had received their authority 'from the grace of God' (*dei gratia*). As Christ's deputies they were obliged to perform their duties in a devout and just way. They were not seen as a sovereign legislator who created and enacted new law. Rather than being 'founders' of new law, they were 'finders' of old law, recognising and sanctioning law that already existed. Law was seen as representing and expressing perennial norms contained in tradition, ethical values, and religious prescriptions; changes in the law were thought of, not as a purposeful creation, but as a 'reformation' of still binding traditional norms and rules, tacitly accepted in a given society (Axtmann 1992; Passerin d'Entrèves 1967: 85–6). Keeping the peace and providing justice under the rule of God as well as under the rule of law were the main responsibilities and justifications of royal authority well into the fifteenth century. The provision of peace and justice (*pax et justitia*) was to result in order (*tranquillitas*). But as the developments in the Holy Roman Empire of German Nations, France, the Netherlands and elsewhere in Europe showed during the sixteenth and seventeenth centuries, it was the attempt to enforce religious conformity after the Reformation that in effect undermined the establishment of *tranquillitas* in the course of the religious wars that swept across Europe in those centuries. As a result of these wars, political necessities and the concern with the maintenance of the political and geographical integrity of the territory came to inform the policies of the secular authorities in the course of the sixteenth century (Oestreich 1982). The notion of *raison d'état* reflected and legitimised this change and brought about the detheo-logisation and deconfessionalisation of political theory: religious issues became subordinated to secular concerns with the stability and order of the *political* commonwealth. For the French philosopher Jean Bodin and the group of political thinkers known as *les politiques* in the late sixteenth century, for example, maintaining political order through the consolidation of the power of the state had precedence over the enforcement of religious uniformity and conformity (Franklin 1973; King 1974). The notion of *raison d'état* undermined the conceptualisation of the political commonwealth as a *respublica christiana* in which the state-objective (and the duty of the ruler) was defined as the protection of the 'true' faith in order to provide for the best possible precondition for the subjects to attain eternal salvation. Instead of this religious-transcendental foundation of the state-objective, the notion of *raison d'état* focused on the endogenous and autonomous determination of politics, and thus explicitly highlighted the tension between religious ethics and secular political prudence.

This shift in the meaning of monarchical authority found its most significant expression in the increase in the legislative activity of the ruler. The ruler now established himself as law-maker. But this very activity generated theoretical endeavours to assess more precisely the nature of that activity, the kind of power which it both presupposed and entailed. The notion of 'sovereignty' in the sense of *superioritas* became central in the context of these reflections. It issued out of the basic assumption that there is:

> somewhere in the community, whether in the people or in the prince, or in both the prince and the people united in one body, a *summa potestas*, a power which is the very essence of the State. The decisive contribution of the [rediscovered] Roman [law] doctrine was the new conception of law as an expression of this power, as an instrument which could be used and adapted in accordance with the changing needs of society, as a system of rules that were valid and effective as long as there existed behind them the control of a supreme will: a will which, in virtue of its supremacy, was

155

legibus solutus, because it was not accountable to any but itself. (Passerin d'Entrèves 1967: 93)

It became one of the major concerns of political and juridical thinking to identify the 'will which legally commands and is not commanded by others' (d'Entrèves 1967: 93). Jean Bodin and Thomas Hobbes conceptualised the king as the source of the law, and it was Hobbes who moved most decisively away from the notion of a sacred foundation of the ruler's legitimacy of rule derived from 'divine right' to a secular notion which saw the ruler invested with sovereignty by the people in the 'covenant'.

Jean Bodin provided one influential theoretical account of 'sovereignty' (that is, *maiestas*). Writing in the second half of the sixteenth century during a time of civil war in France when Calvinist Huguenots and the Catholic monarchy confronted each other, Bodin asserted that there must exist within a state a clearly recognisable, legitimate supreme power which cannot be subordinated to any other power – be it within the state, or be it from without – and which cannot be limited by civil, or positive, or customary law (and is thus *legibus solutus*), but only by divine and natural law: '*maiestas est summa in cives ac legibusque soluta potestas*' (Bodin 1577: I.8 ('*puissance absolue & perpetuelle*');):

> The first prerogative (*marque*) of a sovereign prince is to give law to all in general and each in particular. But this is not sufficient. We have to add 'without the consent of any other, whether greater, equal or below him'. For if the prince is obligated to make no law without the consent of a superior, he is clearly a subject; if of an equal, he has an associate; if of subjects, such as the senate or the people, he is not sovereign. (Bodin, Book 10, chapter 10: 56]; see, for example, Engster 1996; Franklin 1973; Hueglin 1999: 42–8, 169–70, 175, 178, 181; King 1974; Lewis 1968; Quaritsch 1970: 41, 107–9, 266–7, 510–11; Salmon 1996)

'Externally', *maiestas* signifies a particular form of independence and autonomy: a 'sovereign' state (or ruler) is not subject to the *lex* of other powers, be it the Pope and the Catholic Church, the Emperor, or any other kind of 'sovereign'. All sovereign states are, therefore, each others' equals in international law. 'Domestically', *maiestas* determined the constitution of the polity in three respects. First, it is the sovereign, and only the sovereign, who has the competency to determine those enforceable rules which bind the subjects in their behaviour. Secondly, law is valid because it issues from the will of the sovereign. It is binding, not because it is 'good' or 'just' law or within the orbit of customary law, but because it has been issued by the 'sovereign' law-giver – on the basis of respect for divine and natural law. While the sovereign may alter the law as he pleases, positive law itself is unchallengeable and as such releases the sovereign from the need to justify it. This law is valid for all the members or groups within the polity: '. . . *le Prince ou Duc, qui a puissance de donner loy à tous ses subiects en general, & à chacun en particulier*'. Thirdly, while the unity of sovereignty needs to be preserved, a distinction needs nevertheless to be made between the possession of sovereignty or the actual form of state and the form of administration, between *maiestas* and *gubernatio*. All intermediate powers are radically excluded from 'sovereignty', which is one and indivisible; *administratio* can, however, be delegated to corporate bodies or individuals. Hueglin (1999: 47) sums up Bodin's position well: 'unitary concentration of sovereign powers, but decentralised administration by mandated agents or representatives'.

Thomas Hobbes developed his political theory during the revolutionary upheavals in seventeenth-century England. For Hobbes, the state was constituted on the basis of a social contract. Hobbes's starting-point was the 'state of nature' (*societas naturalis*) which was populated by (hypothetically) free and equal individuals. In the 'state of nature', 'the weakest has strength enough to kill the strongest, either by secret machinations, or by confederacy with others, that are in the same danger than himselfe': there is always 'warre, as if of every man, against every man':

> [T]here is no place for Industry; because the fruit thereof is uncertain: and consequently no Culture of the Earth; no Navigation, nor use of the commodities that may be imported by Sea; no commodious Building; no instruments of moving, and removing such things as require much force; no Knowledge of the face of the Earth; no account of Time; no Arts; no Letters; no Society; and which is worst of all, continuall feare, and danger of violent death: And the life of man, solitary, poore, nasty, brutish, and short. (Hobbes [1651] 1991: 89)

The 'state of nature' is thus a state of lawlessness, a state in which individuals are not bound by the force of any agreed human laws. Hence, it is a condition in which there is a 'full and absolute Libertie in every Particular man' (Hobbes [1651] 1991: 149). To escape from this violent, dangerous, and unsociable 'state of nature', men constitute a civil society through mutual agreement. By covenanting to become subjects of a commonwealth, the individuals put themselves under the authority of the civil laws. In a sense, the individuals forfeit liberty in an act of subjection: 'But Civil Law is an Obligation, and takes from us the Liberty which the law of Nature gave us. Nature gave a Right to every man to secure himselfe by his own strength, and to invade a suspected neighbour, by way of prevention; but the Civil Law takes away that Liberty, in all cases where the protection of the Law may be safely stayd for' (Hobbes [1651] 1991: 200).

In the commonwealth based on the social contract, all men are subjects, except he on whom all have agreed to confer power and who thereby becomes sovereign over them. The rights of individuals and the sovereignty of the 'people' were dissolved in the *potestas* of the *Leviathan*, save the right of self-preservation; whatever the sovereign does is by virtue of the powers men have unconditionally conferred on him. For Hobbes, the sovereignty of the state presupposed, on the one hand, the eradication of internal contenders for supremacy. On the other hand, the 'idea' of sovereignty was premised on the notion of 'unity'. In Hobbes's classical formulation, without a common power man remains in a 'state of nature' in which his life is 'solitary, poore, nasty, brutish, and short' and men are nothing but a 'confusion of a disunited Multitude' (Hobbes [1651] 1991: 89, 122). 'Sovereignty' means the reduction of all individual wills 'unto one Will', thus establishing 'a reall Unitie of them all, in one and the same Person', and 'the Multitude so united in one Person, is called a Common-Wealth, in latine CIVITAS' (120). The sovereign, thus established, 'is the publique Soule, giving Life and Motion to the Common-Wealth' (230). The sovereign is the 'very able Architect' who designs 'one firme and lasting edifice' by abolishing diversity and irregularities or by explicitly sanctioning them (221): 'Where there be divers Provinces, within the Dominion of a Common-Wealth, and in those Provinces diversity of Lawes . . . [they] are now Lawes, not by vertue of the Praescription of time, but by the Constitutions of their present Soveraigns' (186). As far as individuals are concerned, they must be forced into uniformity:

> [T]here is in mens aptnesse to Society, a diversity of nature, rising from their diversity of Affections; not unlike to that we see in stones brought together for a building of an Aedifice. For as that stone which by the asperity, and irregularity of Figure, takes more room from others, that it selfe fills; and for the hardnesse, cannot be easily made plain, and thereby hindereth the building, is by the builders cast away as unprofitable, and troublesome: so also, a man that by asperity of Nature, will strive to retain those things which to himself are superfluous, and to others necessary; and

for the stubbornness of his Passions, cannot be corrected, is to be left, or cast out of Society, as cumbersome thereunto. (Hobbes [1651] 1991: 106)

The notion of 'unity' and 'uniformity' of a commonwealth was not unique to Hobbes's political philosophy. Two decades or so after Hobbes's *Leviathan*, Samuel Pufendorf, reflecting above all on the constitution of the Holy Roman Empire of the German Nation, argued against 'irregular' forms of government [*respublica irregularis*] 'in which we do not find that unity which is the essence of a state so completely established, not because of a disease or fault in the administration of the country, but because the irregularity of its form has been as it were legitimated by public law and custom' (Pufendorf [1673] 1991: 144). Such an 'irregular' form of government is defined by the fact that:

the parts of the supreme sovereignty belong separately and independently to different persons and bodies of the same commonwealth, so that individuals hold whatever part they have by their own right and administer it according to their own judgment, whereas they are like subjects in regard to the remaining parts of sovereignty. (Pufendorf [1672] 1994: VII.5.13)

Compared with such an 'irregular' form, a 'perfect and regular' state is defined by a union of the sort 'through which all things pertaining to its rule seem, as it were, to proceed from one soul' (Pufendorf [1672] 1994: VII.5.13; see also Boucher 2001; Roeck 1984). As we shall see shortly, Pufendorf's position can be understood as a critique of Johann Althusius's theory.

To return to Hobbes, we should recall that for Hobbes '. . . the Authority of the Law . . . consisteth in the Command of the Soveraign only' (Hobbes [1651] 1991: 189). As he asserted in the *Dialogue*, 'a Law is the Command of him, or them that have the Soveraign Power, given to those that be his or their Subjects, declaring Publickly, and plainly what every of them may do and what they must forbear to do' (Hobbes [1681] 1971: 71). Hobbes's sovereign is thus above the law and his laws are anterior to justice; indeed, his laws define what justice is. Neither justice nor the idea that laws were reasonable gave them legitimacy, but only the fact that they were the expression of the legislative will of the sovereign: '[I]t is manifest that before there was a law, there could be no Injustice, and therefore Laws are in their Nature Antecedent to Justice and Injustice, and you cannot deny but there must be Law-makers before there were any Laws, and Consequently before there was any Justice, I speak of Humane Justice' (Hobbes [1681] 1971: 72–3).

Hobbes drove this point home in his discussion of the idea of fundamental law. Rather than perceive fundamental law as 'constituting' a limit to the sovereign's legislative will, he understood it as referring to the stability and maintenance of the foundation of the commonwealth:

> For a Fundamentall Law in every Common-wealth is that, which being taken away, the Common-wealth faileth, and is utterly dissolved; as a building without Foundation is destroyed. And therefore a Fundamentall Law is that, by which subjects are bound to uphold whatsoever power is given to the Soveraign . . . without which the Common-wealth cannot stand; such as is the power of War and Peace, of Judicature, of Election of Officers, and of doing whatsoever he shall think necessary for the Publique good. (Hobbes [1651] 1991: 200)

He expressed the same thought succinctly in *Behemoth* (Hobbes [1682] 1840: 248–9): 'I understand not how one law can be more fundamental than another, except only that law of nature that binds us all to obey him, whosoever he be, whom lawfully and for our own safety, we have promised to obey; nor any other fundamental law to a King but *salus populi*, the safety and well-being of his people.' This was a position contrary to that taken by Bodin who had recognised the constraining power of the '*leges imperiales*' (Burns 1959). Hence, for Hobbes, sovereignty was above all the basic fact of political power; it was as Yale (1972: 155) stresses, 'the very political fact of effective power to command obedience'.

Whereas Jean Bodin acknowledged divine and natural law as limitations to the power of the sovereign, Hobbes's sovereign was unlimited by natural, divine, or customary law. His sovereign exercised above all epistemic power, establishing hegemony over the political discourse of society by determining what was to be considered to be 'good' or 'bad'. Bodin had acknowledged the existence of intermediate groups or corporations and tried to tie them into a hierarchical system with delegated administration. Hobbes's vision sees society populated, not by factions, groups, or traditional 'orders', but by ('possessive') individuals. His theory perceives of 'a unitary state presiding over and regulating an individualized society, held together no longer by a network of group formations with their own spheres of thought and action . . . but by a hegemonic public discourse about the rules of the game' (Hueglin 1999: 53).

Manifestly, Hobbes's position was ultimately revolutionary. Against Hobbes's ideas regarding law and supreme power, Chief

Justice Matthew Hale's '*Reflections on Mr. Hobbes His Dialogue of the Lawe*' marshalled the counter-arguments on the basis of English common law. Against Hobbes's intellectual constructions aimed at generating general and universal propositions, Hale upheld the view of politics and law-making as a practical activity which was embedded in customs and traditions and rooted in time and place: 'The Lawes of England . . . are Institutions introduced by the will of and Consent of others implicitely by Custome and usage, or Explicitely by written laws or Acts of Parlem[t1] (Hale 1945: 505). The laws of England do indeed 'teach us, that the King is the only Supreame Governour of this Realme', so that none but he can make laws 'oblidgeing the Subjects of this Realme' (508). Yet, 'there is a Certaine Solemnitie and Qualification of that Power, namely with the advice and assent of the 2 houses of Parlem[t] w[th]out which no Law can be made' (508). Nor can the king repeal a law without the like consent (509). It was this understanding that Hobbes's conceptualisation of sovereignty aimed to dislodge.

Hobbes's conceptualisation was embraced most fully in the nineteenth century (Francis 1980). Among Victorian jurists, A. V. Dicey has been particularly influential. Pursuing Hobbes's argument about law as command, he saw Parliament as the sovereign law-maker: 'Parliament does constitute such a supreme legislative authority or sovereign power as . . . must exist in every civilised state' (Dicey [1885] 1915: 59). The sovereignty of the 'Queen-in-Parliament' manifests itself in Parliament's possessing 'the right to make or unmake any law whatsoever; and, further, that no person or body is recognised . . . as having the right to override or set aside the legislation of Parliament' (Dicey [1885] 1915: 37–8). The debate in the United Kingdom on the application of human rights conventions or the binding force of European Union legislation on the United Kingdom Parliament is systematically linked to the Diceyean argument of the unrestricted right of Parliament to make or unmake any law whatsoever. We should note, then, that just as in Hobbes, we can observe in Dicey's position 'a deep-seated political belief in the need for a strong central power able to make authoritative decisions' (Loughlin 2000: 138).

Hobbes's contractual theory of rule was couched in secular terms. Yet, contractualism did not necessarily have to be secular. During the period of politico-religious conflicts in France, the Netherlands, and Scotland in the second half of the sixteenth century, Calvinist political theorists developed theories of contractual rule in which the notion of *princeps legibus solutus* was challenged by the idea that it was not the ruler but the people who were freed from legal constraint, *populus legibus solutus*. The contractual theory of these Calvinist '*monarchomachs*' was dominated by the idea of a reciprocal bond between ruler and people. This idea was founded on the biblical doctrine of the covenant, the Old Testament *foedus duplex* between God and the people, on the one hand, and between the king and the people, on the other hand (Oestreich 1982: 168). By distinguishing between these two pacts – as was the case in the core text of the Calvinist monarchomachs, *Vindiciae contra tyrannos* (1574–9) – the political rulers were now denied that immediate divine right which the Reformation had initially tended to ensure them. The law and the contract were now seen to intervene between God and the monarch, and the royal acts were considered to be subjected to the test of mere human reason; should the ruler not fulfil his obligation to ensure piety and provide justice, the people could not be held to obey him (Allen 1951: 302–32; Oestreich 1982: 135–54). In the setting of the Holy Roman Empire, it was Johannes Althusius who systematically developed the monarchomachs' notion of popular sovereignty, grounding it in natural law.

While the 'sovereignty' discourse is intricately linked to the formation of the territorial state, there has been an 'alternative' tradition which grew out of reflections on the constitutional structure of the Holy Roman Empire. As Thomas Hueglin (1999) has recently demonstrated, the political theory of Johannes Althusius (1557–1638) is still of considerable importance. Althusius developed a political theory 'based on pluralized governance committed to the autonomy of partial societies with distinct objectives and beliefs' (Hueglin 1999: 9). Contemporary theories of territorial and societal federalism, multi-level governance and consociational democracy may be seen as pursuing perspectives already to be found in Althusius' political theory (Hueglin 1999; see also: Krawietz 1988).

Althusius described political society as an ascending series of corporate groups. Carl J. Friedrich (1965: ix–x) summarised Althusius's architecture of political society succinctly:

> Beginning with the family as . . . a natural and co-organic entity, he suggested that on successive levels of political community those who live together in order and harmony and whom he called 'symbiotes' are united by a pact, expressed or implied, to share things in pursuit of common interests and utility. The village was for him a federal union of families, as was the guild; the town a union of guilds; the province a union of towns and cities; the kingdom or state a union of such provinces; and the empire

a union of such states and free cities . . . Thus, when we arrive at the top, the members of a state are neither individual persons nor families, but are politically organized collectivities, namely, the provinces and cities . . . [The union] is . . . the institutionalized framework of an existential communal reality. This reality consists in the sharing of values, interests, and beliefs . . . it transcends the wilful determination of the participants, it comes into being as part of their very nature, and merely needs to be recognized and consciously organized in the *pactum* or bond of union which makes it explicit.

The question then arises where in this state – understood as a consociation of consociations established on the basis of a compact (or covenant), not between individuals but among communities – does sovereignty reside? Althusius ascribed the *ius maiestatis* to the universal consociational community as a whole: the *populus universus in corpus unum symbioticum consociatus* was the actual bearer of *maiestas*. The *summus magistratus* was simply the administrator and executor of its power together with a conciliar body of the so-called ephors as the representatives of the commonwealth. *Vis-à-vis* the ephors individually, the *summus magistratus* was considered to be superior; *vis-à-vis* the whole body of ephors, however, he was considered inferior. Althusius mapped this distinction onto the fundamental distinction between the *ius regis* and the *ius populi*: 'The *ius regis* was temporary and personal, whereas the *ius populi* was permanent; the king possessed the *ius regis* as a revokable mandate, whereas the *ius populi* belonged to the consociation and could not be alienated by it' (Gross 1964: 172; see also Hofmann 1988; Hoke 1988: 246–7). For Althusius, the sovereign power of the people was premised, however, upon their prior covenant with God, who alone was the true sovereign (Gross 1964: 113). After all, Althusius was a Calvinist. Hueglin (1999: 4) speaks of a 'confederal sovereignty', 'a kind of co-sovereignty shared among partially autonomous collectivities consenting to its exercise on their behalf and within the general confines of this consent requirement.'

We have noted above that Bodin's endeavour to create political stability through legal security veered towards legal positivism as a result of the sovereign's position as above civil or positive law (*legibus solutus*). Althusius took issue with Bodin's position:

Our question is whether the power and office of whoever is said to have supreme power should be subjected to civil law and jurisdiction. Bodin says no, and many agree with him. In their judgement, supreme power is above civil law and not limited by it. But that is not what I would say. For to be free power from civil law is to release it somewhat from the bonds of natural and divine law. There is no civil law, however, nor can there be any, which would not contain a certain degree of that immutable equity which is both natural and divine . . . hence, if a general civil law given by a prince is fair and just, who is to free him from the obligation of this very law? On the contrary, it should be in the judgement of the supreme legislator that whatever we may wish that others do to us, we should also do to them. (Althusius [Politica]: IX.21, quoted and translated in Hueglin 1999: 173–4; see also: Scupin 1965; 1988)

Althusius thus limited the exercise of 'supreme power' in two ways. First, he insisted on the mandated quality of the power of the *summus magistratus* and asserted that 'for greater is the authority and power in the many than in the one who has been constituted by the many and is less than they are' (Althusius [Politica]: XXXIII.20, translated and quoted by Hueglin 1999: 186). Secondly, he perceived of a constitutional link between natural and positive law that bestows legitimacy upon the posited law.

Historically, the development of state sovereignty was accelerated as a result of agreements between states in the Treaties of Westphalia in 1648 at the end of the Thirty Years' War. Then, governments recognised each others' autonomy from external interference in the most important matter of the time, religious belief. No longer, so governments pledged, would they support foreign co-religionists in conflict with their states. This agreement changed the balance of power between territorial authority and confessional groups in favour of the state. It created the precondition for the build-up of an effective system of control and supervision by the state over the population. We should be clear, however, about the characteristics of the sovereignty as defined in the settlements of the Thirty Years' War. In the Westphalian Peace Treaties of 1648, all electors, princes, and estates of the Holy Roman Empire had their old rights, prerogatives, liberties, and privileges confirmed together with their *superioritas territorialis* in all matters spiritual and secular (*libero iuris territorialis tam in ecclesiasticis quam politicis exercisio*) (IPO, Article VIII, §1). This *ius territorialis* included the right to levy taxes, to legislate for their subjects, and to raise an army. Article VIII, §2, also confirmed their right to enter into alliances among themselves and with foreign powers to ensure their own preservation and security, as long as such alliances would not be directed against the emperor, the empire, or the peace treaties. As a result of this provision, one of the constitutive parts of the empire, the Imperial Estates, became subjects in international law. Eventually, these two provisions would allow the larger and more powerful territorial princes to claim (and achieve) 'sovereignty'. However, *ius territorialis* was not identical with 'sovereignty'. Only if, and as long as, territorial laws did not contradict imperial legislation, did the rule of non-intervention and non-interference apply. To that extent Westphalian *ius territorialis* did not constitute a highest, ultimate authority but retained the principle of the subjection of all members of the Holy Roman Empire to the emperor and the institutions of the *Reich*. The two supreme courts of the empire did not only guarantee the subjects of the territorial rulers, that is, of the Imperial Estates, protection against arbitrary treatment and perversion of justice, but they also supervised and scrutinised territorial legislation. Through their norm-setting rulings, the Supreme Imperial courts reinforced the limits to *ius territorialis* and erected a barrier against the appropriation of full sovereignty by the estates. What was being reinforced in the treaties was a system of shared *superioritas*. This principle of shared *superioritas* is not identical with the notion of 'sovereignty as non-intervention', which is normally understood to have been laid down in the Westphalian Peace Treaties. Krasner is right to stress that this idea of sovereignty as non-intervention was first formulated as a principle by Emer de Vattel in the eighteenth century.

Since the mid-seventeenth century in continental Europe the purpose of the state was seen, both by the rulers themselves and the majority of political theorists, as going beyond the confines of preserving *pax et iustitia*; it now comprised the task of actively promoting the secular and material welfare of the state and its population. The promotion of this-worldly happiness of the population replaced the ruler's traditional duty to assist in its other-worldly salvation. Hence, to an ever greater extent, justification for monarchical rule was based on the claim that it would bring about and enhance the secular and material welfare of the state and its citizens. This 'state-objective' was particularly characteristic of the political regime of 'enlightened' absolutism that was embraced by rulers across continental Europe in the eighteenth century. This was the type of regime against which Immanuel Kant formulated his republican theory. Looking back on the changes in the justification of monarchical domination, we notice that the magical and religious-sacral elements of the beliefs that legitimated domination as a 'divine right of kings' were replaced by the secular notions of safety, security, and welfare which the rulers strove, and were expected, to provide for their subjects.

THE SOVEREIGNTY OF THE PEOPLE

In the late eighteenth century, the idea of 'popular sovereignty' came to challenge this notion of the legitimacy of rule, grounded as that notion was in the rulers' performing their tasks and functions well. It was during the struggle of the American colonies for independence from Britain and during the crisis and revolutionary overthrow of the French monarchy in the last third of the eighteenth century that a new principle for the political legitimisation of political authority became firmly established: the state is legitimate only insofar as it enacts the people's will and is, thereby, responsive and accountable to 'the public'. Not only had the people of France abolished, or overthrown, an established political order; they had also established a new political principle in that they replaced the idea of the state's authority to define public right and 'welfare' with their claim to a popular mandate to rule.

The idea of 'popular sovereignty' postulated that political authority was legitimate only if it was bestowed, and willed, by the people, and not because of the 'state-objectives', however defined, which it strove to achieve. The people, not the king, were seen as the source of the law. The Virginia Bill of Rights of 1776 made this point very succinctly: 'All power is vested in, and consequently derived from, the people . . . [M]agistrates are their trustees and servants, and at all times amenable to them' (Article 2; in Morison 1965: 149–51). A related idea was the assertion in the French Declaration of the Rights and Duties of Man and Citizen of 1789 that 'The source of all sovereignty is essentially in the nation; no body, no individual can exercise authority that does not proceed from it in plain terms' ('*Le principe de toute souveranité residé essentiellement dans la Nation; nul corps, nul individu ne peut exercer d'autorité qui n'en émane expressément*'; in Anderson (ed) 1904: 59).

'The sovereignty of the people' was understood as being inalienable, that it could not be revoked by, or ceded to, some other body or person. The first and decisive act of exercising this sovereignty was believed to consist in the people giving themselves a constitution under which they agree to live together. In designing a constitution, so it was thought, the people create a government and give it powers, but they also regulate and restrain the powers so given. 'Popular sovereignty' is thus one particular attempt to address the problem of legitimacy of political institutions. 'The people', understood as the whole body of a territory's legal inhabitants, are imagined as the collective source of the state's authority, determining how this authority should be constructed and employed (Yack 2001). In this sense, 'popular sovereignty' expresses itself in the 'constituent sovereignty' of the people. This conceptualisation raises the following issue. Given that 'the people' establish the political institutions and thus create a political community in the first place, how can the body of 'the people' be defined? Who are 'the people'? As Yack (2001: 523) succinctly states: 'An appeal to the people is an appeal beyond the constituted authority of states actors and institutions to the community that lends them their authority. And if the appeal to the people is an appeal beyond the state, why should we imagine peoples as limited by the contingent borders that a history of accident, force, and fraud have [sic] established for states?' According to Yack, the answer to the question of the 'prepolitical' characteristics of 'the people' is provided by 'the nation': 'in order to conjure up an image of the people as standing apart from and prior to the establishment of political authority, you have to think of its members as sharing something more than political relationships' (Yack 2001: 525).

Clearly, Yack refers to a central problem. Robert Dahl (1989: 193) formulated this problem concisely: 'To say that all people . . . are entitled to the democratic process begs a prior question. When does a collection of persons constitute an entity – a 'people' – entitled to govern itself democratically?' Yack's reference to the idea of the 'nation' is one possible answer. During the first few decades after the French Revolution the notion of the 'nation' state came to stand for the idea that legitimate government could be based only upon the principle of national self-determination and that, at least ideally, state and nation ought to be identical with one another. In the imagery of the 'nation', the plurality and antagonisms of 'society' were moulded into a political entity. The nation became the 'unitary' body in which sovereignty resided. Yet, who or what was to constitute the nation? In the French tradition, the nation was constituted as a unity of individuals who willed to form a voluntary association between themselves and who, as citizens, enjoyed civil equality and equal political citizenship rights as 'of right'. French nationhood is thus state-centred and constituted by political unity. At the same time, the concept of the 'general will' and the notion of *la République une et indivisible* have imparted on this conceptualisation of nationhood a strong sense of uniformity and universality that is adverse to all (ethno-political or cultural) particularisms. As a logical consequence, and in the tradition of the absolutist state, the centralised post-revolutionary Jacobin state embarked upon a policy of centralisation, assimilation, and the eradication of regional and other differences.

This assimilationist tendency is not unique to the French conceptualisation of nation. It can also be found in that tradition that sees a nation, not as a bearer of universal political values, but as a predetermined community bound by blood and heredity. In this tradition, of which Germany has historically been the main representative, the nation is conceptualised as an organic cultural, linguistic, or racial community. Ethno-cultural commonalities form the basis for the integration of a collectivity of individuals into a nation. In this conceptualisation of nationhood, membership in the nation, defined as a community of descent with common culture and language, is the presupposition of citizenship in the nation's state. Territorial boundaries are determined by considerations of ethnic homogeneity; citizenship rights are premised upon membership in the ethno-cultural group; one main objective of the state is the welfare of the ethno-cultural community; and ethno-cultural conflicts, including those of a religious or linguistic kind, are politically more sensitive and more important than those linked to socio-economic inequality or gender issues, for example.

Clearly, these two conceptualisations of the 'nation' do emphasise important differences. But to the extent that belonging to a nation is understood to translate into the entitlement to the acquisition of citizenship in the political community, the difference should not be exaggerated. Across Europe, 'the vast majority of citizens simply inherit their status from their parents: it comes to them as a matter of birth, like a title to family property' (Canovan 2000: 426; 2005). This is the first of three 'typical' routes to citizenship: by descent, that is, having parents who are already citizens (*ius sanguinis*). The second is by virtue of having been born in the country (*ius soli*). Finally, there is the route via petitioning for, and being granted, citizenship. Particularly in the case of *ius soli*, there is a manifest element of the accidental to citizenship status – above all in those cases where the parents themselves are not citizens of the state whose citizenship the new-born child acquires. It also makes the composition of the political community itself 'accidental' or 'contingent'. In the case of the United States, for example, the Fourteenth Amendment established 'nativity' as the foundation for determining membership in the political community: '[I]t allows for the vast majority of the American population to attain equal political status, thereby enabling democratic self-governance and individual self-determination. In this way, the arbitrary and accidental nature of citizenship is precisely that which is celebrated' (Nyers 2006: 34). Yet, as Nyers argues, there is a vociferous political debate in the United States that perceives of 'birthright' citizenship of individuals born on US territory to non-citizen parents as 'accidental citizenship' that lacks affective qualities or affective ties of allegiance, leading to citizenship becoming a purely instrumental calculation and thus justifying revoking it because of its not being 'essential'. Yet, '[i]f birthright is always at risk of being exposed as a birth accident, then the sovereign body politic equally risks being revealed as arbitrary and capricious. When the subject form of citizenship is the accident form, citizenship is exposed as being incidental and contingent, not essential and enduring' (Nyers 2006: 26).

Even if we leave the contested issue of transnational migration and citizenship to one side (and we shall address some aspects of this issue in Chapter 5), then we should nevertheless recognise, first, the contingent character of the territorial boundaries of a state and, secondly, the contingent composition of 'its' people. Who wins power to delimit the boundaries of the political community tends to depend upon the outcome of violent conflicts, wars, and civil wars. The contingent composition of the 'people' as well as the mix of *ius soli* and *ius sanguinis* citizenship put a premium on perceiving the constitution-making body and the 'people' as the collectivity of citizens who, in a Habermasian reading, wish to recognise each other as free and equal, and thus as equally entitled to an equal possession of private and public autonomy.

Yet, any idea of a 'pre-political' (pre-constitutional) body of individuals presupposes an abstract, ultimately 'unhistorical' understanding of constitutional processes. Such an understanding is paradigmatically manifested by Thomas Paine, the British-born radical pamphleteer of the American Revolution. He argued in *The Rights of Man* (1791) that a constitution was 'a thing antecedent to the government, and always distinct therefrom' ([1791] 1985: 192); 'formed by the people in their original character', the constitution served 'not only as an authority, but as a law of control to the government' ([1791] 1985: 187). In the revolutionary period, the idea was reinforced that the rule of law meant that the state, as much as the citizens, had to submit to the laws of the land; that, in effect, not only had law to be independent of the state, constituting, as it were, an autonomous realm, but it had also to be superior to it: then, and only then, could it be conceived of as binding, not only for the subjects or citizens, but for the state itself. This was the core idea behind revolutionary constitutional politics: political rule was established through a constitution and, once established, also limited by it.

'Formed by the people in their original character': in this phrase is summed up the innovative, novel characteristics of the 'modern' constitution. The sovereign people exist in a pre-constitutional, or pre-political condition, as equal individuals in an 'uncivil' state – an idea that we have already encountered in our discussion of Kant's political theory in Chapter 1, and of Hobbes's position in this chapter. If we follow Althusius, however, we should assert that the people are already constituted, and have a constitution in the corporations to which they belong and societal and political federalism that arises out of the structured interdependencies of these political and civil corporations. In his study on constitutionalism, McIlwain quotes Viscount Bolingbroke who, in 1733, upheld the idea of an 'ancient' constitution – a constitutional idea equally removed from Paine as it is from Hobbes; an idea as close in spirit to Althusius as it is sympathetic to Hale's stance:

> By 'constitution' we mean, whenever we speak with propriety and exactness, that assemblage of laws, institutions and customs, derived from certain fixed principles of reason, directed to certain fixed objects of the public good, that compose the general system, according to which the community hath agreed to be governed. (Bolingbroke, quoted in: McIlwain 1947: 3)

In this understanding, a 'constitution' is 'the recognition of how the people are already constituted by their assemblage of fundamental laws, institutions and customs' (Tully 1995: 60). The 'modern' constitution, on the other hand, appears to be the result of a wilful imposition of a people that has freed itself of its history and tradition. McIlwain concisely restated the basic ideas underpinning Paine's conceptualisation of the 'modern' constitution:

> [T]here is a fundamental difference between a people's government and that people's constitution, whether the government happens to be entrusted to a king or to a representative assembly . . . this constitution is 'antecedent' to the government . . . it defines the authority which the people commits to its government, and in doing so thereby limits it . . . any exercise of authority beyond these limits by any government is an exercise of 'power without right' . . . in any state in which the distinction is not actually observed between the constitution and the government there is in reality no constitution, because the will of the government has no check upon it, and that state is in fact a despotism. (McIlwain 1947: 9)

In a sense, part of the debate between the 'Federalists' as the defender of the proposed new constitution of the United States in the debates of the late 1780s and their 'antifederalist' critics was to do with this basic 'constitutional' distinction: did the 'constituent sovereignty' reside in the states of the American confederation, or in 'the people' 'in their original character'? Who, in this invocation of 'We, the People', were the people? As James Wilson, a forceful defender of the federalist case stated: '[I]f there are errors in government, the people have the right not only to correct and amend them, but likewise totally to change and reject its form . . . I view the States as made *for* the people as well as *by* them, and not the people as made for the States. The people, therefore, have a right . . . to form either general government, or state governments in what manner they please' (James Wilson, in: McMaster/Stone (eds), I: 230, 317).[2] It was a debate in which it was argued that an 'unconstituted' people, rather than constituted states, exercised constituent sovereignty as their due and could deploy it as they pleased, and in which the sovereignty of the states that made up the Confederation was seen by the Federalists as possessing delegated 'sovereignty' only, mandated by the people. The question as to where 'sovereignty' was considered to reside – 'We, the people' or 'We, the states' – was not just a matter of the most appropriate institutional arrangement devised by the constitution, but arose also in the context of the debate about who had the 'sovereign' right to ratify the constitution. The argument in favour of the states legislatures was forcefully presented by Oliver Elsworth. He observed that:

> a new sett [sic] of ideas seemed to have crept in since the articles of Confederation were established. Conventions of the people, or with power derived expressly from the people, were not then thought of. The Legislatures were considered as competent . . . The fact is that we exist at present . . . as a federal Society, united by a charter one article of which is that alterations therein may be made by the Legislative authority of the States. (in Farrand II: 91)

James Madison, on the other hand, upheld the idea of 'constituent sovereignty'. He argued that:

> the Legislatures were incompetent to the proposed changes. These changes would make essential inroads on the State Constitutions, and it would be a novel & dangerous doctrine that a Legislature could change the constitution under which it held its existence . . . He considered the difference to be between a system founded on the Legislatures only, and one founded on the people, to be the true difference between a *league* or *treaty*, and a *Constitution*. (Farrand II: 92–3)

Once sovereignty of the people had been established as the principle of legitimate political authority, the question had to be confronted whether there could be any limits to their sovereignty. Benjamin Constant classically formulated this concern with the limitations of popular sovereignty from a liberal perspective. For him, the principle of the sovereignty of the people expressed the idea that there exists 'the supremacy of the general will over any particular will' (Constant [1815] 1988: 175). On the basis of popular sovereignty, the law is the expression of the will of all, rather than the will of some. Yet, unless this sovereignty is limited, 'liberty may be lost notwithstanding that principle, or even through it' ([1815] 1988: 175):

> The universality of the citizens is sovereign in the sense that no individual, no faction, no partial association can arrogate sovereignty to itself, unless it has been delegated to it. But it does not follow from this that the universality of the citizens, or those who are invested with the sovereignty by them, can dispose sovereignly of the existence of individuals . . . At the point where independence and individual existence begin, the jurisdiction of sovereignty ends. (Constant [1815] 1988: 176–7)

The rights of the citizens to individual freedom, to religious freedom, to freedom of opinion and freedom of expression, to the enjoyment of property, and the freedom not to be subjected to arbitrary power: these are individual rights that citizens possess independently of all social and political authority. Whichever authority violates these rights becomes illegitimate: '[T]here are wills which neither the people, nor its delegates, have a right to have' (Constant [1815] 1988: 180). The argument in favour of limiting the sovereignty of the people (of any sovereignty, in fact) is, therefore, grounded in the claim that the individual is a bearer of inalienable rights. A political community must, therefore, be constituted in such a way that these rights are upheld.

Constant ties in this argument with the famous distinction he makes between the liberty of 'the ancients' and that of 'the moderns'. The 'liberty of the ancients' consisted, according to Constant, 'in an active and constant participation in collective power' (Constant [1819] 1988: 316). Public deliberation by the citizens on all matters that concerned them and the holding to account of all office bearers in public meetings are, for Constant, the hallmark of 'ancient liberty'. In his emphasis on the importance attached to the direct participation of the citizens in ruling the polis, Constant rehearses a theme that was central to Pericles's famous 'Funeral Oration', as Thucydides recounted it in his *History of the Peloponnesian War*, written around 400 BCE. In his eulogy to the war dead of Athens in the opening year of the Peloponnesian War, Pericles (at least in the words of Thucydides) spoke of Athens as a paradigmatic community whose constitution was called a 'democracy because power is in the hands not of a minority but of the whole people' – or at least of those men who had obtained the status of citizen: slaves, women, *metics* did not belong to them (Thucydides 1972 (trans.): 145). In this democratic community:

> each individual is interested not only in his own affairs but in the affairs of the state as well: even those who are mostly occupied with their own business are extremely well-informed on general politics – this is a peculiarity of ours: we do not say that a man who takes no interest in politics is a man who minds his own business; we say that he has no business here at all. (Thucydides 1972 (trans.): 147)

For Pericles, direct participation of the citizen in the public affairs of the polis and the observance of the law went hand-in-hand with an acceptance of diversity in the public sphere: 'We are free and tolerant in our private lives' (Thucydides 1972 (trans.): 145). Yet this was precisely a claim that Constant refuted. According to him:

> [a]ll private actions were submitted to a severe surveillance. No importance was given to individual independence, neither in relation to opinion, nor to labour, nor, above all, to religion . . . In the domains which seem to us the most useful, the authority of the social body interposed itself and obstructed the will of the individual. (Constant [1819] 1988: 311)

'Ancient liberty' was hence a form of liberty which Constant was loath to embrace as a normative ideal. Fortunately, so he suggested, the material conditions that grounded 'ancient liberty' had disappeared in modern times: the small size of the territory of the polis; the bellicosity between small-scale political communities constantly in fear of each other; the precedence of war over commerce; and slavery as an institution that allowed citizens the leisure of active citizenship. All these factors contributed to giving the individual a sense of personal importance and real influence as a citizen. Alas, the share which in antiquity everyone held in 'national sovereignty' has become, according to Constant, an abstract presumption in modern times:

> This compensation no longer exists for us today. Lost in the multitude, the individual can almost never perceive the influence he exercises. Never does his will impress itself upon the whole; nothing confirms in his eyes his own cooperation. The exercise of political rights, therefore, offers us but a part of the pleasures that the ancients found in it, while at the same time the

progress of civilization, the commercial tendency of the age, the communication amongst peoples, have infinitely multiplied and varied the means of personal happiness. (Constant [1819] 1988: 316)

The aim of the 'modern' citizen is thus 'the enjoyment of security in private pleasures' (Constant [1819] 1988: 317). The congenial political system for the defence and pursuit of such 'private pleasures' is representative government. In 1794, Maximilien Robespierre, the firebrand of the French Revolution, had declared that '[d]emocracy is not a state in which the people, continuously assembled, regulates by itself all public affairs . . . Democracy is a state in which the sovereign people, guided by laws which are its own work, does by itself all it can do well, and by delegates all that it could not' (quoted in: Dunn 2005: 116). Twenty-five years later, the 'liberal' Constant expressed his support for the representative system in virtually identical words: it is 'nothing but an organization by means of which a nation charges a few individuals to do what it cannot do or does not wish to do herself'; it is 'a proxy given to a certain number of men by the mass of the people who wish their interests to be defended and who nevertheless do not have the time to defend them themselves' (Constant [1819] 1988: 325–6). Political liberty for the 'modern' citizen consists in remaining vigilant and alert so that his representative will not alienate the power delegated to him for a certain length of time. The enjoyment of one's private independence and the pursuit of one's particular interests need thus to be balanced by public vigilance but not by the direct participation of the citizen in political rule.

We will now pursue the two themes that Constant played up – individual rights and representation in connection with the principle of popular sovereignty – in somewhat greater detail.

For Constant, it was evident that there are certain areas of individual behaviour over which even 'the people' have no right to exercise control. Frequently, such a claim was supported through references to natural rights, rights of man, or human rights – as we have observed in the previous chapters. These rights have been seen as a barrier against the exertions of the sovereign people. The Virginia Bill of Rights of 1776 (Article 1) claimed that:

all men are by nature equally free and independent, and have certain inherent rights, of which, when they enter into a state of society, they cannot by any compact deprive or divest their posterity; namely the enjoyment of life and liberty, with the means of acquiring and possessing property, and pursuing and obtaining happiness and safety.

The Declaration of Independence a few weeks later expressed the same thoughts in the following famous words:

> We hold these truths to be self-evident, that all men are created equal, that they are endowed by their Creator with certain unalienable rights, that among these are life, liberty, and the pursuit of happiness. That to secure these rights, governments are instituted among men, deriving their just powers from the consent of the governed. That whenever any form of government becomes destructive of these ends, it is the right of the people to alter or to abolish it. (Morison 1965: 157)

The Declaration thus put the defence of the rights and liberties of individuals against government at the very centre of the foundation of a new political commonwealth. Liberty and property as the natural rights of man had already been discussed in the political philosophy of John Locke. He had argued that God's natural law provided that 'no one ought to harm another in his life, health, liberty or possessions' and that, derived from this law, each person had a natural right to his life, liberty, and property as well as the 'executive right of nature' to protect his natural rights by whatever means necessary. The exercise of this 'executive right' was seen by him as a source of conflict in a state of nature and, as a consequence, men would seek peace by handing it over to a common authority. Through this transferral of the 'executive right', men established a political community (Locke [1689] 1989). Locke argued that men do not give up their rights when they enter into a political community. Rather, the primary function of a political community, or government, was the maintenance and protection of these rights. If government violated these rights, it forfeited the trust its citizens had put in it and could be legitimately overthrown. This conceptualisation of inalienable natural rights was quite distinct from the political philosophy of Thomas Hobbes. As we have seen, for Hobbes the 'state of nature' was a place of violence and devastation in which the life of man was 'solitary, poore, nasty, brutish, and short'; but once they entered into civil and political society, they surrendered their virtually unlimited rights almost totally to the ruler, or government: only through men divesting themselves of their natural rights could political authority be instituted and peace be achieved. For Locke, on the other hand, the 'state of nature', though lacking security, was potentially a place of civilisation and progress in which adult, male, property-owning individuals, who are each others' equals, enjoy freedom to dispose of their powers and possessions as they choose. It is here that individuals as bearers of 'inalienable' rights, capable of living within the bounds of natural law, realise their freedom.

Hobbes and Locke shared, however, a conception of 'negative' liberty. For Hobbes, a free man is a person who 'in those things, which by his strength and wit he is able to do, is not hindered to doe what he has a will to' and who performs his actions freely, in that he 'may refuse to do it if he will' (Hobbes [1651] 1991: 146). In his 'Essay concerning human understanding' (chapter 21), Locke ([1690] 1975) embraced this view: 'Liberty, 'tis plain, consists in a power to do or not to do; to do or forbear doing as we will. This cannot be denied.' And for both Locke and Hobbes:

> the law preserves our liberty essentially by coercing other people. It prevents them from interfering with my acknowledged rights, helps me to draw around myself a circle within which they may not trespass, and prevents me at the same time from interfering with their freedom in just the same way. (Skinner 1990: 305)

We should beware the import of this particular political philosophy. For what we encounter here is a condensed summary of the position of classical political liberalism – a position of which Constant's argument is a typical exemplar. According to Locke, men enjoy equal rights under the law of nature; therefore, no one can exercise authority over another except by that other person's consent. Political authority in a liberal polity, therefore, rests on the freely given consent of the governed. Furthermore, governments are instituted by popular consent in order to protect life, liberty, and property of the individual. Government finds its legitimacy as well as its limits in the performance of this, and only this, function. It is within the context of this political philosophy that liberalism since the late eighteenth century strove to lay down constitutional provisions that protected citizens from the interference by the state and to stipulate the rights that citizens have in the private sphere and 'civil society'. There was recognition of a separation between 'public' and 'private' spheres, between the 'state' and 'civil society'. Individuals were considered to be more than citizens with political interests, rights and duties; they were seen as possessing capacities and interests of a non-political nature which they were at liberty to express and pursue without the state's interference. Out of this thinking issued a conceptualisation of the constitution as that mechanism that established the state as a guarantor of individual liberty and societal autonomy, while, at the same time, limiting the state to that function. The (classical) liberal constitutional model thus aimed to combine an endorsement of the coercive role of the state as the enforcer of civil peace and collectively binding decisions (the Hobbesian tradition) with an endorsement of the right of protection of individuals and social groups against the agency of the state (the Lockean tradition).

We should pause for a moment and review the argument put forward so far. The starting point of our current discussion has been the idea of 'popular sovereignty'. In our analysis of Hobbes's argument concerning authority, we emphasised Hobbes's conceptualisation of law as the command issued by the sovereign. *Auctoritas non veritas facit legem*: law is grounded in authority, not in truth; it is the expression of the authoritative sovereign will. This view informed John Austin's influential conceptualisation of law as commands of the supreme political authority which are obeyed by citizens (or subjects) because infringement of the rules carries the threat of coercive sanctions (Austin [1832] 1995). As Martin Loughlin rightly asserts – and our reference to A. V. Dicey earlier in the chapter bears out this assertion – law as command:

> fits particularly well with modern ideas of representative democracy. We the people engage in a form of self-government by establishing a Parliament in which our representatives deliberate and make laws. These laws – Acts of Parliament – are the highest expressions of the will of the people and, in order to sustain a self-governing order, must be obeyed. (Loughlin 2000: 9)

'Law as command' is legitimate if it issues out of institutions backed up by the principle of popular sovereignty.

We have, however, also encountered another conceptualisation of law: 'law as right'. Whereas 'law as command' is the outcome of a political process, 'law as right' establishes the preconditions for the conduct of politics: 'Politics', so Kant asserted, 'must bend the knee before right' (*Perpetual Peace*). Loughlin sums up the difference between 'law as command' and 'law as right':

> If democracy is the modern legitimating principle for the idea of law as command, it is liberty or autonomy which provides the normative criterion of law as right . . . Law as right aims at no less than the elimination of the idea of the (political) sovereign and its replacement with the sovereignty of law. (Loughlin 2000: 223, 224)

Yet, we have encountered in Habermas's model of deliberative democracy, which he put forward on the basis of his discourse theory, an argument that would deny that there is such a strong and decisive separation between 'democracy' (out of which issues 'law as command') and 'law as right' (on the basis of which popular sovereignty is curtailed). As we recall, Habermas did not accept as sensible a question that aimed to determine what comes first: 'the individual liberties of the members of the modern market society or the rights of democratic citizens to political participation?' (Habermas 2001: 767). For Habermas, there is no choice to be made between Constant's 'liberty of the ancients' and 'liberty of the moderns'. There is a co-originality of the two forms of autonomy such that private and political autonomy require each other:

> Citizens can make an *appropriate* use of their public autonomy, as guaranteed by political rights, only if they are sufficiently independent in virtue of an equally protected private autonomy in their life conduct. But members of society actually enjoy their equal private autonomy to an equal extent – that is, equally distributed individual liberties have 'equal value' for them – only if as citizens they make an appropriate use of their political autonomy. (Habermas 2001: 767; see also: MacCormick 1993)

In his discussion of the forms of law, Loughlin distinguishes a third concept of law, 'law as custom', which we have encountered when we discussed Hale's critique of Hobbes. This conceptualisation of 'law as custom' also underpins Edmund Burke's critique of Thomas Paine's *Rights of Man*. Against, as he saw it, the abstract and metaphysical idea of natural law which he perceived to inform Paine's support for the rationalistic design of a constitution, he held up the concrete, 'real' English liberties grounded in history. These liberties are 'an *entailed inheritance* derived to us from our forefathers, and to be transmitted to our posterity; as an estate specially belonging to the people of this kingdom without any reference whatever to any other more general or prior right' (Burke [1790] 1968: 119; italics in original). In this conceptualisation, law is 'a set of conventional practices which frame, but do not establish, political order' (Loughlin 2000: 218). Law is understood as sedimented experience, a cultural code inscribed in the body politic. If legislation is the *modus vivendi* of law as command and proclamation the *modus vivendi* of law as right, law as custom lives through the art of rhetoric (Loughlin 2000: 217–27). Both 'law as right' and 'law as custom' may curtail, in political praxis, the sovereign will behind 'law as command'.

While 'popular sovereignty' is 'constrained' by (as well as grounded in) the 'rights' discourse, the institution of representation mediates 'popular rule' which remains nevertheless grounded in the will of the people. In the political writings and debates of the late eighteenth century, 'popular sovereignty' and 'representative government' were welded together. This was a point forcefully put forward by Constant as we have noticed above. The connection between 'popular sovereignty' and 'representation' had already been a central cause of disagreement in the debate on the American constitution. 'Different interests necessarily exist in different classes of citizens', argued James Madison, one of the 'Founding Fathers' of the American constitution:

> A zeal for different opinions concerning religion, concerning government, and many other points, as well of speculation as of practice; an attachment to different leaders ambitiously contending for pre-eminence and power . . . have, in turn, divided mankind into parties, inflamed them with mutual animosity, and rendered them much more disposed to vex and oppress each other than to co-operate for their common good . . . The most common and durable source of factions has been the various and unequal distribution of property. Those who hold and those who are without property have ever formed distinct interests in society. (Federalist Papers: no. 10)

Madison recognised that society was composed of different alliances, groupings, and parties, all of them pursuing a plurality of interests. He accepted factionalism and political conflict as an inherent aspect of a political community. Much as we take this view for granted in our time, when Madison and the other 'Federalists' espoused this point, they were taking their leave from a long tradition in political thinking that can be traced back to ancient Greece. The question of 'democracy' had been raised for the first time in the Greek polis in the first half of the fifth century BC. It was there that the idea was formulated and institutionalised that a substantial number of free, adult males should be entitled to participate in governing the political community.

However, the classical Greek notion of democracy was premised on the assumption that, in order for democratic rule to uphold the common good of the political community, the citizen body had to be highly homogeneous in order to avoid conflict and disagreements over the common good. A shared sense of the common good was seen to require a citizen body that was harmonious in its interests. Homogeneity and uniformity of interests and opinions was the prerequisite of democracy; democracy was not seen as that institutional arrangement that would create harmony out of diversity, but as the 'rule of the many' sharing a common understanding of the common weal. It was argued that heterogeneity of interests and opinions could be avoided only in a small city-state. Only in the polis could citizens acquire the knowledge of their city and their fellow citizens by direct observation, experience, or discussion that would allow them to gain an understanding of the common good. Furthermore, it was only in the polis that citizens could assemble in public, decide directly on the laws and policies, and participate actively in the administration of the city. Hence, the direct and active participation of the citizens in law-making, law-execution, and law-adjudication was seen as the core element of democracy. The idea that citizens could be 'represented' by other people was quite alien to classical democratic thinking. Only through this direct and active participation in public matters for the common good, could human beings realise their 'nature' and be good, 'virtuous' citizens (Dahl 1989).

The conviction that this kind of 'democracy' could only be viable in small republics was received wisdom well into the eighteenth century. In *The Spirit of the Laws*, Montesquieu ([1748] 1989) still endorsed that view, much as he also embraced the idea of the active citizen. He was, therefore, sceptical that direct and active 'democracy' could be established in the consolidated, large territorial states of his time. This view was widely accepted in the American colonies. 'A [Pennsylvanian] Farmer' expressed this view cogently in the debate on the new constitution:

> In order that a republic may preserve its liberty, it must not only have a good form of government, but it must be of a small extent; for if it possess extensive territory, it would be ruined by internal imperfection. The authority of government in a large republic does not equally pervade all parts; nor are the political advantages equally enjoyed by the citizens remote from the capital as by those in the vicinity; combinations consequently prevail among the members of the legislature, and this introduces corruption and is destructive of that confidence in government without which a free republic cannot be supported . . . in short, the diversity of the situation, habits, manners, and interests of the people in an extensive dominion, subjects the government to a thousand accidents, which would embarrass a republican government. (in Storing III: 3.14.9, 185; see also Brutus in: Storing II: 2.9.16, 369–70)

'A Farmer' asserted that, since a republic, given its size, is liable to be destroyed by external force, it is necessary to form 'a confederation of republics, as the only method to preserve internal freedom, together with external strength and respectability' (in Storing III: 3.14.10). Such a 'federal republic' or 'empire of states' is built upon the recognition of the sovereign equality of its members, but does not constitute the delegation of sovereignty to a 'national government' nor its alienation by a central body (A [Pennsylvanian] Farmer, April 1788, in: Storing III: 3.14.6, 183–4).

Madison turned these arguments on their head. For him, in large republics, there is a greater variety of parties and interests which makes it difficult for permanent majorities to emerge; small republics are particularly susceptible to oppression by a majoritarian faction, whereas in a large republic, the factions are more likely to balance each other off (Pitkin 1967: 190–8).

These concerns with the political effects of the diversity of interests and of factions were central to Madison's political theory. His conceptual distinction between a 'pure democracy' and a 'republic' is premised upon these concerns. A 'pure democracy', Madison insisted, is:

> a Society, consisting of a small number of citizens, who assemble and administer the Government in person, can admit of no cure for the mischief of faction. A common passion or interest will, in almost every case, be felt by a majority of the whole; a communication and concert results from the form of Government itself; and there is nothing to check the inducements to sacrifice the weaker party, or an obnoxious individual. (Federalist Papers: no. 10)

A 'pure democracy' does not, therefore, allow for factions but aims, according to Madison, at uniformity and homogenisation. He expressed this thought forcefully in a letter of October 1787:

> Those who contend for a simple Democracy, or a pure republic, activated by the sense of the majority, and operating within narrow limits, assume or suppose a case which is altogether fictitious. They found their reasoning on the idea, that the people composing Society, enjoy not only an equality of political rights; but that they have all precisely the same interests, and the same feelings in every respect. Were this in reality the case, their reasoning would be conclusive . . . The interest of the majority would be that of the minority also . . . We know however that no Society ever did or can consist of so homogeneous a mass of Citizens . . . In all civilized Societies, distinctions are various and unavoidable . . . There will be rich and poor; creditors and debtors; a landed interest, a mercantile interest, a manufacturing interest . . . (quoted in Dunn 2005: 214, n. 16)

Madison's solution to these problems was 'republican government' in which 'the delegation of the Government . . . to a small number of citizens' obtained. He defined a 'republic' as a form of government 'in which the scheme of representation takes place' (Federalist Papers: no. 10). In the case of Madison, then, the acceptance of the reality, and even legitimacy, of conflicting interests and competing factions went hand-in-hand with an attempt at devising an institutional structure that would secure the protection of minorities and the containment of factions. Let us look at the proposed institutional solutions in greater detail.

The proposed federation of the American states is one institutional solution. Jon Roper summed up succinctly one strand of Madison's and Hamilton's argument:

> [A] kaleidoscope of different alliances, groupings and interests across the diverse union would constantly form and reform. Minority groups could gain allies to transform themselves into temporary majorities. Majorities would lose friends, and be relegated to a subordinate influence. Such a democracy was energetic, shifting, changing, such that the prospects of a permanent majority, uniting for unworthy or even benign reasons, or of a regional hegemony were unlikely. (Roper 1989: 58)

This idea of countervailing factions and interests was complemented by the conviction that, in line with Montesquieu's political theory, an institutionalised separation and balance of powers within the state had to be created. The 'Federalists' argued that political authority had to be dispersed and many power centres had to be created to prevent the wholesale capture of authority by any one particular interest. It became accepted that in republican regimes there was a need for designing institutional mechanisms to prevent the concentration of power within the state. In the past, forms of 'mixed government' had been advocated in which the interests of 'the one', 'the few' and 'the many' (in the Aristotelian sense) could be represented and pursued. The British constitution with its institutional separation of the monarchy, the aristocratic upper chamber, and the lower house of commons was one of the longest established forms of government in Europe. Underlying its constitution was the idea that the exercise of power by one section had to be checked by the exercise of a countervailing power by other sections. However, the 'Federalists' developed this idea of the need to check power with power into the concept of the institutional separation of powers. Already in 1776, the Constitution of Virginia had stated unequivocally that 'The legislative, executive, and judiciary departments shall be separate and distinct, so that neither exercises the powers properly belonging to the other' (Morison 1965: 151–7). The Federal Constitution of 1787 entrenched a division of powers between the national government and the state governments, and within the national government between the three main functions of legislature, executive, and judiciary. Through the establishment of the House of Representatives and the Senate, there was a further balance within the legislature, allowing for the interests of 'the people' and those of the individual states to be pursued in different, though closely articulated institutional settings. This separation of powers was, however, not fully institutionalised. Given, for example, the involvement of both the executive (President) and the legislature in the appointment of Supreme Court judges, and given also the judicial politics of the Supreme Court through the institution of judicial review, we may be entitled to see powers as not so much clearly separated as closely interconnected and articulated. Still, the idea that legislative, executive, and judicial powers should not be exercised by one person or one group of people or one assembly, but should be institutionally disaggregated has become firmly entrenched in the constitutional and political self-understanding of Western liberal democracy.

However, Madison identified yet another safeguard of the common good. He was adamant that for a large-scale community, direct democracy was impossible as the people could not meet as a legislative body and had, therefore, to choose, or elect, representatives to do what they, as citizens, could not do themselves. The Constitution of Massachusetts of 1780 had already stated that 'the people of this commonwealth are not controllable by any other laws, than those to which their constitutional representative body have given their consent' (Article 10; in: Peters 1978: 48). Contained in this conceptualisation of representative government is the idea that law is positive, enacted law; it is reasoned law issuing out of the deliberations of an assembly of individuals who act as the representatives of the people. As we have already mentioned, Madison made this notion of representative government central to his political theory by defining a republic as 'a government in which the scheme of representation takes place' (Federalist Papers: no. 10). As he saw it, the delegation of the government to a small number of citizens elected by the rest had the positive effect to:

> refine and enlarge the public views by passing them through the medium of a chosen body of citizens, whose wisdom may but discern the true interest of their country and whose patriotism and love of justice will be least likely to sacrifice it to temporary or partial considerations. Under such a

183

regulation it may well happen that the public voice, pronounced by the representatives of the people, will be more consonant to the public good than if pronounced by the people themselves, convened for the purpose. (Federalist Papers: no. 10)

As 'proper guardians of the public weal', these representatives cannot be mere delegates or servants of their constituents. 'Representation' was thus conceived as that mechanism through which an 'extended republic' could be governed, and proper representational arrangements would ensure that 'temperate and respectable men', standing for 'reason, justice and truth' (Federalist Papers: no. 63), would be elected, men of 'more cool and sedate reflection' (Federalist Papers: no. 71). A 'virtuous' elite, striving for the common good, was to replace the 'virtuous' citizen. Indeed, in the words of Madison, in order to allow for 'republican' rule in an 'extensive territory', *the total exclusion of the people in their collective capacity*, from any share [in government]' was imperative (Federalist Papers: no. 62; italics in the original).

This view of representation did not go unchallenged. The 'anti-federalist' opponents of the draft constitution of the United States took issue with the idea of the 'virtuous representative'. Many of them, standing as they did in the classical tradition, would have preferred to have no representatives at all, but a 'direct democracy'. Liberty, for them, still referred to the direct political participation in public affairs. But if representation was to be institutionalised, then it should be of a different kind from the Federalists' idea. One 'anti-federalist' argued that:

> the idea that naturally suggests itself to our minds, when we speak of representatives, is that they resemble those they represent. They should be a true picture of the people, possess a knowledge of their circumstances and their wants, sympathise in all their distress, and be disposed to seek their true interests. (Melancton Smith, quoted in: Kramnick 1987: 44)

Smith insisted that a representative system ought not to seek 'brilliant talents', but 'a sameness, as to residence and interests, between the representative and his constituent' (Kramnick 1987: 44). In advocating short terms of office for representatives, he, and other anti-federalists, aimed also for a much greater control over the political office-holders, making them much more like mandated delegates than independent representatives.

But while there were these differences between 'Federalists' and 'Anti-Federalists' regarding the qualitative character of representation, they were agreed on one thing: if there was to be representation, it had to be 'actual', not 'virtual'. To put it differently, they were united in their opposition to the idea of representation as developed in the British constitution. The Americans shared the republican premise that 'the many' can judge and express the common good; within the British tradition, it was maintained that only the 'virtuous few' could do so. The Members of Parliament, as an important part of these 'virtuous few', were seen in the British tradition as representing not a particular place, or the idiosyncratic 'interests' of an individual or a group of individuals, but the whole nation. In his famous 'Speech at the Conclusion of the Poll to the Electors in Bristol', the British-Irish politician and political thinker, Edmund Burke said in 1774 that:

> Parliament is not a *congress* of ambassadors from different and hostile interests, which interests each must maintain, as an agent and advocate, against other agents and advocates; but Parliament is a *deliberative* assembly of *one* nation, with one interest, that of the whole – where not local purposes, not local prejudices, ought to guide, but the general good, resulting from the general reason of the whole. (Burke in: Hill 1975: 158)

Hence, according to Burke, it was not, for example, the 'interest' of the 'common people' that would be 'represented' *vis-à-vis* the king; nor the 'interest' of conflicting or antagonistic classes or status groups which would aim for some kind of peaceful accommodation of these 'interests' in a deliberative assembly. Rather, what was being represented was the common interest of the nation as a whole; and it was in the debate of free individuals that this common national interest could be recognised. It is the duty of Members of Parliament to reason and judge about the good of the whole, and 'the selfish wishes of parts of the nation, the wills of individual voters have nothing to do with it' (Pitkin 1967: 170–1). Samuel Beer has summarised Burke's position well, emphasising the close connection between the idea of 'representation' and 'parliamentary sovereignty':

> If the many had been enfranchised and deference abolished, the rule of the virtuous few would have collapsed into popular government. The great interests of realm and empire and the various ranks and orders of the governing class would have no longer been assured of their proper weight and voice in government. For that reason, sovereign authority could not be vested in the people but only in that complex body, the parliament, which, including king, lords, and commons, brought all virtues and all interests into a common deliberation in their proper ordering. (Beer 1993: 145)

Burke further argued that representation did not have to be an 'actual' one, in the sense that a constituency elects a Member of Parliament. He argued that disenfranchised groups or localities, which did not send a member to Parliament, may be 'virtually' represented by some member from some other constituency. This was for the simple reason that Members of Parliament were considered by Burke to represent unattached interests – 'interests to which no particular persons were so specially related that they could claim to be privileged to define the interest' (Pitkin 1967: 210). The agricultural interest, the trading interest, and the manufacturing interest, for example, were identified by Burke as such objective, 'fixed' interests which could be 'virtually' represented. This means, for example, that:

> [a]lthough the city of Birmingham elects no members to Parliament, it can still be virtually represented there because Bristol sends members; and these are really representatives of the trading interest, of which Birmingham, too, is a part. Although a member may be called the Representative of Bristol since he is elected there, he really represents Bristol's interest, which may also be the interest of many other cities like Bristol. (Pitkin 1967: 174)

This idea of 'virtual representation' was, manifestly, based on the assumption that one (or some) of the constituencies that do elect members share the interest of the disenfranchised group. Burke acknowledged that such an assumption could not always be made. Both in the case of the Irish Catholics and the American colonists, Burke asserted that no constituency that was 'actually' represented shared the interest of these excluded groups and he concluded that they had, therefore, to be represented 'actually' (Pitkin 1967: 177–8). The American colonists had, of course, also proclaimed that their interests had not been represented in Parliament when they demanded 'No taxation without representation'. But as the conflict with the imperial centre progressed, 'independence' from Britain, rather than 'actual' representation in the British Parliament, became the political objective of the American colonists.

In France, too, the question of representation caused much controversy. Could the sovereignty of the people be exercised in ways other than through the direct and immediate participation of all citizens in public affairs? After all, the revolutionary rhetoric had put forward the idea that a multiplicity of individuals was made one, not by the absolute and irrevocable submission to the (individual) person of the monarch, but to the single, unitary (collective) person of the body of citizens as a whole (Baker 1990: 253; Singer 1986: 61–7, 71, 89). In Hobbes's political philosophy, unity was brought to the 'many' members of society by their consent in the covenant to the transferral of sovereignty to the 'Leviathan'. It was the sovereign state that 'represented' the people: 'The Soveraign, in every Commonwealth, is the absolute Representative of all Subjects' (Hobbes [1651] 1991: chapter 22; also: chapter 16; Baumgold 1988: chapter 3; Pitkin 1967: chapter 2; Skinner 2005). For Jean-Jacques Rousseau, on the other hand, the people themselves were sovereign and could not be 'represented'; legislative power as the expression of their *summa potestas* had to remain with them. For Hobbes, the common good found expression and manifestation through the sovereign state; for Rousseau, the 'general will' manifested itself in the collective person of the body of citizens as a whole. But there was an ambivalence in Rousseau's thinking. In *The Social Contract*, he argued that the 'general will' was indivisible and could, therefore, not be 'represented' or 'delegated' (Rousseau [1762] 1968: Book II, chapter 1). In his *Considérations sur le gouvernement de Pologne*, on the other hand, he accepted that in a large state like Poland, legislative power could only be exercised through representative institutions (Rousseau [1772] 1953). However, in order to uphold the idea of direct democracy in the best way possible, he defined the representatives as delegates with a binding mandate, instructed to express, not their personal opinions, but the will of the nation (Baker 1990: 236–7). This ambivalence also informed the arguments of the radical Rousseauian politicians in the National Assembly in 1789. They, too, accepted, grudgingly, the idea of representation but still aimed to ensure the direct participation of all citizens by imposing a binding mandate on their representatives. In the early phase of the Revolution they, therefore, endorsed the idea of a suspensive veto of the monarch on the legislation of the representative assembly. Since they did not expect the representatives to always be the organ of the 'general will' of the nation, they construed the suspensive veto of the executive authority of the Crown as the means of enabling the reassertion of the 'general will' because the veto had to be followed by an appeal to the people and its direct vote on the disputed piece of legislation. In short, in this theoretical perspective, 'the unity of general will exists prior to representation, and that, as a result, representation is not to produce a unified political will above society, but simply to mirror the larger unity of purpose present within a politicized social totality' (Singer 1986: 158).

However, this Rousseauian notion of direct democracy and representation was challenged from a variety of theoretical perspectives. Among those who were committed to the revolutionary transferral of sovereignty from the monarchy to the people, the arguments of the Abbé Sieyès were particularly cogent (Singer 1986: 93–108; 153–7). He was quite adamant that in a large, populous state like France popular sovereignty could find its manifestation only in the deliberations of a unitary legislative assembly: 'The people can have but one voice, that of the national legislature. . . . In a country that is not a [direct] democracy – and France cannot be one – the people . . . can speak or act only through its representatives' (Sieyès, in Baker 1990: 249). The deputies were seen as representatives of not just their localities where they had been elected, but of the entire nation, transcending the necessarily 'particular will' of their constituencies. To be a 'mandated delegate' of his constituency would make the deputy a carrier of that particular will and would not allow him to be the representative of the nation. For Sieyès, representatives were sent to the assembly to discover the national will through deliberations. The deputies came to 'propose, listen, take counsel together, modify [their] opinions, and finally to form in common a common will' (Sieyès, in Baker 1990: 299). Hence, representation was not seen as a mechanism for the aggregation of particular wills; the 'general will' was more than the sum of particular wills (Forsyth 1987: chapter 7).

In his phamphlet *What is the Third Estate?* (1789), in which he put forward the initial political programme of the Revolution, Abbé Sieyès had already discussed at some length the idea of a *répresentation nationale*. For him, the representative assembly of the nation had to address matters of common concern: common security; common liberty; and the common welfare. He did not suggest that there was no diversity of interests among individuals; but he did not consider personal interest, 'whereby everyone stands apart, thinking of himself only' as dangerous 'since it is insulated. To each man his own. In its diversity lies its own cure' (Sieyès [1789] 1963: 158, 159). Hence, individual personal interests will balance each other off, cancel each other out. However, he saw the major difficulty springing from the interest 'by which a citizen allies himself with just a few others. This type of interest leads to conspiracy and collusion; through it anti-social schemes are plotted; through it the most formidable enemies of the People mobilise themselves' (Sieyès [1789] 1963: 159). It is thus organised interests which Sièyes detested; or rather, he detested the representation of 'interests' through corporate orders as it had been institutionalised in the *ancien régime*. He negated the political legiti-macy of all corporate bodies and the Revolution dissolved them all, 'leaving in their place individuals whose rights were protected by their membership in a nation-state' (Kates 1990: 112). Following Singer (1986: 154–5) we can say that for Sieyès, 'representation is always partial. . . . [T]he political will . . . does not represent the particulars but only what is common to them, leaving, as it were, a stratum of particularity unrepresented . . . Ultimately what is represented are not the individual wills . . . but the national will that the representation is to produce.' But in any case, as far as the assembly of a nation was concerned, he argued that it should be constituted in such a way that each personal interest it contained was insulated; it should ensure 'that the will of its majority is always consistent with the general good' (Sieyès [1789] 1963: 158; also: Hont 1994: 192–205).

We know that in the revolutionary upheavals in France, there was no final constitutional settlement of many of the contentious political issues. However, both the American Revolution and the French Revolution embraced the idea that 'the many' are capable of self-rule. They came to accept the necessity for this self-rule to be exercised by representatives who were seen as responsible for the common welfare of the people and accountable to the people through elections. They differed on the legitimacy of the representation of particular interests. In France, the idea of a unified or united nation went hand-in-hand with the belief that any idiosyncratic particular interests of individuals, groups, or corporations had to be submitted, if need be by force, to the national will: '[T]he French did not conceive of repre-sentation in terms of separate interests; only a unitary national will could be the ultimate political expression of French sovereignty' (Kates 1990: 114). And it was the National Assembly that was considered to embody the will of the nation – just as it was in the British Parliament that, according to Burke, the national interest was recognised. This reasoning was instrumental in entrenching the notion of parliamentary sovereignty. In America, on the other hand, the legitimacy of particular interests was acknowledged. There, politics became conceptualised as that process in which the interests became represented in the deliberative and decision-making political assem-blies in which, in turn, negotiations between particular and divergent ideas and interests of individuals, groups, and parties would result, if successful, in the tentative, and fragile, definition of the common weal.

There emerged one further commonality in some of the political thinking of the French and American Revolutions; and it was a

189

commonality that also included Burke and other defenders of the British constitution. For all of them, political rule was exercised as government by deliberation. It was through deliberations in parliamentary assemblies that the 'public good' or the 'general will' was defined. It was defined as a result of political contestation and thus as permanently amenable to redefinition – although the respective degree of openness distinguished the American, French, and British systems.

In the course of time, the idea of representation became linked to the notion of a reasoning public which, exercising the rights of assembly, petition, and association formed political associations, political clubs and political parties and, with the help of a free press, deliberated on the issues concerning the political community. The link between this 'reasoning public' and the parliamentary assembly was the electoral process through which parliamentarians were chosen to serve as representatives of public opinion(s). Representation was thus premised on rights of political participation. To that extent, the constitutional provisions that aimed to protect citizens from the interference of the state and gave them rights to be left alone, were complemented by rights to be involved in the political process.

Democratic government could thus be conceptualised as representative government circumscribed by constitutional constraints. Government was seen to be accountable to the people through the mediation of their representatives assembled in parliament. But parliament itself was also held accountable through the institution of periodical elections. This allowed for both the control and sanctioning of parliament by the public and the adjustment of parliament to changes that occurred in the distribution of political preferences within the public. Parliament, as a deliberative assembly, has thus become part of the reasoning public, in that it both processes and circulates information emanating from society and also produces information for society. Insofar as parliament manifests the idea of the essentially open-ended, contingent nature of politics in Western democracies, it is premised on the acceptance of a fluid and varied public opinion and, hence on the acceptance of public contestation and the legitimacy of opposition. We should note, however, that political science is still centrally concerned with analysing the extent to which 'reality' deviates from this 'ideal', and with explaining such divergence.

One form that 'representative democracy' took was 'liberal democracy'. In a 'liberal' democracy, it is the people who have the 'undisputed right to determine the framework of rules, regulations and policies within a given territory and to govern accordingly' (Held 1991: 150). Liberal democracy is premised on the acceptance of the notion of popular sovereignty and its institutionalisation in citizenship rights. Sovereignty has been transferred from the (monarchical) ruler to the people, and the people have been defined as the sum of the legally equal citizens.

Let us look more closely at the principles that underlie this type of democracy. Liberalism, as a political philosophy and a political ideology, revolves around the key assumption of the inalienable liberty of the individual, its autonomy and self-determination. It stipulates that an individual must be free to decide for her or himself what goals he or she wishes to pursue in life. It upholds the idea that each person is to have an equal opportunity to enjoy liberty, and that no person's liberty is more important or valuable than any other's. Liberalism aims to create a society in which conditions obtain that enable the individual to exercise her or his capacity of self-rule. In that respect, its key concern is with curtailing the power of other individuals as well as that of government to interfere with an individual's freedom. The democratic idea centres upon the assumption of the capacity of individuals as citizens to govern themselves, or, to put it differently, to determine for themselves their collective life. It is assumed, first, that every adult individual can rightly be considered, in principle, to be sufficiently well qualified to participate in the democratic process of governing the state to whose laws they are subjected. Also it is further assumed that 'among adults no persons are so definitely better qualified than others that they should be entrusted with the complete and final authority over the government of the state' (Dahl 1998: 75–8).

However, we should note that, as a matter of fact, in Western 'liberal' democracies, individuals must be members of the state, must be its 'nationals', in order to possess citizenship rights. In contrast to the conceptualisation of popular sovereignty as the self-rule of nationals in their capacity as citizens, the 'radical' (republican) democratic principle stipulates that everyone who is permanently subjected to rule and domination in a legal order must have a part in the exercise of the sovereignty that ultimately legitimates that rule (Dahl 1989: chapter 9). Citizenship status would, therefore, be distinct from nationality and would adhere to all permanent residents, who would be subject to the same qualifications as the 'nationals'. Such a disjuncture of citizenship and nationality is, however, alien to the political reality of 'liberal' democracy – with even European Union citizenship still premised upon the possession of the status of a citizen in one of the member states. The collective 'self' whose autonomous determination liberalism aims to ensure in the democratic process is the politically organised nation. Offering *Considerations on Representative Government*, John Stuart Mill made these connections quite explicit. 'Free institutions', Mill ([1861] 1991: 428) argued, 'are next to impossible in a country made up of different nationalities. Among a people without fellow-feeling, especially if they read and speak different languages, the united opinion, necessary to the working of representative government, cannot exist.' He maintained that 'it is in general a necessary condition of free institutions, that the boundaries of governments should coincide in the main with those of nationalities' (Mill [1861] 1991: 430). His reference to the Habsburg Empire in the explication of this thesis makes it plain that Mill favours the political independence and self-determination of nationalities which are ruled and dominated by an imperial centre. But this 'liberal' endorsement of national emancipation is accompanied by an equally 'liberal' proposition that free institutions and representative government within a state are premised upon the 'blending of nationalities' (Mill [1861] 1991: 434). In a 'liberal' democracy, such a systemic linkage between democracy and nation-state is presupposed. Democratic rule by the sovereign people is exercised by citizens in the sovereign, territorially consolidated nation-state. Since it is assumed that only in a sovereign state can the people's will command without being commanded by others, 'state sovereignty' and 'popular sovereignty' are inextricably intertwined in 'liberal' democracy.

'Liberal' democracy is premised upon an acceptance of this dual notion of self-determination: the capacity of the individual to govern herself or himself, and the capacity of individuals as citizens to govern themselves as a political community. 'Liberal' democracy further assumes that in large territorial states the political self-rule of autonomous and competent individuals in their capacity as citizens cannot be exercised in the form of a 'direct democracy'. Along Madisonian lines, 'liberal' democracy assumes that in geographically expansive territorial states with a numerically large population and pronounced social, economic, political, and cultural heterogeneities, the only possible form of democracy is 'representative democracy': political rule is exercised by officials whose power derives from their election by the citizens and whose power is constrained by their accountability to the citizens as voters. Modern democracy is, therefore, a system of self-rule in which the principle of representation obtains and where representation is grounded in the institution of election based on universal adult suffrage: political decision-makers are chosen in frequent and fairly conducted competitive elections. Electoral competition, in turn, presupposes the institutionalisation of a number of other principles. Associational autonomy allows for the formation of organised political groups, such as political parties or interest groups. This is only possible in a political community that upholds civil liberties and, in particular, the freedom of expression, of movement, and of association as well as free access to sources of information that are not controlled by political power holders (Dahl 1998: 84–99).

To sum up, democratic rule is exercised in the sovereign, territorially consolidated nation-state. In a bounded territory, people's sovereignty is the basis upon which democratic decision-making takes place; and 'the people' are the addressees, or the constituents, of the political decisions. The territorially consolidated democratic polity, which is clearly demarcated from other political communities, is seen as rightly governing itself and determining its own future through the interplay between forces operating within its boundaries. Only in a sovereign state, possessing both 'domestic' and 'Westphalian/Vattelian' sovereignty, can the will of the people command without being commanded by others.

As we saw in Chapter 3, a political system approximating this 'ideal-typical' model of liberal-representative democracy, grounded in the idea of individual autonomy protected by 'liberal' human rights, on the one hand, and collective self-legislation, on the other hand (with both of these elements firmly embedded and supported by the institutions of market capitalism), provided the blueprint for democracy promotion. We saw how this promotion of a new 'standard of civilisation' went hand-in-hand with a political disregard for the institution of sovereignty (if deemed advisable) of certain states (perceived to be deficient in the norms, values, and institutions embraced by the 'West'). We also noted the intellectual and scholarly endeavour to redefine sovereignty in such a way that such attacks on the legal institution of sovereignty could be justified legally and morally. We saw how such policies and justifications led to a 'liberal anti-pluralism' (Gerry Simpson), in which 'failed states' and 'outlaw states' are singled out for special treatment by 'the international community' composed by 'state alliances of the willing'. We have also noted that one should be quite sceptical about the possibility of bringing, imposing, or promoting democracy – if we leave aside the politically fraught issue as to whether what is being promoted is what is actually being desired by those at the receiving end. 'Building democracy' is a time-consuming, even hazardous, undertaking with uncertain outcome. Whether the institutionalisation of 'neotrustee-ships' or other forms of Western tutelage are conducive to democratisation is as unclear as the success of imposing conditionalities of an economic or political nature in pursuit of 'good governance'.

We have been looking from 'the West' with 'its' constitutionally embedded human rights and democratic institutions into the 'the Rest'. Yet we must look at some of the forces that challenge the liberal-democratic model in the West. Both 'popular sovereignty' and 'state sovereignty' have become problematical 'at home'.

Notes

1 These arguments could now be pursued further into areas of international relations and the whole *problematique* of the politics of humanitarian intervention, its history and legal–philosophical justifications. Such an analysis is beyond the scope of the current discussion, but a good starting point for gaining an overview of the literature is Chandler 2002, Holzgrefe and Keohane 2003; Roth 1993; Roth 1999; Slaughter 1995; and Welsh 2004. The following articles engage directly with the report of the International Commission on Intervention and State Sovereignty: Mac-Farlane et al. 2004; Warner 2003; Weiss 2004; and Welsh 2002. As we saw, intervention is both patchy (and frequently determined by specific 'great power' interests) and there is an uneasy mixture of justifications based on self-defence and humanitarian concerns. For Habermas and Rawls (as well as the authors of the UN reports and many other writers hoisting the flag of human rights), intervention is – in principle – welcome and a first step towards the bright future of a global domestic politics with its own international police force. For others, such a policy of intervention continues the century-old tradition of Western imperialism and a struggle for hegemony under the ideology of humanitarianism (see, for example, Chandler 2002 and Zolo 2002).

2 For reasons of the reader's convenience, the contributions to the constitutional debate are quoted by reference to one of the following three edited collections: McMaster/Stone (Pennsylvania and the Federal Constitution); Farrand (The Records of the Federal Convention); and Storing (The Complete Anti-Federalist). Roman numerals refer to volume number.

5

Liberal Democracy between Multiculturalism and Globalisation

From 'Demos' to 'Demoi': Multiculturalism and Democracy

We have seen in previous chapters that both 'domestic' and 'West-phalian' sovereignty have come under attack. However, it is not only 'state' sovereignty that has been assailed, but also 'popular sover-eignty'. The idea of a 'homogeneous' or 'uniform' people that informed the notion of the 'demos' is no longer convincing. If we define 'democracy' in accordance with Abraham Lincoln's Gettysburg Address as 'government of the people, by the people, for the people', we must recognise that 'the people' (in the singular) has vanished (if it ever existed). We should better speak of 'demoi'. In the last few decades, the definition of the 'demos' has become ever more problematic and has raised questions about political integration and political rule in general: we could witness that in an increasing number of countries (historical) national and ethnic (immigrant) communities with distinct languages, histories and traditions have demanded the recognition and support for their cultural identity. At stake in these struggles is the demand by these 'minorities' for group-differentiated rights, powers, status or immunities that go beyond the common rights of citizenship. These claims may encompass demands for territorial autonomy – ranging in its form from federalism to devolution to the status of 'autonomous' region; for self-government in certain key policy areas such as education, health or family law; for guaranteed representation in the political institutions of the larger society on the basis of quota systems favourable to the group and guaranteed veto powers over legislation and policies that centrally affect the respective 'minorities'; and for group-specific legal exemptions. These demands are premised upon the belief that only by possessing and exercising these rights, powers, and immunities will it be possible for these communities to ensure the full and free development of their culture and the retention of their 'identity'. Manifestly, demands for secession of 'national minorities' are part of the repertoire of 'minority' politics. The domestic politics of states such as the United Kingdom (Scotland, Wales, and Northern Ireland), Spain, Belgium, Canada (Quebec) as well as those in southeast Europe have been dominated by the political mobilisation of 'internal' nationalities and the need to recognise the 'multinational' and 'multi-ethnic' character of many 'nation'-states.

At the same time, we have also witnessed the political struggle of indigenous peoples in white settler states (such as Canada, Australia, and New Zealand, but also, to an extent, in the United States) for recognition as free, equal and self-governing peoples under international law. We saw these struggles reflected in some of the human rights covenants and statements discussed in Chapter 2. As 'nations within', 'stateless nations' (such as the Catalans, Scots or Québécois) and 'indigenous peoples' share the historical experience of an existence of complete and functioning societies on their historic homeland prior to their being incorporated into a larger state. However, there are two major differences between these 'minority groups' in democratic states (Kymlicka 1995; 2000). First, indigenous peoples in white settler societies were subjected to *de facto* 'genocidal' policies and generally threatened in their very physical survival to an extent quite incomparable to anything experienced by most 'stateless nations'. Secondly, most 'stateless nations' embrace a form of 'civic' or 'post-ethnic' nationalism (where group identities and membership are held to be fluid, hybridic and multiple), a form a nationalism they tend to share with the 'majority nation'. 'Indigenous peoples', on the other hand, are typically mobilising around a more static, descent-based, and culturally exclusive conception of group identity and membership. Through their reluctance to speak the language of 'liberal democracy' and 'liberal nationalism', as well as through their demands for official apologies for past atrocities and humiliations, they challenge the assumption that their claims can be accommodated through the institutional arrangement of liberal democracy.

The demands put forward by the 'stateless nations' and the 'indigenous peoples' challenge us to rethink our conception of democracy and popular sovereignty. The question they pose is this: 'must we redefine democracy so that it should no longer be seen as an affair of a singular body of citizens who together constitute a singular people, but rather as an affair of citizens who constitute a plurality of diverse peoples, groups and associations?' (see Hindess 2001: 100–4). The demands of transmigrant communities add to the urgency for addressing this question. Yet, it is the political demands for 'self-determination' and 'self-government' put forward by the 'stateless nations' and 'indigenous peoples' that raises the issue of 'sovereignty' to a degree that the demands of transmigrant ethnic communities do not.

Iris Marion Young concisely identified the problem:

> Internally, the idea of sovereignty entails that a state has ultimate authority to regulate all the activities taking place within a specific territorial jurisdiction. This often seems to mean, by implication, that the same form of law, regulation and administration ought to apply to all the peoples and locales within the territory. Both these aspects of internal sovereignty are morally questionable, however, because they do not sufficiently recognise and accommodate the rights and needs of national and cultural minorities. (Young 2000: 251; see also Tully 2000)

For 'indigenous peoples', the exercise of self-determination consists of decolonisation and the recognition of indigenous peoples as free, equal, and self-governing under international law. Few indigenous peoples mobilise for secession and independent statehood, but seek significant self-government rights. Their claim to 'sovereignty without secession' develops the idea of 'nested sovereignty', which demands the right of self-determination over those jurisdictions of direct relevance to the indigenous peoples while at the same time acknowledging a shared jurisdiction over certain lands and resources on the basis of mutual consent. As Maaka and Floras (2000: 89) stated: 'The politics of indigeneity resonate with references to sovereignty and self-determination. Particular emphasis is focused on indigenous peoples as fundamentally autonomous political communities, each of which is sovereign in its own right, yet sharing in the sovereignty of society through multiple, yet interlocking, jurisdictions.' While the differences between 'stateless nations' and 'indigenous peoples' lead to different political dynamics with regard to formulating and implementing institutional solutions to the problem of self-government, it would appear that territorial or community 'concessions', or possibly some combination of the two, are the two broad channels of action that are available to governments (Urwin 2001). Territorial accommodation involves power being 'ceded' to one or more geographical regions, that is, some form of devolution – with the most pronounced form of devolution taking the form of full-scale and constitutional federalisation, as was the case, for example, in Belgium between 1958 and 1994. Community concessions may take the form of consociational accommodation, of which we have already spoken in a previous chapter and whose first sustained intellectual formulation we have found in the political theory of Johannes Althusius. In such a consociational approach, 'some form of proportionality [is applied] to how access to power, decision-making and other kinds of public goods is distributed among distinctive or conflicting ethnonational groups' (Urwin 2001: 68).

This is not the place to review the varied history of institutional reform in multinational democracies (see Gagnon and Tully: 2001). We should, however, emphasise that, while it is undeniable that national 'minorities' and 'indigenous peoples' do, in effect, act in many respects like interest groups when putting forward their claims, it is not just the distribution of material goods that is at stake but the group's expectation to have its unique culture and identity recognised. These are struggles for both resources and recognition. Such contests over the appropriate form of recognition 'constitute an enduring dimension of modern politics: the public disclosure of misrecognized identities and the demand that other members acknowledge these and respond' (Tully 2001: 6). Arguably, 'identities' – and the 'cultures' out of which they draw their substance – are not fixed once and for all. 'Culture' is a notoriously difficult concept to define, but Bhikhu Parekh (2000: 2–3) highlights key aspects of any definition when he understands culture as 'a body of belief and practices in terms of which a group of people understand themselves and the world and organize their individual and collective lives'. There are a number of reasons for the fluidity of a culture:

All beliefs are necessarily general and articulated in terms of inherently indeterminate concepts, and need to be reinterpreted in the light of new situations and knowledge. Although practices are more specific, they too need to be adapted to new and unexpected circumstances. Their adherents cannot therefore avoid stretching the boundaries of the prevailing system of beliefs and practices and opening up new interpretative possibilities, sometimes with consequences they neither intend nor approve of. Culture is thus not a passive inheritance but an active process of creating meaning, not given but constantly redefined and reconstituted. (Parekh 2000: 152–3)

These reinterpretations of culture take place within two sets of constraints. First, to the extent that culture legitimises and sustains a particular kind of social order, it operates as a system of power necessarily interlocked with other power systems. Furthermore, a culture is 'far from being a transparent and univocal system of meaning claiming spontaneous allegiance of its members'; it is rather the case that 'every culture is subject to contestation, and its dominant meaning tends to reflect the balance of power between its different groups' (Parekh 2000: 79). If this balance of power shifts, the system of meaning and practices may shift, too. Secondly, 'cultures are formed through complex dialogues and interactions with other cultures' (Benhabib 2002: 184). Cultures are in a constant dialogue with their own traditions and self-understandings as well as in frequent confrontation with other 'cultures' and 'identities'. One reason why intercultural dialogue is always potentially achievable is precisely the fluidity – if not hybridity – of cultures.

Such confrontation is not a recent phenomenon. Yet, arguably, it is a key aspect of the contemporary stage of global interconnectedness that concrete societies situate themselves in the context of a world complex of societies, that they conceptualise themselves as part of a global order. As a result of this global self-reflection, the criteria for societal change and conduct tend to become 'matters of inter-societal, inter-continental, inter-civilizational, and inter-doctrinal interpretations and debate' (Robertson and Chirico 1985: 237). Such a situating of societies may engender strains and even discontent within societies. It heightens the significance of the problem of societal order in relation to global order and is thus likely to give rise to a large number of political-ideological and religious movements with conflicting definitions of the location of their society in relation to the rest of the world and the global circumstances as a whole. Nationalism and religious fundamentalism may be seen as two answers. The global discourse on human rights is another moment where a 'cultural' mediation between the 'local' and the 'global' takes place with profound implications for cultural self-interpretations. We find here the moment of the formation of a 'global consciousness'. We are challenged to develop in such cultural encounters an 'enlarged mentality' which may, however, express itself as much in cosmopolitan virtues and visions as it does in patriotism.

If we follow the logic of this argument, then there are no 'fixed' identities whose 'equal representation' has to be institutionally ensured. Rather, identities need presence in the public sphere in order to pursue their cause of 'self-understanding'. Such 'presence' and 'engagement' is all the more warranted, as we argued, because identities do not just develop 'endogenously' over time, but change as a result of their openness to 'exogenous' (socio-) cultural influences. The politics of recognition is thus a continuous activity. A demand is presented, others respond, the demand is reformulated in response, others respond to this, and an agreement is either reached or it is not and this in turn gives rise to dissent and a new demand (Tully 2001). If we follow James Tully in this understanding of identity and the politics of recognition, then there arises a straightforward question: what form of democracy enables the politics of recognition to be played out freely from generation to generation, with as little domination as possible? At stake is not the 'once and for all' institutional solution to demands for recognition, but the institutionalisation of a form of democracy that makes such a politics possible and allows for institutional change. In the terminology used in Chapter 1, such politics presupposes the embrace of 'local patriotism' and 'cosmopolitan virtues': a willingness to live together as free and equal citizens and as members of equal peoples, groups, and associations in conjunction with a willingness to embark on an intercultural dialogue within the shared polity.

The urgency of this task is further highlighted by the presence of 'transmigrant communities' in most Western states. Mobility is one of the hallmarks of our global age. For example, there is the global flow of visual images and information. There are few inhabited places on earth that are without television and radio; and the internet and other communication systems such as mobile phones allow ever more people the free exchange of opinions and information unobstructed by censorship. The capitalist mode of production currently has hardly any rival and its products are no longer bound by geographical constraints. Capital faces few boundaries nowadays and can be transferred from one end of the globe to the other almost instantaneously. The fact that business has become global does not only create increasing flows of products, but it also necessitates the mobility of managers, specialists, and those persons who actually transport both these people and the products. Yet, it is not just members of the transnational economic and political elites and tourists from the rich 'West' that are 'on the move'. David Held et al. (1999: 303) have summarised the major migration patterns:

> The contemporary era is witnessing a very complex pattern of overlapping and interacting global and regional migratory flows of both an economic and non-economic nature. At the centre of these global flows have been economically driven migrations to OECD countries initially at a regional level, from poorer to richer Western states, predominantly to Western Europe, but they subsequently shifted to North America and Australia. In addition, global migrations have focused on the Middle East. The other large migratory flows have been regional and have developed apace from the 1960s within South East Asia, western and southern Africa, Latin America and within the Middle East.

Let us concentrate on migration away from poor countries in the 'south' into the 'west'. According to Held et al. (1999: 312), the estimated total for post-1945 migration to OECD countries was well over 100 million people, which is more than triple the great transatlantic migrations between the 1880s and 1920. The majority of these post-war migration movements took place in the thirty years between 1965 and 1995. Owing to the influx of labour migrants and their families, refugees, and asylum seekers and their settlement in nearly all highly developed countries – as well as in many parts of the less developed regions – populations have become ever more heterogeneous and culturally diverse.

With immigration having become unavoidably part and parcel of our global age, governments, first and foremost those of liberal democratic 'welfare' states, must determine whether they accept the presence of considerable numbers of aliens on their territory who are essentially left to fend for themselves at the very margins of society, and thus create a very visible group of new paupers, or whether they devise creative policies by which to prevent this from happening. In order to deal politically and administratively with second generation immigrants, many OECD states have created systems of quasi-citizenship. In their study *Citizenship and Migration* (2000), Stephen Castles and Alistair Davidson argue that quasi-citizens enjoy neither political rights nor a complete equality of social rights. They distinguish between 'denizens' – 'who are foreign citizens with a legal and permanent resident status' – and 'margizens' – long-term immigrants without secure residence status. These 'margizens' 'include illegal workers, unauthorized family entrants, asylum-seekers, refused asylum-seekers who have not (yet) been deported, former legal residents who have lost this status . . . the long-term unemployed who may be subject to deportation in some countries, and people classed as temporary workers who are in fact permanently integrated into the workforce' (Castles and Davidson 2000: 95–6). How to deal with these 'margizens', who are truly living on the margins of prosperous Western societies, is as politically fraught a question as that about the political and social inclusion of 'denizens'.

As a matter of fact, at issue is a reconsideration of routes to citizenship. In Chapter 4, we distinguished between three routes: by descent (*ius sanguinis*); by virtue of having been born in the country (*ius soli*); or by virtue of petitioning for, and being granted, citizenship. Castles and Davidson suggest that the socio-political pressures exerted by immigration will result in yet another mechanism gaining increasing significance: 'that of *ius domicili* (law of residence), according to which people may gain an entitlement to citizenship through residence in the territory of a country' (Castles and Davidson 2000: 85). This *ius domicili* provides an option of naturalisation to young people of immigrant origin, which means we are likely to see mixed types of citizenship entitlements combining several routes to citizenship.

Manifestly, what is at stake here is the political and legal status of immigrants in liberal democracies. In a sense, the challenge is to decide whether immigrants should be seen as 'ethnic minorities' or as 'ethnic communities' (Castles and Miller 1993). Understood as 'ethnic minorities', 'immigrants are excluded and marginalised, so that they live on the fringes of society', without, ultimately, a rightful place in the political community. As 'ethnic communities', on the other hand, 'the immigrants and their descendants are seen as an integral part of a multicultural society which is willing to reshape its culture and identity' (Castles and Miller 1993: 195). To the extent that immigration has led to ethnic community formations, political inclusion of immigrant communities must be achieved without aiming for cultural assimilation. This is the challenge of multiculturalism.

In some academic literature in recent years, it has been claimed that a new type of citizenship, 'post-national' in character, has been forming, linked to the intensification of transnational migration. David Jacobson (1996: 8–9) has argued that:

> [t]ransnational migration is steadily eroding the traditional basis of nation-state membership, namely citizenship. As rights have come to be predicated on residency, not citizen status, the distinction between 'citizen' and 'alien' has eroded. The devaluation of citizenship has contributed to the increasing importance of international human rights codes, with its premise of universal 'personhood' . . . States must increasingly take account of persons *qua* persons as opposed to limiting state responsibilities to its own citizens.

Yasemin Soysal declared that national citizenship was losing ground to a more universal model of membership that is anchored in deterritorialised notions of person's rights: 'In the postnational model, universal personhood replaces nationhood; and universal human rights replace national rights . . . The rights and claims of individuals are legitimated by ideologies grounded in a transnational community, through international codes, conventions, and laws on human rights, independent of their citizenship in a nation-state. Hence, the individual transcends the citizen' (Soysal 1994: 142; Soysal 2000; Hollifield 1992: 222–6). As a result of this process, the role and character of the

state have changed, and the state is now charged with the institutionalisation of international human rights. The basis of state legitimacy
has undergone a shift 'from an exclusive emphasis on the sovereignty
of the people and right to self-determination . . . to rights of individuals regardless of nationality' (Sassen 1996: 95). We have discussed
certain aspects of these developments in previous chapters.

There is no denying the political importance of discourses on human
rights and the legal significance of human rights in international law
and through it, in municipal law. Yet, a number of reservations may
be raised against the notion of a 'post-national' citizenship model.
Joppke (1999a: 273) is right to point out that 'individual rights are not
external to, but part and parcel of liberal states. Otherwise one could
not explain why human-rights constraints are more urgently felt in the
states of the West than, for example, in the migrant-receiving states in
the Middle East.' He is also right to remind us that most civil rights –
such as freedom of speech or the right to ownership – and social rights
– such as entitlement to social 'benefits' – have never been dependent
upon 'political' citizenship, but upon lawful residence in the territory
of the state and, frequently, labour market participation. It was the
political right to participation in the process of collective self-determination that had been reserved exclusively to the citizen. The important qualification with regard to civil rights pertains to residence
and free movement in a state's territory that did not extend to persons,
but were reserved to citizens:

> The dramatic moment in the evolution of migrant rights was the decou-
> pling of resident and free-movement rights from citizenship. Only, this was
> not a postnational moment driven by abstract human-rights considera-
> tions. Instead, it was a crypto-national moment that equated long-term
> residency with *de facto* membership in the national community . . . The
> underlying motif is communitarian, not universalist: migrants are not
> conceived of as abstract holders of human rights, but as particular
> members of a community with historically derived entitlements to due
> consideration and protection. (Joppke 1999a: 272)

Finally, national citizenship in their 'host' country matters for many
immigrants. Indeed, it matters so much that many would wish to
possess double citizenship, both in their 'home' country and in their
'host' country. 'National', not 'post-national' citizenship is a status
that many immigrants value and crave. As long as this interest prevails
among immigrant populations, and as long as there are no autonomous institutional structures that could enforce entitlements that

individuals hold on the basis of human rights, 'post-national' member-ship is not a viable alternative to 'national' citizenship (Joppke 1999a, 1999b). Rather, 'national' citizenship needs to be conceptualised as 'multicultural' citizenship.

Will Kymlicka has made one of the most important recent con-tributions to the discussion of 'multicultural citizenship'. Kymlicka (1990: chapter 6) suggests that a key idea of liberalism is the self-determination of the individual. For him, individual autonomy means that, first, we must be free to lead our life from the inside, in accordance with our idiosyncratic beliefs about what gives value to life; that is, it must be left to the individual to choose a particular way of life as approximating most closely to what an individual considers the 'good' life. Secondly, the individual must be free to question those beliefs and reassess whether a chosen social practice or involvement in a social relationship retains its imputed value; that is, I determine in a process of practical reasoning which ends I want to pursue and which values I want to cherish. Yet, this value pluralism, this process of evaluating distinct 'good' ways of life, is supported by a cultural structure. We choose among various options that our culture pro-vides, and it is through this cultural mediation that the options are meaningful to us. It is through membership in cultural communities with their shared memories and values and their common institutions and practices that individuals are provided with meaningful ways of life across the full range of human activities:

> Whether or not a course of action has any significance for us depends on whether, and how, our language renders vivid to us the point of that activity. And the way in which language renders vivid these activities is shaped by our history, our 'traditions and conventions'. Understanding these cultural narratives is a precondition of making intelligent judgements about how to lead our lives. (Kymlicka 1995: 83)

Kymlicka suggests, then, that liberalism wants individuals to be free, not in order to go beyond the language, conventions, and history of their community, but to move around within their culture, to distance themselves from particular cultural roles, 'to choose which features of the culture are most worth developing, and which are without value' (Kymlicka 1995: 90–1). It is through this 'moving around' and 'distancing' that individuals gain their individuality. In this perspec-tive, cultural communities are instrumental to the formation and the exercise of the autonomy of the individual, and it is for this reason that they deserve to be protected.

Yet this theoretical justification of the relevancy of cultural groups is inherently problematic. It may easily lead to a position in which only those cultural groups which meet the liberal paradigm of individual self-determination (the principle of autonomy) will find support. Many cultural communities, however, claim group rights so that they can defend their cultural integrity and retain their identity which often does not accord individual self-determination any ultimate value at all. In such circumstances, Kymlicka's foundation of cultural rights in the protection of an individual's freedom autonomously to choose her or his ends prepares the ground for interference with the internal structure of communities in the name of the liberal ideal of autonomy (Kukathas 1995: 239–45). Kymlicka's position stays perilously close to the idea that '[i]ndividual autonomy trumps all' (McDonald 1991: 237). 'Individual autonomy' is upheld as a universal human value that transcends particular cultural contexts. However, this idea is controversial since 'it is difficult to determine whether the claim is truly universal, namely, part of what it means to be human, or simply is a set of beliefs specific to a particular culture disguised by the rhetoric of universality' (Macklem 1993: 1340). In the debate between universalists and cultural relativists, who claim that practices and values of a particular culture cannot be judged by relying on universal standards that transcend such cultural specificity, Kymlicka sides with the universalists.

Most countries today are multicultural states. For Kymlicka (1995: 18) this means that members of such states 'either belong to different nations (a multination state), or have emigrated from different nations (a polyethnic state)'. A multi-nation state is thus composed of more than one historical community which is more or less institutionally complete, occupies a given territory or homeland, and shares a distinct language and culture. A 'polyethnic' state is composed of a number of transnational migrant communities. While these distinctions are useful for analytical purposes, it must not be overlooked that, as a matter of fact, most multi-nation states are at the same time polyethnic states as a result of processes of immigration.

It is central to Kymlicka's argument that 'national' minorities alone can legitimately claim self-government rights. These national minorities already possess a 'societal culture' whose continuance must be ensured for the sake of the freedom and liberty of its members if the community so wishes. Such a societal culture 'provides its members with meaningful ways of life across the full range of human activities, including social, educational, religious, recreational, and economic life, encompassing both public and private spheres' (Kymlicka 1995: 76). As these cultures tend to be territorially concentrated, their protection through self-government rights could possibly take the form of the devolution of power from the centre to smaller political units within a federal or cantonal structure. For example, discussing the Indian tribes/bands in Canada, Kymlicka argues that they have, in effect, become 'a third order of government, with a collection of powers that is carved out of both federal and state/provincial jurisdiction' (Kymlicka 1995: 30). It is their increasing control over health, education, family law, policing, criminal justice, and resource development that empowers them to protect their societal culture.

Kymlicka thus accepts the claim of national minorities to self-government and the protection of their societal culture. However, he is quite clear that '[a] national minority which rules in an illiberal way acts unjustly' (Kymlicka 1995: 168) – and liberals have 'a right and a responsibility' to speak out against such injustice and offer incentives for liberal reform. In the context of the discussion in previous chapters, it is interesting to note that Kymlicka suggests emulation of the foreign policy of 'Western democracies' to push for liberal reforms in post-1989 eastern Europe and elsewhere in domestic politics: 'Obviously, there are many analogous opportunities for a majority nation to encourage national minorities, in a non-coercive way, to liberalize their internal constitutions' (Kymlicka 1995: 168). As a liberal, Kymlicka also endorses a policy of pushing for the development and strengthening of international mechanisms for protecting human rights: minority nations may be more inclined to accept an international review of their practices than being subjected to the liberal constitution of the majority nations which may have imposed their rule as conquerors and colonisers (Kymlicka 1995: 169). While he argues for 'peaceful negotiation' between majority and minority nations in cases of conflict over 'basic principles', nowhere does Kymlicka suggest that such negotiation may be directed at changing the 'societal culture' of the majority nation – as long as it is a 'liberal' culture.

In Kymlicka's theory, immigrant communities have a status that is quite different from that of 'minority nations' (Kymlicka 1995: 95–6). According to Kymlicka, immigrants have uprooted themselves and have thus voluntarily relinquished some of the rights that go along with their original national membership. When they made the free decision to emigrate, they could know that they would settle in a country which was likely to have a different societal culture. In these circumstances, the expectation of the host country that immigrants should integrate into mainstream society is not unjust. It would also be wrong to compare immigrants with colonists such as the English and French nations in Canada or the United States:

> There was a fundamentally different set of expectations accompanying colonization and immigration – the former resulted from a deliberate policy aimed at the systematic re-creation of an entire society in a new land; the latter resulted from individual and familial choices to leave their society and join another existing society. (Kymlicka 1995: 95)

Kymlicka sums up his position succinctly: in the case of immigrant groups, it is 'legitimate to compel respect for liberal principles . . . I do not think it is wrong for liberal states to insist that immigration entails accepting the legitimacy of state enforcement of liberal principles, so long as immigrants know this in advance, and none the less voluntarily choose to come' (Kymlicka 1995: 170).

Both arguments are flawed. Kymlicka himself accepts the fact that the world order is unjust and that international inequality is a cause behind international migration. What does 'voluntary' migration mean in this context? How do we deal with those immigrants who, for example, as 'involuntary' refugees, have settled in foreign countries? Furthermore, the second argument would appear to be blatantly 'imperialist'. It amounts to saying that, if people come as a colonial vanguard that overpowers and dispossesses indigenous peoples with the intention of creating the new country and society in the image of the one left behind, then they are entitled to the re-creation and maintenance of their societal culture. But if they arrive peaceably as immigrants as a result of 'free' individual and familial choices, then they do not have such entitlements.

While they are not entitled to re-create their societal culture, immigrants can rightfully insist on maintaining some of their heritage (Kymlicka 1995: 97). To this end, they may be granted 'polyethnic' rights:

> For example, Jews and Muslims in Britain have sought exemption from Sunday closing and animal slaughtering legislation; Sikh men in Canada have sought exemption from motorcycle helmet laws and from the official dress-codes of police forces, so that they can wear their turban; Orthodox Jews in the United States have sought the right to wear the yarmulka during military service; and Muslim girls in France have sought exemption from school dress-codes so that they can wear the *chador*. (Kymlicka 1995: 31)

Such 'polyethnic' rights – for example, the right to maintain their languages, the right not be discriminated against, to be exempt from those laws that unjustly disadvantage them – support the demand by ethnic groups for the manifestation and recognition of their identity and the public acceptance of the value of polyethnicity. They are thus conducive to their integration into the dominant society. While the public sphere is affected in some ways by the granting of 'polyethnic' rights and their exercise by ethnic groups, these rights are primarily designed to affirm 'the right of immigrants to maintain their ethnic heritage in the private sphere' (Kymlicka 1995: 78). They can be defended by arguing that to treat people justly requires treating equal cases equally and different cases differently. Equality must not be equated with uniformity. Yet, there is an unresolved tension in Kymlicka's argument. He has argued that individual freedom and the capacity to form meaningful identities is premised on a strong, comprehensive cultural context. For such a culture to be socially relevant, 'it must be institutionally embodied – in schools, media, economy, government' (Kymlicka 1995: 76). This means, that unless a culture is a 'societal culture', '[it] will be reduced to ever-decreasing marginalization' (Kymlicka 1995: 80). However, as we saw, Kymlicka would not accept that immigrants/ethnic groups have a right to re-creating a societal culture. Inevitably, therefore, with the decline in the vitality of their own culture they will have to assimilate into the dominant 'societal culture' in order to be 'free'. The 'polyethnic' rights which Kymlicka grants ethnic groups would appear not to be strong enough to stall the evaporation of the cultural traditions of these groups.

In previous chapters, we have noted the liberal anti-pluralism that informs the Western promotion of human rights and democracy around the world. In Kymlicka's theory of multicultural citizenship we observe yet another instance of a 'liberal' limitation to pluralism. Such limitations are also explicitly acknowledged by John Rawls, whose eagerness to use and justify the category of 'outlaw state' we have already encountered in Chapter 1. He accepts that in a 'modern democratic society' there will always (and of necessity) be 'a pluralism of incompatible yet reasonable comprehensive doctrines'; such a pluralism 'is the normal result of the exercise of human reason within a framework of the free institutions of a constitutional regime' (Rawls 1993/2005: xvi; see for succinct summaries and comments on Rawls's 'political liberalism': Jones 1995; Sandel 1993–4). It is the hallmark of a reasonable comprehensive doctrine that 'it does not reject the essentials of a democratic regime. Of course, a society may also contain unreasonable and irrational, even mad, comprehensive doctrines' (Rawls 1993/2005: xvi–xvii). In such a case where doctrines reject 'one or more democratic freedoms' the practical tasks consist of containing them – 'like war and disease' (Rawls 1993/2005: 64, fn. 19). Not only does Rawls exclude from political society everyone who does not embrace the 'essentials' of democratic constitutionalism, but he also insists that certain matters must be 'taken off the political agenda once and for all' (Rawls 1993/2005: 152, fn. 16) – matters which violate 'the fundamental ideas we seem to share through the public political culture' (Rawls 1993/2005: 150). Of course, the 'liberal' bias of Rawls's 'political liberalism' is already embedded in his distinctly liberal conceptualisation of human beings. In effect, this conceptualisation constitutes – despite Rawls's claims to the contrary – a 'comprehensive doctrine'. Starting within the tradition of (liberal) democratic thought, Rawls thinks of citizens as free and equal persons:

> The basic idea is that in virtue of their two moral powers (a capacity for a sense of justice and for a conception of the good) and the powers of reason (of judgment, thought, and inference connected with these powers), persons are free. Their having these powers to the requisite minimum degree to be fully cooperating members of society makes persons equal. (Rawls 1993/2005: 19)

Whether human beings as moral persons are adequately or appropriately defined in those terms is precisely one of the contested issues among 'comprehensive doctrines' – yet Rawls takes this contestation off the 'public agenda'.

In contrast to John Rawls, Jürgen Habermas insists – as we have already observed in previous chapters – that there are no legitimate 'gag rules' for keeping issues off the agenda that could be taken as 'ontologically private' (Habermas 1995: 851). He assumes that a constitutional democratic culture of any community is 'ethically impregnated' in the sense of its principles being interpreted from the point of view of a common, yet particular civic identity to whose formation the constitutional culture in turn contributes. In practical-political terms, this argument results in the expectation that:

> Immigrants should be obliged to assent to the principles of the constitution as interpreted within the scope of the political culture; that is, the ethical-political self-understanding of the citizenry of the receiving country. Once they become citizens themselves, they in turn get a voice in public debates,

which may then shift the established interpretation of the constitutional principles. The obligation to accept the political culture may not, however, extend to assimilation to the way of life of the majority culture. A legally required *political* socialization may not have an impact on other aspects of the collective identity of the immigrants' culture of origin. (Habermas 1995: 853; see on Habermas's notion of 'constitutional patriotism', to which this passage refers, Booth 1999; Cronin 2003; Markell 2000)

Habermas thus assumes that it is possible to decouple a (shared) political-constitutional culture from both the majority culture and the cultures of (immigrant) 'minorities'. In a sense, Habermas's model of deliberative democracy presupposes such an assumption and allows, at the same time, for the reflective modification of one's own culture in the process of public deliberation and the struggle for recognition:

> Democratic politics must take the form of a 'politics of recognition' that protects the integrity of individuals in the life contexts in which their identities are formed. But the price of participation in a politics of recognition in a pluralistic society is that, in seeking recognition for their distinctive culture and identity, members of religious, ethnic and other cultural groups expose themselves to the corresponding demands for recognition of other groups, and hence to the pressure to revise intolerant and discriminatory aspects of their own self-understanding. (Cronin 2003: 11)

The constraints which Habermas's position thus imposes on groups and individuals are the 'modern' expectation of self-reflectivity and the willingness to embrace the idea of 'enlarged thinking'. While the 'interpretation' of constitutional principles may be affected by public deliberation, it is pivotal to Habermas's theory that any such changes must stay within the horizon of liberal human rights.

Globalisation and Democracy

We have seen in previous chapters how the 'globalisation of democracy' has been embedded in the worldwide promotion of human rights and the idea of an entitlement to democratic governance. Indeed, we saw how the notion of 'good governance' comprised the ideas of representative democracy based on fundamental human rights and of free-market capitalism. If states uphold the norms of this type of 'liberal' good governance, then their 'juridical' and 'Westphalian' sovereignty do not become a matter of concern for the 'international community'. However, states reluctant to embrace those liberal norms may have 'conditionalities' imposed upon them to enforce compliance, or may be subject to external intervention to bring about change. Peter Gowan (2003: 52) sums up this 'new liberal cosmopolitanism' in terms very similar to those deployed in previous chapters: '[S]overeignty is reconceived as a partial and conditional licence, granted by the "international community", which can be withdrawn should any state fail to meet the domestic or foreign standards laid down by the requirements of liberal governance.' The sustained endeavour by Western states to impose these standards of liberal 'civilisation' on non-Western, developing countries is a matter of record. But we must also remain cognisant of the fact that in many Western states a similar policy of 'neoliberal' restructuring has been going on since the 1980s. Reflecting on 'democracy's future', Philippe Schmitter summarises these policies:

> Privatization of public enterprises; removal of state regulations; liberalization of financial flows; conversions of political demands into claims based on rights; replacement of collective entitlements by individual contributions; sacralization of property rights; downsizing of public bureaucracies and emoluments; discrediting of 'politicians' in favour of 'entrepreneurs'; enhancement of the power of 'neutral technical' institutions, like central banks, at the expense of 'biased political' ones – all these modifications have two features in common: 1) they diminish popular expectations from public choices; and 2) they make it harder to assemble majorities to overcome the resistance of minorities, especially well-entrenched and privileged ones. (Schmitter 1995, quoted in Gowan 2003: 62; see also Crouch 2004 and Patterson 2004)

For Schmitter, these developments constitute a process of de-democractisation: a substantial set of subject-matters that are central to any notion of the 'common good' has been removed from the opinion and will formation of the citizens. Referring back to the argument we encountered in Chapter 2 regarding the relationship between 'negative' and 'positive' liberties, it is evident that such policies may arguably (and controversially) be justified by a claim that they enhance the ('negative') liberty of the individual. It cannot be doubted, however, that they do not enhance democratic self-determination. This is the paradox, then: policies are being recommended to, or actively imposed on, non-Western states under the banner of human rights and democracy which, if implemented, would limit democratic self-legislation to a relatively narrow band of policy issues as the experience of those Western countries shows where such policies have triggered a process of de-democratisation.

There is a second paradox: many elites in Western democracies which argue in favour of the global spread of democracy and human rights (above all in the form of civil and political 'fundamental' rights) attempt to convince their populations and citizens that, while these policies that lead to de-democratisation are regrettable, in a globalising world they are also inevitable. 'Globalisation', so the argument goes, has changed the environment within which states have to compete to ensure prosperity, security, and survival. There is no agreed-upon understanding of what is meant by 'globalisation' (see the discussions in Held et al. 1999 and Scholte 2000). At a 'descriptive' level, 'globalisation' gestures towards the following developments. We live in an era of ever increasing interconnectedness of peoples, places, capital, goods, and services. We are also witnessing an increase, and intensification, of political, economic, social, and cultural interactions across territorial borders. Globalisation as a multifaceted process manifests itself in such diverse forms as global tourism, mass migration, and the global reach of nuclear, environmental and health risks. Arguably, however, it has been economic changes and technological innovations in transport and information systems and their worldwide diffusion that have conjured up visions of a 'global' world. All states and societies – and, increasingly, individuals as well – have become entangled in a complex (and 'global') system of mutual dependencies. The 'globalisation hypothesis' posits that these interconnections and dependencies lead to the receding of the constraints of space and time on social and cultural arrangements in such a way that there occurs the 'spatial' and 'temporal' shrinking of the world. This process is accompanied by the development of a 'global' consciousness that perceives the world as 'one place'. It is this reality of worldwide interdependence, its emergence and its dynamics as well as its effects on states, societies, and individuals that the word 'globalisation' aims to sum up.

We discussed in Chapter 3 the four meanings of sovereignty that Stephen Krasner (1999) distinguished. What he calls 'interdependence sovereignty' is germane to any discussion on globalisation, and helps us to find the focus for our reflections in the current chapter. According to Krasner, 'interdependence sovereignty' relates to the control aspect of sovereignty (rather than its authority dimension). 'Interdependence sovereignty' refers to 'the ability of public authorities to regulate the flow of information, ideas, goods, people, pollutants, or capital across the borders of their state' (Krasner 1999: 4). It is one major claim in the globalisation literature that public authorities have lost control over ever more (types of) transborder movements. International political and economic inter-dependence has undermined the capacity of governments to attain their objectives through individual action, as Robert Keohane (1993) suggests. Anne-Marie Slaughter (2004b: 284) explicitly links these two concerns for control and capability when she asserts that '[a] state's ability to control its own territory without external interference is no longer sufficient to allow it to govern its people effectively – to provide security, economic stability and a measure of prosperity, clean air and water, and even minimum health standards' (see also Slaughter 2004a).

Kjell Goldmann, whose conceptual distinctions of the term 'sovereignty' we have also encountered in Chapter 3, has analysed the structural transformation of the European nation-state discerning three 'master' processes of internationalisation (a term he prefers to 'globalisation' and 'interdependence'). First, the 'internationalisation of problems' means that many of the political problems that a country faces come (increasingly) from abroad. Examples include environmental problems or crime. Secondly, the intensification of all kinds of human relations across nation-state borders manifests societal internationalisation: the 'internationalisation of societies' comprises an increasing exchange of goods, services, people, information, and ideas. Thirdly, there is an increase in the 'internationality' of political decision-making. This internationalisation expresses itself in the 'intensity' of decision-making, running from consultation with other states prior to national decisions to negotiated international agreements, on to decision-making by intergovernmental organisations, and, finally, to supranational decision-making. The 'scope' of internationalised decision-making has also changed insofar as we witness the proliferation of international decision-making to new, and ever-expanding, policy areas (Goldmann 2001: 8–17).

We should pursue Goldmann's line of argument a step further. If we look at the international position of states, we notice that they have been losing the monopoly which they had acquired over the last two hundred years or so of representing 'their' people in the 'international' arena, and their dominant position within this arena has been increasingly challenged (Rosenau 1997). International governmental organisations (IGOs) such as NATO, the UN, the International Labor Organization, the International Monetary Fund, the World Bank or the World Trade Organization constitute distinctive collective political actors which are firmly entrenched in decision-making procedures. These IGOs add to the complexity of the 'international' system that had formed around the power-political interests of states.

However, as associations of states based on multilateral treaties in accordance with international law these organisations, despite an increase in their 'political' independence, do not ultimately diminish the dominance of states in the 'international' system. Rather, they complement the power of (some) states. Indeed, IGOs can usefully be understood as manifestations of the efforts by states to claw back some competencies regarding the control of societal interactions across borders by going 'international' and opting for 'international' co-operation. In Krasner's terminology, IGOs potentially diminish the 'Westphalian' sovereignty of states and thus potentially impair a state's 'authority'; yet this 'cost' may be recouped through an increase in a state's capacity to 'control'.

Yet, as we are well aware, many more actors populate global politics, among them ever more prominently non-governmental organisations (NGOs). In the middle of the last decade, it was calculated that there were well over 15,000 recognisable NGOs operating in three or more countries and which drew their finances in more than one country (Gordenker and Weiss 1995: 357). Based on developments in communication and transport infrastructure, an increasingly dense network structure that connects NGOs globally has come to be established. Mary Kaldor referred to both empirical processes and one way of evaluating these processes in a normative political theory when she pointed out that:

> Whether we are talking about isolated dissidents in repressive regimes, landless labourers in Central America or Asia, global campaigns against land mines or third world debt, or even religious fundamentalists and fanatic nationalists, what has changed are the opportunities for linking up with other like-minded groups in different parts of the world, and for addressing demands not just to the state but to global institutions and other states . . . a new form of politics, which we call civil society, is both an outcome and an agent of global interconnectedness. (Kaldor 2003: 2)

For Kaldor, global civil society expands the sphere of 'active citizenship'; it refers to 'growing self-organization outside formal political circles, and expanded space in which individual citizens can influence the conditions in which they live both directly through self-organization and through political pressure' (Kaldor 2003: 8). However, these new actors in global civil society 'do not take decisions. Nor should they have a formal role in decision-making' – after all, 'they are voluntarily constituted and represent nobody but their own opinions' (Kaldor 2003: 108). Global civil society provides a way to supplement 'traditional' democracy, creating new channels for global deliberation and offering 'the possibility for the voices of the victims of globalisation to be heard if not the votes' (Kaldor 2003: 148; see also p. 141 where Kaldor speaks of global civil society being 'an alternative vehicle for . . . introducing normative concerns, for raising the interests of the individual and not just the state'). It is above all these developments, and their normative evaluations, that underpin the debates on the emergence of a 'global civil society' and a new system of 'global governance'.

The last few decades have seen the formation of movements that do not limit their activities to any one particular territory. These movements responded, for example, to the perceived threats to the survival of the human race posed by nuclear, biological and chemical warfare and by dangers of an eco-catastrophe, and concerned themselves with political and social injustice worldwide, be it with political prisoners, discrimination based on race or gender, or 'Third World' poverty. For these activists – for example, in the environmental and peace movements, in the women's movement, the movement of 'indigenous peoples' or the more recent 'anti-globalisation movements' – the 'one world' has become their point of reference. Such a global orientation is also becoming prominent within religious organisations and movements. The participants in these movements act on the basis of a global consciousness:

> [Their] ethos implies a reorientation of citizenship in order to go beyond loyalty and diligent participation in the collective life of a territorially delimited society that qualifies as a sovereign state. The citizen sensitive to the claims of this emergent ethos needs to extend his or her notions of participation in dimensions of both space (beyond the territory of any particular state) and time (beyond the present, reclaiming past wisdom and safeguarding future generations). (Falk 1992: 153–4, 1995: 212; Kaldor 2003: 111–12; see also Keane 2003: 57–65 on activists' nurturing their identities and publicising their concerns in 'translocalities'.)

'Think globally, act locally' as much as 'Think locally, act globally' is the core of this ethos that is 'necessarily deferential to the local and the diverse' (Falk 1992: 153). These 'citizen-pilgrims' are participating, so it is argued, in the creation of a 'global' civil society.

Alejandro Colás (2002) has highlighted two aspects of the debate on 'global civil society'. First, the growing economic, technological, and cultural integration of a globalising world is believed to impel a deeper and more extensive co-operation among socio-political activists across the globe. This extension of social movement activity beyond state boundaries is considered to be opening up previously closed arenas of global politics, thereby gradually replacing the sovereign nation-state as the major locus of political power. Secondly, concomitantly with this wave of transnational movement activity, we witness the formation of a structure of global governance. The international governmental organisations that have been the building blocks of the multilateral arrangements entered into by sovereign states are being drawn into a system of 'complex multilateralism' where international non-governmental organisations, citizens' movements, and multinational corporations together with states share in the task of governance.

James Rosenau provides one prominent understanding of 'global governance'. In his analysis of the 'turbulent world' of the late twentieth century, Rosenau understands global governance as the (mainly) unintended consequence of the conscious pursuit of goals by distinctive collective actors through the exercise of control mechanisms that have transnational repercussions:

> To assess global governance . . . is to trace the various ways in which the processes of governance are aggregated. The cumulation encompasses individuals, their skills and orientations, no less than private and public collectivities at the local, provincial, national, transnational, international, and global levels . . . Global governance is not so much a label for a high degree of integration and order as it is a summary term for highly complex and widely disparate activities that culminate in a modicum of worldwide coherence. (Rosenau, 1997: 10–11; also Rosenau 1998)

In this world, governance is no longer the exclusive domain of national governments and the state. Rather, the sites out of which authority is exercised and compliance generated have been dispersed and authority has been relocated 'outwards to transnational and supranational organizations, sidewards to social movements and NGOs, and inwards to subnational groups' (Rosenau 1997: 43–4). Rosenau pays scant attention to the question of what makes for *democratic* 'global governance'. He organises his thoughts on democracy around the idea of 'checks and balances':

> The decentralization of rule systems in disparate and localized sites has greatly inhibited the coalescence of hierarchical and autocratic centers of power . . . authority is so widely dispersed that neither tyrannical majorities nor autocratic leaders are likely to gain much of a foothold in this emergent domain and, if they do, the constraints against their tyranny are

likely to be too numerous and resistant for them to expand the scope of their power. (Rosenau, 1997: 40–1)

This rather mechanistic model with its emphasis on the dispersal of power among a multiplicity of groups and collective actors is reminiscent of American pluralist political theory of the 1950s and 1960s. In this line of analysis, there is no sustained discussion of the obvious power differentials that exist between, say, transnational corporations on one side and, say, Oxfam, on the other. Rosenau does not discuss how such power differentials affect the distribution of power in the global governance structure; nor does he have an adequate theoretical framework that would allow him to do so. Colás (2002: 152) rightly suggests that such a conceptualisation of 'global governance', and of 'global civil society' as an important part of its material infrastructure, is dominant in the mainstream International Relations and International Law literature (see, for example, Charnovitz 2001/02; Guzman 2004; McGinnis and Movsesian 2004 on international law discussions on the role of the WTO in global governance). 'Transnational', or 'global', civil society is seen as a fairly homogeneous, non-hierarchical and disinterested counterpoint to the power-driven system of states representing an otherwise marginalised or disenfranchised 'global citizenry'.

Against such an understanding of 'global civil society', Colás raises a series of pertinent questions. Empirically, he points to the fact that 'global civil society is what states make of it' (2002: 153). Many NGOs are organised by governments (GONGOs), are quasi non-governmental organisations (QUANGOs) or are even government-run or initiated (GRINGOs). Their participation in conferences organised by international governmental organisations such as the UN is premised on their state-approved accreditation (Friedmann et al. 2005). This observation raises the question about the adequacy of a 'liberal' conceptualisation of ('global') civil society as pitted against the domestic 'state' (and the states in the inter-state system) and points us to a hypothesis that posits the state as a significant component of international social movement activity (Colás, 2002: 75–83; see also Halliday 2000; Sassen 2003). Furthermore, a considerable number of NGOs have been boosters, and often willing executioners, of neo-liberal policies, more concerned with spreading, and entrenching, a particular form of capitalism rather than promoting democracy (Petras 1997). More generally, NGOs as 'functional' organisations represent the interests of their members rather than a nascent global 'demos'. That there are, in the various 'anti-globalisation movements', forces that struggle against the logic of global capitalist accumulation and its political and cultural ramifications, cannot be doubted – although fighting against capitalism in itself does not make a social movement democratic.

It is worth distinguishing two lines of argument in the literature on global governance and/or civil society. As we have seen with regard to Kaldor, Keane and Falk, for example, a normative theory of politics grounds their concern with global civil society. A second line of enquiry starts from the empirical observation of a multiplicity of actors at the global stage and the (alleged) incapacity of states as the traditional international actors to solve global problems on their own. Following on from the empirical investigation, a necessity for setting-up decentralised and plural mechanisms of political co-operation and regulation that brings together public and private actors is stipulated. Hence, supporters of the idea of 'global governance' do not argue in favour of establishing a sovereign, centralised institution at the global level that could authoritatively impose order, if need be through coercive means.

These developments and their theoretical-normative reflections have put emphasis upon the need to understand the location of democracy in such a complex world. In the past, the sovereign nation-state was considered to be the 'ultimate power' that could impose, and enforce, order within a territory. Political rule in general, and the regulatory, steering and co-ordinating capacities of the state in particular, have been territorially bounded in their reach. The success of the nation-state in the last two hundred years or so, as well as its universality and legitimacy, were premised on its claim to be able to guarantee the economic well-being, the physical security, and the cultural identity of the people who constitute its citizens. However, ever more societal interactions cross borders, becoming transnational and hence detached from a particular territory. The links between the citizens and the nation-state are becoming ever more problematic. The citizens demand political representation, physical protection, economic security, and cultural certainty. Yet, we are moving into a world of diffused and decentralised power. In this world that is made up of states (politically organised), regions, international and supranational organisations, non-governmental organisations, and transnational corporations, the nation-state finds it increasingly difficult to accommodate these interests and mediate between its citizens and the rest of the world.

In the current age, then, the conception of the state's *summa potestas* has become problematical. Also, as we have seen, so has the notion of the sovereignty of the people as a united, homogeneous body legitimating the sovereign power of 'its' state through a constitution that manifests the principle of *voluntas populi suprema lex* (that is, 'the will of the people be the highest law'). In this complex and fragmented world, where is the place of 'democracy'? If there is no longer a *summa potestas*, who, then, can be held accountable by the 'people'? Moreover, if we, as individuals and members of groups and communities, are 'embedded' in a plethora of cross-border or transnational power networks, bringing us into relationships of dominance and dependency with alternating sets of individuals, groups, and communities, who is the 'people', and who or what 'constituency' can legitimately claim the democratic right of control and participation? In a global world, has the concern with the creation and maintenance of citizenship and rights attached to membership in a national community become anachronistic?

Furthermore, as a result of the increasing transnationalisation of a wide range of societal interactions, the effective political solution of ever more societal problems is being sought at a level above or outside the nation-state. However, many transnational interactions, and the transnationalisation of economic action in particular, have hurried ahead of the current possibilities for their political regulation. At the same time, the structures and mechanisms of international regulatory policy-making – such as IGOs – are, in turn, more advanced than the institutions for their democratic control. This creates a tension between the effectiveness of political problem-solving at the 'international' level, on the one hand, and democratic legitimacy which remains embedded in 'domestic' political institutional arrangements, on the other hand. This tension is aggravated by the repercussions of international policy-making on domestic societies. Democratic politics at the nation-state level is increasingly curtailed as a result of the binding force of international political agreements. While 'democracy beyond the nation-state' remains weak, 'democracy within the nation-state' is weakened as well. International policy agreements restrict the range of democratically contested domestic policy options. The human rights regime since 1948, which we discussed in Chapter 2, may serve as an example. For better or worse, human rights qualify the notion of the rightful authority of the state: 'How a state treats its own citizens, and even what legal and constitutional arrangements it has, can thus no longer be regarded as a purely internal matter for the government concerned' (Beetham 1998: 61–2).

According to David Held, one of the foremost analysts of these developments, globalisation poses the question as to how to combine adequately the system of territorially rooted democratic governance with the transnational and global organisation of social and economic life. Held pinpoints the problem succinctly:

> National boundaries have traditionally demarcated the basis on which individuals are included and excluded from participation in decisions affecting their lives; but if many socio-economic processes, and the outcomes of decisions about them, stretch beyond national frontiers, then the implications of this are serious, not only for the categories of consent and legitimacy but for all the key ideas of democracy. At issue is the nature of a constituency (how should the proper boundaries of a constituency be drawn?), the meaning of representation (who should represent whom and on what basis?), and the proper form and scope of political participation (who should participate and in what way?). As fundamental processes of governance escape the categories of the nation-state, the traditional national resolutions of the key questions of democratic theory and practice are open to doubt (Held 2000: 28).

We face the challenge, so Held argues, to create and entrench democratic institutions at regional and global levels – complementing those at the nation-state level – which would enable the peoples of the world to express and deliberate upon their aims and objectives in a progressively more interconnected global order (Held 1995a: chapters 10–12).[1]

For Held, the concept of 'cosmopolitan democracy' refers to 'a model of political organisation in which citizens, wherever they are located in the world, have a voice, input and political representation in international affairs, in parallel with and independently of their own governments' (Held 1995b: 13). Transnational socio-political movements and NGOs, that is, civil society actors, are to play a vital role in this process of global democratisation (Porta et al. 1999; Smith et al. 1997). Held's model does not aim for a world government or a federal world state. He favours a global and divided authority system, 'a system of diverse and overlapping power centres, shaped and delimited by democratic law' (Held 1995a: 234–5). For Held, cosmopolitan law 'demands the subordination of regional, national and local "sovereignties" to an overarching legal framework, but within this framework associations may be self-governing at diverse levels' (Held 1995a: 234). He accepts that democracy must be institutionalised on many levels, ranging from the local/municipal to the sub-national and national levels and through the regional level to the global level. His goal is thus to strengthen democracy 'within' communities and civil associations 'by elaborating and reinforcing democracy from "outside" through a network of regional and international agencies and assemblies that cut across spatially delimited locales' (Held 1995a: 237). Held frankly concedes that, 'in the first instance', it would be those democratic states and civil societies 'that are able to muster the necessary political judgement and to learn how political practices and institutions must change and adapt in the new regional and global circumstances' that would promulgate and defend cosmopolitan democratic law (Held 1995a: 232). Cosmopolitan law would thus start out as law pronounced by Western liberal democracies.

Yet, such endorsement of democracy at nation-state level does not involve a full embrace of the idea of 'popular sovereignty'. Andrew Linklater argues that cosmopolitan concerns and considerations ultimately override the democratically expressed will of national citizens: he advocates a 'break with the supposition that national populations have the sovereign right to withhold consent' if cosmopolitan demands 'clash with their conception of national interests' (Linklater 1998b: 192). Arguably, there is the distinct danger that an emphasis on the need for designing a cosmopolitan legal order, of which human rights are a constituent element, risks ultimately marginalising political participation and popular will – and, *in extremis*, vaporising popular sovereignty in impersonal and decentred, yet mutually interlocking and overlapping, networks and associations of deliberation, contestation, and argumentation – networks that constitute the public sphere of an Habermasian 'deliberative' democracy.

Some of Held's institutional innovations are defined as long-term, others as short-term objectives (Held 2004: 110–14). The short-term objectives aim, for example, at the reform of the United Nations with a modification of the veto arrangement in the Security Council and a reconsideration of representation on it to allow for adequate regional accountability; the creation of regional parliaments (for example, in Latin America and Africa) as well as the enhancement of the role and power of such bodies where they already exist (as in the case of the European Union); the creation of a new, international Human Rights Court; and the establishment of an effective, accountable military force. Within the UN context, Held proposes the establishment of an independent assembly of democratic peoples, directly elected by them and accountable to them, whose rule would have been agreed upon in an international constitutional convention involving states, IGOs, INGOs, citizen groups, and social movements. This new assembly could become an authoritative centre for the examination of the most pressing global problems: '[H]ealth and disease, food supply and distribution, the debt burden of the "Third World", the instability of the hundred of billions of dollars that circulate the globe daily, global warming, and the reduction of risks of nuclear and chemical warfare' (Held 1995a: 274). IGOs such as the WTO, IMF, and the World Bank would be opened up to public examination and agenda setting. General referenda cutting across nations and nation-states at regional or global levels would be introduced in those cases where priorities concerning the implementation of core cosmopolitan concerns are contested (Held 2003: 477).

How convincing is Held's model of 'cosmopolitan democracy'? We may offer a number of critical reflections.

(1) Held foresees that the new democratic political institutions would override states in clearly defined spheres of activity 'where those activities have demonstrable transnational and international consequences, require regional or global initiatives in the interests of effectiveness and depend on such initiatives for democratic legitimacy' (Held 1998: 24; see also Held 2003: 475). This is an exceedingly vague statement. In the 'age of globalisation', which activities do *not* have demonstrable trans- and international consequences? Who, or which bodies, decide whether regional or global initiatives are warranted? Who enforces the appropriation of decision-making powers by regional or global bodies? As Held himself argues, states are reluctant to submit their disputes with other states to arbitration by a 'supreme authority': who then enforces the decisions taken by these bodies (Held 1995a: 276)? How realistic is it to stipulate – as either a short-term or long-term objective – the formation of an 'effective' and 'accountable' international military force (Held 2003: 478)? In particular, it is inconceivable that the rich states of the North are willing to submit to any political will that is counter to their core political interests. Held boldly asserts that 'the possibility of cosmopolitan democracy would be enhanced if the UN system actually lived up to its Charter' (Held 2003: 475). He does not mean that the UN system should re-assert the equal sovereignty of states. For him, being true to the UN Charter consists in implementing 'key elements of the rights Conventions, and enforcing the prohibition on the discretionary right to use force' (Held 2003: 475). We have seen in previous chapters what consequences such a policy has.

(2) There is woefully little analysis of the 'prerequisites' of 'cosmopolitan democracy'. Philip Resnick has argued that prospects for global democracy are held back by uneven economic development, diverging political traditions, cultural and ethnic identities, and solidarities that are primarily local or national in character (Resnick 1998: 126–43). Above all, issues of economic and social equality will have to be put back on to the agenda if we wished to create the conditions for global democracy. The extreme inequality of living conditions between North and South must be addressed. Resnick is right to point out that 'the very parameters of global economic development further the concentration of wealth and power in the core countries' (Resnick 1998: 131). IGOs such as the International Monetary Fund, the World Bank or the World Trade Organisation have played an important role in shaping national public policies and creating a political and legal institutional infrastructure for global capitalism. They have been very much under the control of the richest and most powerful countries and have been implicated in retaining structures of inequality. To address these concerns adequately, Held would have to integrate economic issues as areas of severe political struggles more profoundly than has so far happened into his model of 'cosmopolitan democracy'.

In his model, Held has listed under short-term objectives the 'foundation of a new co-ordinating economic agency at regional and global levels' and the 'introduction of strict limits to private ownership of key "public-shaping" institutions' such as the media (Held 1995a: 279–80). The long-term objectives include the 'establishment of the accountability of international and transnational economic agencies to parliaments and assemblies at regional and global levels' as well as a 'guaranteed basic income for all adults, irrespective of whether they are engaged in market or household activities'. Held would have to show how these objectives of a global 'social market' capitalism are likely to be achieved; how they could possibly be justified (for example, in terms of global justice); and whether capitalism as an inherently inegalitarian system organised around the profit motive can ever be the appropriate means of overcoming the division of the world as well as the divisions within its constituent states and societies into 'rich' and 'poor'. More broadly, he would have to theorise the connection between economic development and cosmopolitan democracy, or, to put it another way, the connection between democracy and economic power.

(3) Furthermore, while a call for the establishment of regional

parliaments appears to be unproblematic from within a democratic position, efforts at parliamentarisation in the politically most advanced region, Europe, show that this is by no means the case. In the first instance, political development in the past has shown that it is around the conflict and cleavage structure within the bounded territory of the nation-state that intermediary institutions such as political parties, interest groups, voluntary associations, trade unions, or the mass media have been organised. Citizens tend to avail themselves of the national intermediary institutions as the means of their political participation. To put it differently, the role of the citizen has been firmly institutionalised at the level of the nation-state.

Even after fifty years of European integration, we still find that intermediary structures remain 'nationalised'. As yet, there is no European party system that would aggregate and articulate social and political interests on a Europe-wide level. So far, political parties are national actors that, at best, aim to translate the interests of their *national* constituencies into the European political system. The degree of 'Europeanisation' of other than business interests has been low. With citizens still directing their interests, concerns and demands to their national, or subnational, government not to 'Brussels', there is no European public opinion. Given that the intermediary structures necessary for interest and opinion formation are not in place, whom or what could a European Parliament possibly represent? Only if there is a genuine process of Europe-wide, transnational interest formation does it become necessary for reasons of democratic legitimacy to institute the European Parliament as that mechanism through which diverse interests have to be channelled, reconciled, and acted upon. Indeed, as the recent experience with the drafting and confirmation of a 'constitution' of the European Union has shown many citizens in member states across the Union remain unconvinced of the need and desirability of such a 'constitution'.

Further, a key feature of parliamentary rule is policy-making on the basis of decisions taken by a parliamentary majority. Yet the principle of majority rule does not suffice to generate legitimacy of the political system as a whole. The application of majority rule as a legitimating principle is premised on a socio-political and socio-cultural context that is conducive to the defeated minority's acceptance of the majority decision. The existence of such a congenial context cannot be taken for granted. Democratic legitimacy as an effect of parliamentary majority rule has a number of preconditions. First, there must be no fundamental ethnic, linguistic, religious, ideological, or economic cleavages in a society. Secondly, the political community must have developed a collective identity based on shared citizenship and political equality as well as shared normative orientations so that differences in specific policy areas will not be dramatised into fundamental differences over the institutional order of the political community. In national political systems it is the intermediary institutions that play a central part in the generation of a collective identity as well as in processing conflicts among interests and differences in cultural orientation in such a way that they can be integrated into the political system. Morever, it is the dynamics of the intermediary structure that holds open the promise for minorities of possibly turning their current minority position into a majority position at some point in the future. Neither of these two preconditions for the acceptance of parliamentary majority decisions as legitimate is as yet in place in Europe with its historical, cultural, linguistic, and political-institutional diversity and economic disparities. To expect that decisions by the European Parliament would meet with widespread acceptance under these circumstances would appear to be unwarranted, even foolhardy.[2]

What has just been said about the socio-political and socio-cultural preconditions for the parliamentarisation of the European Union would also apply to David Held's envisaged 'assembly of democratic peoples' within the UN, but also, for example, to Johan Galtung's institutional reform of the UN (Galtung 2000: 153–9). Galtung envisages five UN assemblies: in addition to the General Assembly (UNGA) for governments, the UN People's Assembly (UNPA) would be the ultimate sovereign body and legitimised on the basis of direct elections. There would be a Third Assembly, for economic corporations (UNCA), and a Fourth Assembly for local authorities (UNLAA). The Fifth Assembly of NGOs (CONGO) would have, like UNCA and UNLAA, only consultative status. Whereas it is possible to conceive of UNGA, UNPA, and UNLAA as possessing – in the long term – some degree of democratic legitimacy as a result of their grounding in elections, the same cannot be said of either corporations or NGOs. The former Secretary-General, Boutros Boutros-Ghali, while sharing Galtung's utopian and romantic ideas about political representation, is on firmer ground in terms of legitimacy when he argues for a closer integration of the Inter-Parliamentary Union, the world organisation of parliamentarians, into the UN system (Boutros-Ghali 2000: 113).

These considerations about the place of a supranational parliament within a 'cosmopolitan democracy' turn our attention back to the nation-state and its role within a changing global structure. The effects of globalisation on the modern state (and the effects of state policies on globalisation) have been controversially discussed. We should not assume without detailed argument that globalisation, of necessity, 'weakens' the modern state and undermines, if not destroys, its policy capacity. There are still certain functions and tasks that will have to be performed even in the 'global' world and which are unlikely to be performed well, or at all, by private agencies.

(4) Economic globalisation affects different sectors and regions within each state differently. 'De-industrialisation', for example, is bound to bring disadvantages to the manufacturing industries and industrial regions of advanced capitalist countries, whereas the internationalisation of financial services is likely to benefit other geographical locations and socio-economic groups within these countries. One of the effects of global capitalism on the advanced capitalist countries has been the occurrence of socio-economic and socio-political crises which used to be seen as unique to less-developed countries: for example, rising long-term unemployment, increases in income disparities and in absolute poverty, depopulation of the countryside, decay of urban centres, and an increase in organised crime. Neither for the global system as a whole nor for its constituent units does economic globalisation thus result in homogeneity and overall integration; rather, it is likely to accentuate heterogeneity and fragmentation. Global capitalism is best analysed as a system of structured inequality. There is a need for an agency that integrates society and takes care of the interests individuals share as members of a community. Who else but states (on their own or in co-operation with each other) could take care of this task?

(5) The very real danger of a global eco-catastrophe is an important aspect of globalisation and of the formation of a global consciousness, the idea of a shared fate of humankind on 'Planet Earth'. There can be no doubt that, in the twenty-first century, a new balance will have to be found between the economy and ecology. Achieving 'sustainable development' and hence an economic system that is ecologically safe and socially just presupposes an agency that can instigate reform and see through fundamental changes. Who else but states (on their own or in co-operation with each other) could take care of this task?

(6) We have come to recognise that 'local' (national) decisions may have 'global' effects – for example, policies regarding emission levels for power stations. Likewise, 'global' processes may have a 'local' impact – for example, the global dissemination of Western imagery

through satellite-based communications systems and its effect on 'local' or 'national' cultures. There is a need for an agency that considers the possibly global effect of 'local' decisions, but that also protects 'national' communities as best as possible against the 'local' effects of 'global' forces. Who else but states (on their own or in co-operation with each other) could take care of this task?

(7) International governmental organisations are a vital element in global governance. Furthermore, ever more policies and decisions are being taken in the setting of multilateral negotiations and agreements. Who, if not the state, could bestow legitimacy upon these international organisations and would have the legitimacy to participate in multilateral negotiations, agree to binding policy decisions, and then have the power to guarantee their 'local' implementation?

(8) Around the world, political projects of regional integration are being pursued as an attempt to promote regional economies and create structures of regional political governance. The European Union (EU), the North American Free Trade Agreement (NAFTA), the Asia-Pacific Economic Co-operation (APEC), or the Association of South East Asian Nations (ASEAN) may serve as examples. These projects will put a premium on the co-operation of states. Who else but states could provide a legal and material infrastructure for such a regional, 'supranational' space and contain the political, economic, and social dislocations which will necessarily arise in such an enterprise? As Paul Hirst has argued, *democratic* practices within states make wider institutions both possible and legitimate:

> Democratic governments can credibly speak for their populations, since they are legitimated by majority vote. Democratic governments know that the international commitments they enter into will, by convention, be honoured by successor administrations. Other states know this too and can thus accept such commitments as binding. Democratic states, because they abide by the rule of law internally and accept decisions against them in the domestic courts, also tend to abide by international law and to respect international agreements. Without this lawful behaviour of states as members of the international society, international law would have little force and international governance above the level of the sovereign state would be virtually impossible (Hirst 2001: 271; also Bellamy and Jones 2000: 202–16).

The argument put forward in the previous paragraphs re-focuses the question of democracy. As long as the state retains those functions and is expected to perform those tasks in discharge of its duties *vis-à-vis* its citizens, it is imperative that democratic accountability of state elites is upheld at the level of the nation-state. Indeed, there is an urgent need to enhance the opportunities for political participation and citizen engagement 'at the local level'.

(9) Arguably, a 'strong democratic civil society' (Barber 1998) is a key prerequisite for the transnational movements and (international) non-governmental organisations mentioned above. For the most part, they are formed within national societies and depend for their success, and even frequently their very survival, on other institutions within this national political environment, such as political parties, trade unions, churches, and the media. Also we must not forget that one response to globalisation has been the formation of extreme national and racist movements which have been mobilising for the closing down of democratic spaces in Western societies and elsewhere. A 'global' civil society as part of a 'cosmopolitan' democracy that is built partially around the global linkages of these 'nationally' embedded 'transnational' movements is thus inherently fragile and premised on a national environment supportive of movement politics. It is through citizen participation that such an environment must be nurtured and sustained.

(10) We pointed out in connection with Rosenau's conceptualisation of global governance that his rather mechanistic model with its emphasis on the dispersal of power among a multiplicity of groups and collective actors is reminiscent of American pluralist political theory of the 1950s and 1960s. Let us disregard the obvious question as to whether there are no power differentials between, say, transnational corporations on the one side and Amnesty International on the other, which translate into power differentials in the 'global governance' structure. Let us ask instead: may we reasonably assume that the quality and scope of 'global democracy' would be enhanced should democratic structures and processes obtain within these non-state agencies and organisations implicated in 'global governance'? At issue are questions of intra-organisational democracy, the representativeness, responsiveness, and accountability of organisational elites to the members and supporters of the organisation and the openness of organisations to outside scrutiny. If intra-organisational democracy contributes to the democratic character of global governance, then, arguably, the struggle for extending democracy to 'private' associations or corporations would have to be fought initially at the nation-state level where most of these organisations are 'incorporated'.

(11) Such democratic involvement and struggle at the nation-state level is all the more imperative since economic 'globalisation' has had manifest 'political' roots in the decisions and non-decisions of national

governments over the past three decades or so, mainly in the area of macroeconomic management (Jones 2000: 55–64): globalisation is not the inevitable outcome of 'technologically'-driven processes, but is manifestly a political 'project'. State policies of liberalisation, deregulation, and marketisation that have been presented by national and transnational political and economic elites as a necessary and inevitable 'response' to the 'challenges' of globalisation to the nation-state have propelled globalisation forward. Philip Cerny has analysed these policy changes in the context of a discussion of the transition from the industrial welfare state to the competition state:

> Rather than attempt to take certain economic activities *out* of the market, to 'decommodify' them as the welfare state in particular was organized to do, the competition state has pursued *increased* marketization in order to make economic activities located within the national territory, or which otherwise contribute to national wealth, more competitive in international and transnational terms. The main features of this process have included attempts to reduce government spending in order to minimize the 'crowding out' of private investment by state consumption and the deregulation of economic activities, especially financial markets. (Cerny 2000: 122–3; Jessop 2002, emphasis in original)

Any resistance to such 'national' policies has to be organised 'nationally'. In all the democratic nation-states in western Europe, we find well-developed systems of interest formation and intermediation, of institutionalised conflict management, and institutionalised norms of social justice. Among the forces that have had the greatest impact on the formation of these systems, the political, economic, and cultural struggles around the formation of centralised, and secularised, state structures and of industrial-capitalist national economies stand out. Of course, the precise cleavage structure has been different in each country, and so have the course and outcome of the struggles caused by it. As a result, each country has developed complexes of interest formation and intermediation that are fairly idiosyncratic. In the process of democratisation and the formation of 'mass politics', each country has built up political parties, trade unions, professional associations, voluntary associations, special interest groups, and media for the formation and expression of public opinion. Yet, for example, party systems, structures of industrial relations, the incorporation of interest groups into the political system, or the allocation of jurisdiction and resources to sub-national, regional and municipal bodies, have developed in historically distinct ways in each case. So, for example, has the specific mix of policies through which national welfare states became institutionalised. 'National' economies and national welfare states exhibit distinct structures and institutional features that influence the degree to which they are able to respond to 'globalisation'. Furthermore, public welfare services must be wanted, and demanded, by the citizens, and the citizens must be willing to pay for them. Such solidaristic values and attitudes must be embedded in a national political culture; but for them to be sustained, and acted upon, it needs political mobilisation and citizens' involvement at the 'local' level (Hirst and Thompson 1999: chapter 6). More generally, the 'local' (ill-) effects of 'global' processes need 'local' responses from within a 'strong' democratic civil society. Because of the historical path-dependency of state form and policy formation, political struggle over policies must be organised 'nationally' and co-ordinated 'internationally'.

We live in a world of value conflicts. For example, some people may believe that 'global' capitalism is conducive to reducing world poverty and excessive environmental concerns and regulations will not only unduly restrict economic development but also result in 'global injustice'. Even if we accepted that there is a 'global' consensus on certain elements of a 'global ethic' (such as 'human rights'), there are then still conflicts over the specific policies necessary (or appropriate) to enact such rights. We may think, for example, in the case of abortion how the (human) rights of the mother are best balanced with the (human) right of the unborn child. Politics finds one expression in the authoritative allocation of values for a political community as a whole – even under conditions of multiculturalism. Given value conflicts, such allocation is, of necessity, contentious. Democracy aims to prevent the authoritarian or dictatorial allocation of such values by institutionalising mechanisms of popular participation in, and control over, political decision-making. The argument of this section of the chapter has been that the establishment of such democratic institutions and mechanisms at the level 'beyond the nation-state' is sub-optimal compared to the expansion of democracy at the level of the nation-state. The institutional framing, or balancing (if not the settlement), of value clashes above the level of the nation-state needs the mediation of the democratic nation-state.

A criticism of Held's model of 'cosmopolitan democracy' still leaves the possibility of embracing the more modest claim that individuals ought to work for global goals and that the agendas of citizens within a state increasingly ought to include global concerns.[3] Global goals such as the protection of human rights, peace, the reduction of poverty or caring for the environment, and action such as working for Oxfam, joining an Amnesty International letter writing campaign, or standing in vigil for peace at a time of war may serve as examples of global commitment and forms of action geared towards achieving them (Dower 2000; Erskine 2002). Bhikhu Parekh (2003: 12–17) has eloquently argued the case for a 'globally oriented national citizenship'. Such a type of citizenship has three important components: it involves (1) 'constantly examining the policies of one's country and ensuring that they do not damage and, within the limits of its resources, promote the interests of humankind at large'; (2) 'an active interest in the affairs of other countries'; and (3) 'an active commitment to create a just world order' (Parekh 2003: 12–13). One way of understanding Parekh's definition of globally-oriented citizenship is to see it as embracing Kant's local and global patriotisms. On the one hand, we may expect 'those who strongly identify with their community and feel a sense of responsibility for its action [to be] the most likely to feel ashamed and protest when it behaves badly'. On the other hand, accepting that 'human well-being everywhere should be matter of moral concern to us', the globally-oriented citizens think it their duty 'to protest and mobilise international public opinion when governments in other parts of the world engage in genocide or ethnic cleansing, oppress their citizens or those in neighbouring countries, deny them rights, and in general damage their ability to lead the good life' (Parekh 2003: 13). The globally-oriented citizen thus possesses the characteristics of Kant's patriotic cosmopolitan.

Notes

1 On 'global democracy' see also: Archibugi (2003); Archibugi and Held (1995); Archibugi (1998); Archibugi, Held and Köhler (1998); Falk (1995); (1996: 353–60), (1998); Held et al. (1999); Holden (2000); Hutchings and Dannreuther (1999); Linklater (1996), (1998a), (1998b), (1999). Held stipulates eight 'cosmopolitan principles' which constitute the basis of the new internationalism (Held 2004: 170–8): (1) the equal worth and dignity of each individual and hence the individual as the ultimate unit of moral concern; (2) active agency or individual self-determination based on self-conscious, self-reflective reasoning; (3) personal responsibility and accountability; (4) consent as the basis of non-coercive collective agreement and governance; (5) collective decision-making about public matters through voting procedures; (6) inclusiveness and subsidiarity so that all who are affected by a decision are involved in the decision-making process; (7) avoidance of serious harm; and (8) sustainability. All of these principles are solidly 'liberal' and do not make it necessary for Western states to make any major changes in their institutional make-up.

2 Held's assumption that a (strengthened) European Parliament is imperative for a more democratic European Union – a notion he shares with
many academic and political commentators – would appear to be based
upon the supposition of the state-like character of the European Union.
However, as Schmitter (2000) has forcefully reminded his readers, unless
the European Union is understood as a polity *sui generis* one fails
adequately to talk about the challenges one faces concerning its democratisation. Schmitter puts forward a whole raft of institutional proposals
to address the political problem of democratic representation. They range
from the insertion of direct advisory referenda into existing European
elections and the creation of a special status for European denizens to the
institutionalisation of functionally differentiated representation in 'functional subparliaments' whose membership would be made up of representatives from those countries which had accepted the full *acquis* in the
respective functional domain and 'whose decisions would be automatically
given the imprimatur of the [EU] parliament as a whole' (Schmitter 2000:
57). He proposes semi-public status for those (non-profit-making) interest
associations and social movements which have members and some degree
of organisation in several European countries and which would commit
themselves to participating in the deliberation of European issues, while
agreeing 'to obey a common set of norms and submit themselves potentially to the jurisdiction of the ECJ (as well as be prepared to operate within
the legal norms of whatever member country they might find themselves
in' (Schmitter 2000: 60). Such 'incorporation' would aim at establishing a
'Charter of Rights and Obligations' for European associations and movements which would thereby be recognised as 'secondary (organizational)
citizen of Europe' (Schmitter 2000: 60).
  Whatever one may think about the appropriateness of such a semi-
corporatist model of representation at EU level, it is clear that the institutionalisation of democratic representation cannot just proceed along the lines
of liberal-representative democracy at the nation-state level. For Schmitter,
institutional innovation must come from the European elites: the national
demoi are spectators on the sidelines. That not all citizens in member states
share such an elitist conceptualisation of democracy became apparent in the
context of the ratification of the draft 'constitution' of the EU.

3 Calhoun (2003); Chandler (2005); Nakano (2006); Urbinati (2003) raise
critical questions for cosmopolitan democrats related to the persistence of
territorially localised political power and globally diffused economic
power and the need for enabling locally embedded political participation.
Miller (1995), (1999); Zolo (1997), for example, emphasise the continuing
importance of (liberal) nationalism and the sovereign state for democracy.
Kurasawa (2004) discusses 'cosmopolitanism from below'. Archibugi
(2004) responds to some critics of cosmopolitan democracy.

Bibliography

Abrahamsen, Rita (2000), *Disciplining Democracy: Development Discourse and Good Governance in Africa*, London and New York: Zed Books.

Achenwall, G. and St. Pütter ([1750] 1995), *Anfangsgründe des Naturrechts [Elementa iuris naturae]*, ed. and trans. J. Schröder (Bibliothek des deutschen Staatsdenkens, vol. 5), Frankfurt a. M. and Leipzig: Reclam.

Allen, J. W. (1951), *A History of Political Thought in the Sixteenth Century*, London: Methuen.

'A More Secure World. Our Shared Responsibility. Report of the High-level Panel on Threats, Challenges and Change', New York: United Nations, 2004.

Anderson, Frank M. (ed.) (1904), *The Constitutions and Other Select Documents Illustrative of the History of France, 1789–1901*, Minneapolis, MN: Wilson Company.

Anderson, Perry (2005), 'Arms and rights. Rawls, Habermas and Bobbio in an age of war', *New Left Review*, 31: 5–40.

Anghie, Antony (2005), *Imperialism, Sovereignty and the Making of International Law* (Cambridge Studies in International and Comparative Law), Cambridge: Cambridge University Press.

Annas, Julia (1993), *The Morality of Happiness*, New York, Oxford: Oxford University Press.

Archibugi, Daniele (1998), 'Principles of cosmopolitan democracy', in Daniele Archibugi, David Held and Martin Köhler (eds) (1998), *Re-Imagining Political Community. Studies in Cosmopolitan Democracy*, Cambridge: Polity Press, pp. 198–228.

Archibugi, Daniele, David Held and Martin Köhler (eds) (1998), *Re-Imagining Political Community. Studies in Cosmopolitan Democracy*, Cambridge: Polity Press.

Archibugi, D. and D. Held (eds) (1995), *Cosmopolitan Democracy*, Cambridge: Polity Press.

Archibugi, Daniele (ed.) (2003), *Debating Cosmopolitics*, London: Verso.

Archibugi, Daniele (2004), 'Cosmopolitan democracy and its critics: a review', *European Journal of International Relations*, 10: 3, 437–73.

Arendt, Hannah (1982), *Lectures on Kant's Political Philosophy*, ed. and with an interpretative essay by Ronald Beiner, Brighton: Harvester Press.

Aristotle (1990), *The Politics* (Cambridge Texts in the History of Political Thought), Cambridge: Cambridge University Press.

Ashford, Douglas (1986), *The Emergence of the Welfare State*, Oxford: Blackwell.

Austin, John ([1832] 1995), *The Province of Jurisprudence Determined*, ed. Wilfrid E. Rumble, Cambridge: Cambridge University Press.

Axtmann, Roland (1992), ' "Police" and the formation of the modern state: legal and ideological assumption on state capacity in the Austrian Lands of the Habsburg Empire, 1500–1800', *German History*, 10: 1, 39–61.

Axtmann, Roland (1993), 'The formation of the modern state: the debate in the social sciences', in Mary Fulbrook (ed.), *National Histories and European History*, London: UCL Press, pp. 21–45.

Baker, Keith Michael (1990), *Inventing the French Revolution. Essays on French Political Culture in the Eighteenth Century*, Cambridge: Cambridge University Press.

Baldry, H. C. (1965), *The Unity of Mankind in Greek Thought*, Cambridge: Cambridge University Press.

Barber, B. (1998), *A Place for Us. How to Make Society Civil and Democracy Strong*, New York: Hill and Wang.

Baumgold, Deborah (1988), *Hobbes's Political Theory*, Cambridge: Cambridge University Press.

Baxi, Upendra (1998), 'Voices of suffering and the future of human rights', *Transnational Law and Contemporary Problems*, 8: 2, 125–69.

Baxi, Upendra (2002), *The Future of Human Rights*, New Delhi: Oxford University Press.

Beer, Samuel H. (1993), *To Make a Nation. The Rediscovery of American Federalism*, Cambridge, MA: Harvard University Press.

Beetham, D. (1998), 'Human rights as a model for cosmopolitan democracy', in Daniele Archibugi, David Held and Martin Köhler (eds), *Re-imagining Political Community. Studies in Cosmopolitan Democracy*, Cambridge: Polity Press, pp. 58–71.

Beitz, Charles R. (2000), 'Rawls's Law of Peoples', *Ethics*, 110: 4, 669–96.

Bell, Daniel A. (2000), *East Meets West. Human Rights and Democracy in East Asia*, Princeton, NJ: Princeton University Press.

Bellamy, R. and R. J. Barry Jones (2000), 'Globalization and democracy – an afterword', in B. Holden (ed.), *Global Democracy. Key Debates*, London: Routledge, pp. 202–16.

Benhabib, Seyla (1992), *Situating the Self. Gender, Community and Postmodernism in Contemporary Ethics*, Cambridge: Polity Press.

Benhabib, Seyla (1994), 'Deliberative rationality and models of democratic legitimacy', *Constellations*, 1: 1, 26–52.

Benhabib, Seyla (2002), *The Claims of Culture. Equality and Diversity in the Global Era*, Princeton, NJ: Princeton University Press.

Benhabib, Seyla (2004), *The Rights of Others. Aliens, Residents and Citizens*, Cambridge: Cambridge University Press.

Bermeo, Nancy (1997), 'Myths of modernization: confrontation and conflict during democratic transitions', *Comparative Politics*, 29: 3, 305–22.

Beutz, Molly (2003), 'Functional democracy: responding to failures of accountability', *Harvard International Law Journal*, 44: 2, 387–431.

Bodin, Jean ([1577] 1992) *On Sovereignty: Four Chapters from 'The Six Books of the Commonwealth'*, ed. and trans. Julian H. Franklin, Cambridge: Cambridge University Press.

Bohman, James (1997), 'The public spheres of the world citizen', in James Bohman and Matthias Lutz-Bachmann (eds), *Perpetual Peace. Essays on Kant's Cosmopolitan Ideal*, Cambridge, MA: MIT Press, pp. 179–200.

Bohman, James (1999), 'International regimes and democratic governance: political equality and influence in global institutions', *International Affairs*, 75: 3, 499–513.

Booth, W. James (1999), 'Communities of memory: on identity, memory, and debt', *American Political Science Review*, 93: 2, 249–63.

Boucher, David (2001), 'Resurrecting Pufendorf and capturing the Westphalian moment', *Review of International Studies*, 27: 4, 557–77.

Boutros-Ghali, B. (2000), 'An agenda for democratization: democratization at the international level', in B. Holden (ed.), *Global Democracy. Key Debates*, London: Routledge, pp. 105–24.

Brown, Chris (2002), 'The construction of a "realistic utopia": John Rawls and international political theory', *Review of International Studies*, 28: 1, 5–21.

Brown, Garrett (2005), 'State sovereignty, federation and Kantian cosmopolitanism', *European Journal of International Relations*, 11: 4, 495–522.

Buchanan, Allen (2000), 'Rawls's "Law of Peoples": rules for a vanished Westphalian world', *Ethics*, 110: 4, 697–721.

Buergenthal, Thomas (1995), *International Human Rights in a Nutshell*, 2nd edn, St. Paul, MN: West Group.

Burke, Edmund ([1790] 1968), *Reflections on the Revolution in France*, Harmondsworth: Penguin Books.

Burke, Edmund ([1791] 1887), 'An appeal from the New to the Old Whigs', *Works of the Right Honourable Edmund Burke*, vol. 4, London: J. C. Nimmo.

Burns, J. H. (1959), 'Sovereign and constitutional law', in Bodin, *Political Studies*, 7: 2, 174–7.

Calhoun, Craig (2003), 'The class consciousness of frequent travellers: towards a critique of actually existing cosmopolitanism', in Daniele Archibugi (ed.), *Debating Cosmopolitics*, London: Verso, pp. 86–116.

Canovan, Margaret (2000), 'Patriotism is not enough', *British Journal of Political Science*, 30: 3, 413–32.

Canovan, Margaret (2005), *The People*, Cambridge: Polity Press.

Caplan, Richard (2002), *A New Trusteeship? The International Administration of War-torn Territories*, Adelphi Papers 341, Oxford: Oxford University Press.

Carothers, Thomas (2002), 'The end of the transition paradigm', *Journal of Democracy*, 13: 1, 5–21.

Castles, Stephen and Alastair Davidson (2000), *Citizenship and Migration: Globalization and the Politics of Belonging*, Basingstoke: Macmillan.

Castles, Stephen and Mark J. Miller (1993), *The Age of Migration: International Population Movements in the Modern World*, Basingstoke: Macmillan.

Cavallar, Georg (2001), 'Kantian perspectives on democratic peace: alternatives to Doyle', *Review of International Studies*, 27: 2, 229–48.

Cerna, Christina M. (1994/95), 'Universality of human rights and cultural diversity: implementation of human rights in different socio-cultural contexts', *Human Rights Quarterly*, 16: 4, 740–52.

Cerna, Christina M. (1994/95), 'Universal democracy: an international legal right or the pipe dream of the West?', *New York University Journal of International Law and Politics*, 27: 2, 289–329.

Cerny, P. (2000), 'Restructuring the political arena: globalization and the paradoxes of the competition state', in R. Germain (ed.), *Globalization and Its Critics. Perspectives from Political Economy*, Basingstoke: Macmillan, pp. 11–38.

Chandler, David (2002), *From Kosovo to Kabul: Human Rights and International Intervention*, London: Pluto Press.

Chandler, David (2005), *Constructing Global Civil Society. Morality and Power in International Relations*, Basingstoke: Palgrave.

Charnovitz, Steve (2001/02), 'WTO cosmopolitics', *New York University Journal of International Law and Politics*, 34: 2, 299–354.

Cicero ([44BC] 1991), *On Duties [De officiis]*, Cambridge: Cambridge University Press.

Cicero ([45BC] 1914), *De Finibus Bonorum et Malorum*, with an English translation by H. Rackham, London: Heinemann (The Loeb Classic Library).

Cicero ([51BC] 1998), *The Republic [De Re Publica]*, trans. Niall Rudd, Oxford: Oxford University Press.

Cohen, Jean and Andrew Arato (1992), *Civil Society and Political Theory*, Cambridge, MA: MIT Press.

Colás, Alejandro (2002), *International Civil Society. Social Movements in World Politics*, Cambridge: Polity Press.

Collier, David and Steven Levitsky (1997), 'Democracy with adjectives. Conceptual innovation in comparative research', *World Politics*, 49: 3, 430–51.

Collier, Ruth Berins (1999), *Paths Toward Democracy. The Working Class and Elites in Western Europe and South America*, Cambridge: Cambridge University Press.

Collini, Stephen (1979), *Liberalism and Sociology: L. T. Hobhouse and Political Argument in England 1880–1914*, Cambridge: Cambridge University Press.

Colomer, Josep M. (1991), 'Transitions by agreement: modelling the Spanish way', *American Political Science Review*, 85: 4, 1283–1302.

Constant, Benjamin ([1815] 1988), 'Principles of politics applicable to all representative governments', in Benjamin Constant, *Political Writings*, ed. B. Fontana, Cambridge: Cambridge University Press, pp. 169–305.

Constant, Benjamin ([1819] 1988), 'The liberty of the ancients compared with that of the moderns', Benjamin Constant, *Political Writings*, ed. B. Fontana, Cambridge: Cambridge University Press, pp. 307–28.

Creveld, Martin van (1999), *The Rise and Decline of the State*, Cambridge: Cambridge University Press.

Cronin, Ciaran (2003), 'Democracy and collective identity: in defence of constitutional patriotism', *European Journal of Philosophy*, 11: 1, 1–28.

Crouch, Colin (2004), *Post-Democracy*, Cambridge: Polity Press.

Dahl, Robert A. (1971), *Polyarchy: Participation and Opposition*, New Haven, CT: Yale University Press.

Dahl, Robert A. (1989), *Democracy and Its Critics*, New Haven, CT: Yale University Press.

Dahl, Robert A. (1998), *On Democracy*, New Haven, CT: Yale University Press.

Davis, Michael C. (1998), 'Constitutionalism and political culture: the debate over human rights and Asian values', *Harvard Human Rights Journal*, 11: 1, 109–47.

Devine, Francis Edward (1970), 'Stoicism on the best regime', *Journal of the History of Ideas*, 31: 3, 323–36.

Diamond, Larry (2002), 'Thinking about hybrid regimes', *Journal of Democracy*, 13: 2, 21–35.

Dicey, A. V. ([1885] 1915), *Introduction to the Study of the Law of the Constitution*, 8th edn, London: Macmillan.

Donnelly, Jack (1998), 'Human rights: a new standard of civilization?', *International Affairs*, 74: 1, 1–24.

Donnelly, Jack (1999), 'Human rights, democracy, and development', *Human Rights Quarterly*, 21: 3, 608–32.

Dower, N. (2000), 'The idea of global citizenship – a sympathetic assessment', *Global Society* 14: 4, 553–67.

Dunn, John (2005), *Setting the People Free. The Story of Democracy*, London: Atlantic Books.

Engle, Karen (1999/2000), 'Culture and human rights: the Asian values debate in context', *New York University Journal of International Law and Politics*, 32: 2, 291–333.

Engster, D. (1996), 'Jean Bodin, scepticism and absolute sovereignty', *History of Political Thought*, 17: 4, 469–99.

Epictetus (1946/1952), *The Discourses as Reported by Arrian, The Manual and Fragments*, with an English translation by W. A. Oldfather, 2 vols, London: Heinemann.

Erskine, Toni (2002), ' "Citizen of nowhere" or "the point where circles intersect"? Impartialist and embedded cosmopolitanisms', *Review of International Studies*, 28: 4, 457–78.

Ertman, Thomas (1998), 'Democracy and dictatorship in interwar Western Europe revisited', *World Politics*, 50: 3, 475–505.

Etzioni-Halevy, Eva (1993), *The Elite Connection: Problems and Potential of Western Democracy*, Cambridge: Polity Press.

Evans, Mark (2005), 'In humanity's name: democracy and the right to wage war', in Mark Evans (ed.), *Just War Theory: A Reappraisal*, Edinburgh: Edinburgh University Press.

Falk, Richard (1992), *Explorations at the Edges of Time. The Prospects for World Order*, Philadelphia, PA: Temple University Press.

Falk, Richard (1995), *On Humane Governance: Toward a New Global Politics*, Cambridge: Polity Press.

Farrand, Max (ed.) (1937), *The Records of the Federal Convention of 1787*, revised edn, 4 vols, New Haven, CT: Yale University Press.

Fearon, James D. and David D. Laitin (2004), 'Neotrusteeship and the problem of weak states', *International Security*, 28: 4, 5–43.

Federalist Papers = Madison, James, Alexander Hamilton and John Jay ([1788] 1987), *The Federalist Papers*, ed. Isaac Kramnick, London: Penguin Books.

Fidler, David P. (2000), 'A kinder, gentler system of capitulations? International law, structural adjustment policies, and the standard of liberal, globalized civilization', *Texas International Law Journal*, 35: 3, 387–413.

Fidler, David P. (2001), 'The return of the standard of civilization', *Chicago Journal of International Law*, 2: 1, 137–57.

Forsyth, Murray (1987), *Reason and Revolution. The Political Thought of the Abbé Sieyès*, Leicester: Leicester University Press.

Fox, Gregory H. (2000), 'The right to political participation in international law', in Gregory H. Fox and Brad R. Roth (eds), *Democratic Governance and International Law*, Cambridge: Cambridge University Press, pp. 48–90.

Fox, Gregory H. (2003), 'International law and the entitlement to democracy after war', *Global Governance*, 9: 2, 179–97.

Fox, Gregory H. and Brad R. Roth (2000), 'Introduction: the spread of liberal democracy and its implications for international law', in Gregory H. Fox and Brad R. Roth (eds), *Democratic Governance and International Law*, Cambridge: Cambridge University Press, pp. 1–22.

Fox, Gregory H. and Brad R. Roth (eds) (2000), *Democratic Governance and International Law*, Cambridge: Cambridge University Press.

Franceschet, Antonio (2000), 'Popular sovereignty or cosmopolitan democracy? Liberalism, Kant and international reform', *European Journal of International Relations*, 6: 2, 277–302.

Francis, Mark (1980), 'The nineteenth century theory of sovereignty and Thomas Hobbes', *History of Political Thought*, 1: 3, 517–40.

Franck, Thomas M. (1992), 'The emerging right to democratic governance', *The American Journal of International Law*, 86: 1, 46–91.

Franck, Thomas M. (1995), *Fairness in International Law and Institutions*, Oxford: Clarendon Press.

Franklin, Julian (1973), *Jean Bodin and the Rise of Absolutist Theory*, Cambridge: Cambridge University Press.

Freeden, Michael (1978), *The New Liberalism. An Ideology of Social Reform*, Oxford: Clarendon Press.

Friedmann, Elisabeth Jay, Kathryn Hochstetler and Ann Marie Clark (2005), *Sovereignty, Democracy, and Global Civil Society. State-Society Relations at UN World Conferences*, Albany, NY: State University of New York Press.

Friedrich, Carl J. (1965), 'Preface', in Johannes Althusius, *The Politics of Johannes Althusius*, an abridged translation of the third edition of *Politica methodice digesta* . . . and including the prefaces to the first and third editions, translated, with an introduction by Frederick S. Carney.

Gagnon, Alain-G. and James Tully, (eds) (2001), *Multinational Democracies*, Cambridge: Cambridge University Press.

Galtung, J. (2000), 'Alternative models for global democracy', in B. Holden (ed.), *Global Democracy. Key Debates*, London: Routledge, pp. 143–61.

Gathii, James Thuo (1999), 'Good governance as a counterinsurgency agenda to oppositional and transformative social projects in international law', *Buffalo Human Rights Law Review*, 5: 1, 107–74.

Gathii, James Thuo (1999/2000), 'Neoliberalism, colonialism and international governance: decentering the international law of governmental legitimacy', *Michigan Law Review*, 98: 6, 1996–2055.

Geiman, Kevin Paul (1996), 'Enlightened cosmopolitanism: the political perspective of the Kantian "sublime"', in James Schmidt (ed.), *What is Enlightenment? Eighteenth-Century Answers and Twentieth-Century Questions*, Berkeley, CA: University of California Press, pp. 517–32.

Gills, Barry, J. Rocamora, and R. Wilson (1993), 'Low intensity democracy', in: B. Gills, J. Rocamora and R. Wilson (eds), *Low Intensity Democracy: Political Power in the New World Order*, London: Pluto Press.

Goldmann, Kjell (2001), *Transforming the European Nation-State: Dynamics of Internationalization*, London: Sage.

Goldsmith, Jack (1999/2000), 'Sovereignty, international relations theory, and international law', *Stanford Law Review*, 52: 4, 959–86.

Goldsmith Jack L. and Eric A. Posner (2005), *The Limits of International Law*, Oxford: Oxford University Press.

Goldstone, Jack A. and Jay Ulfelder (2004), 'How to construct stable democracies', *Washington Quarterly*, 28: 1, 9–20.

Goodman, Ryan (2002), 'Human rights treaties, invalid reservations, and state consent', *The American Journal of International Law*, 96: 3, 531–60.

Gordenker, Leon and Thomas G. Weiss (1995), 'Pluralising global governance: analytical approaches and dimensions', *Third World Quarterly*, 16: 3, 357–87.

Gould, Carol (1988), *Rethinking Democracy. Freedom and Social Co-operation in Politics, Economy, and Society*, Cambridge: Cambridge University Press.

Gowan, Peter (2003), 'The new liberal cosmopolitanism', in Daniele Archibugi (ed.) (2003), *Debating Cosmopolitics*, London: Verso, pp. 51–65.

Green, T. H. ([1881] 1986), 'Liberal legislation and freedom of contract', in T. H. Green, *Lectures on the Principles of Political Obligation, and Other Writings*, eds Paul Harris and John Morrow, Cambridge: Cambridge University Press, pp. 194–212.

Gross, Hanns (1964), *Empire and Sovereignty: A History of the Public Law Literature in the Holy Roman Empire, 1599–1804*, Chicago, IL: University of Chicago Press.

Guttman, Amy and Dennis Thompson (1990), 'Moral conflict and political consensus', *Ethics*, 101: 1, 64–88.

Guzman, Andrew T. (2004), 'Global governance and the WTO', *Harvard International Law Journal*, 45: 2, 303–51.

Habermas, Jürgen (1993), 'Further reflections on the public sphere', in Craig Calhoun (ed.), *Habermas and the Public Sphere*, Cambridge, MA: MIT Press, pp. 421–61.

Habermas, Jürgen (1994), 'Human rights and popular sovereignty: the liberal and republican versions', *Ratio Juris*, 7: 1, 1–13.

Habermas, Jürgen (1995), 'Multiculturalism and the liberal state', *Stanford Law Review*, 47: 5, 849–53.

Habermas, Jürgen (1996), *Between Facts and Norms. Contributions to a Discourse Theory of Law and Democracy*, Cambridge: Polity Press.

Habermas, Jürgen (1997), 'Kant's idea of perpetual peace, with the benefit of two hundred years' hindsight', in James Bohman and Matthias Lutz-Bachmann (eds), *Perpetual Peace. Essays on Kant's Cosmopolitan Ideal*, Cambridge, MA: MIT Press, pp. 113–53.

Habermas, Jürgen (2001), 'Constitutional democracy: a paradoxical union of contradictory principles?', *Political Theory*, 29: 6, 766–81.

Habermas, Jürgen (2002), 'On legitimation through human rights', in Pablo de Greiff and Ciaran Cronin (eds), *Global Justice and Transnational Politics. Essays on the Moral and Political Challenges of Globalization*, Cambridge, MA: MIT Press, pp. 197–214.

Habermas, Jürgen (2004), 'Hat die Konstitutionalisierung des Völkerrechts noch eine Chance?', in Jürgen Habermas, *Der gespaltene Westen. Kleine politische Schriften, vol. 10*, Frankfurt a. M.: Suhrkamp, pp. 113–93.

Hale, Mathew (1945), 'Reflections by the Lrd. Cheife Justice Hale on Mr. Hobbes his Dialogue of the Lawe', in William Holdsworth, *A History of English Law*, 3rd edn, vol. 5, London: Methuen, pp. 500–13.

Halliday, Fred (2000), 'Global governance: prospects and problems', *Citizenship Studies*, 4: 1, 19–33.

Hayek, Friedrich (1960), *The Constitution of Liberty*, London: Macmillan.

Held, David (1991), 'Democracy, the nation-state and the global system', *Economy and Society*, 20: 2, 138–72.

Held, David (1995a), *Democracy and the Global Order. From the Modern State to Cosmopolitan Governance*, Cambridge: Polity Press.

Held, David (1995b), 'Introduction', in D. Archibugi and D. Held (eds), *Cosmopolitan Democracy*, Cambridge: Polity Press.

Held, David (1996), *Models of Democracy*, 2nd edn, Cambridge: Polity Press.

Held, David (1998), 'Democracy and globalization', in Daniele Archibugi, David Held and Martin Köhler (eds.), *Re-imagining Political Community. Studies in Cosmopolitan Democracy*, Cambridge: Polity Press, pp. 11–27.

Held, David (2000), 'The changing contours of political community: rethinking democracy in the context of globalization', in B. Holden (ed.), *Global Democracy. Key Debates*, London: Routledge, pp. 17–31.

Held, David (2003), 'Cosmopolitanism: globalisation tamed?', *Review of International Studies*, 29: 4, 465–80.

Held, David (2004), *Global Covenant. The Social Democratic Alternative to the Washington Consensus*, Cambridge: Polity Press.

Held, David, Anthony McGraw, David Goldblatt, and Jonathan Perraton (1999), *Global Transformations. Politics. Economics. Culture*, Cambridge: Polity Press.

Hill, B. W. (ed.) (1975), *Edmund Burke. On Government, Politics and Society*, Hassocks: Harvester.

Hill, Lisa (2000), 'The two *Republicae* of the Roman Stoics: can a cosmopolite be a patriot?', *Citizenship Studies*, 4: 1, 65–79.

Hindess, Barry (2001), 'Democracy, multiculturalism and the politics of difference', in Roland Axtmann (ed.), *Balancing Democracy*, London: Continuum, pp. 90–106.

Hinsley, F. H. (1986), *Sovereignty*, 2nd edn, Cambridge: Cambridge University Press.

Hirst, P. and G. Thompson (1999), *Globalization in Question*, 2nd edn, Cambridge: Polity Press.

Hirst, Paul (2001), 'Between the local and the global: democracy in the twenty-first century', in Roland Axtmann (ed.), *Balancing Democracy*, London: Continuum, pp. 255–75.

Hobbes, Thomas ([1682] (1840), 'Behemoth: The History of the Causes of the Civil Wars of England', in William Molesworth (ed.), *The English Works of Thomas Hobbs*, vol. 6, London: John Bohn, pp. 161–422.

Hobbes, Thomas ([1651] 1991), *Leviathan*, ed. Richard Tuck, Cambridge: Cambridge University Press.

Hobbes, Thomas ([1681] 1971), *A Dialogue between a Philosopher and a Student of the Common Laws of England*, new edition, edited with an introduction by Joseph Cropsey, Chicago, IL: University of Chicago Press.

Hofmann, Hasso (1988), 'Repräsentation in der Staatslehre der frühen Neuzeit', in Karl-Wilhelm Dahm (ed.), *Politische Theorie des Johannes Althusius*, Berlin: Duncker & Humblot, pp. 513–42.

Hoke, Rudolf (1988), 'Althusius und die Souveränitätstheorie der realen und personalen Majestät', in Karl-Wilhelm Dahm (ed.), *Politische Theorie des Johannes Althusius*, Berlin: Duncker & Humblot, pp. 235–53.

Holden, B. (2000), *Global Democracy. Key Debates*, London: Routledge.

Hollifield, James F. (1992), *Immigrants, Markets, and States: The Political Economy of Postwar Europe*, Cambridge: Cambridge University Press.

Holzgrefe, J. L. and R. O. Keohane (eds) (2003), *Humanitarian Intervention. Ethical, Legal, and Political Dilemmas*, Cambridge: Cambridge University Press.

Hont, Istvan (1994), 'The permanent crisis of a divided mankind: "contemporary crisis of the nation state" in historical perspective', *Political Studies*, 42 (special issue): 166–231.

Hooper, James R. and Paul R. Williams (2002/2003), 'Earned sovereignty: the political dimension', *Denver Journal of International Law and Policy*, 31: 3, 355–72.

Howard-Hassmann, Rhoda (2005), 'The second great transformation: human rights leapfrogging in the era of globalization', *Human Rights Quarterly*, 27: 1, 1–40.

Hudock, A. C. (1999), *NGOs and Civil Society: Democracy by Proxy?*, Cambridge: Polity Press.

Hueglin, Thomas O. (1999), *Early Modern Concepts for a Late Modern World. Althusius on Community and Federalism*, Waterloo: Wilfrid Laurier University Press.

Huntington, Samuel P. (1984), 'Will more countries become democratic?', *Political Science Quarterly*, 99: 2, 193–218.

Huntington, Samuel P. (1991), *The Third Wave: Democratization in the Late Twentieth Century*, Norman, OK: University of Oklahoma Press.

Hutchings, K. and R. Dannreuther (eds) (1999), *Cosmopolitan Citizenship*, Basingstoke: Macmillan.

Ignatieff, Michael (2001), *Human Rights as Politics and Idolatry*, Princeton, NJ: Princeton University Press.

Igoe, Jim (2003), 'Scaling up civil society: donor money, NGOs and the pastoralist land rights movement in Tanzania', *Development and Change*, 34: 5, 863–85.

International Commission on Intervention and State Sovereignty (2001), *The Responsibility to Protect*, Ottawa: International Development Research Centre (at www.idrc.ca).

Jackson, Robert H. (1990), *Quasi-states: Sovereignty, International Relations and the Third World*, Cambridge: Cambridge University Press.

Jacobson, David (1996), *Rights across Borders. Immigration and the Decline of Citizenship*, Baltimore, MD: Johns Hopkins University Press.

Jessop, Bob (2002), *The Future of the Capitalist State*, Cambridge: Polity Press.

Jones, Barry (2000), *The World Turned Upside Down? Globalization and the Future of the State*, Manchester: Manchester University Press.

Jones Peter (1995), 'Two conceptions of liberalism, two conceptions of justice', *British Journal of Political Science*, 25: 4, 515–50.

Joppke, Christian (1999a), *Immigration and the Nation-State: The United States, Germany, and Great Britain*, Oxford: Oxford University Press.

Joppke, Christian (1999b), 'How immigration is changing citizenship: a comparative view, *Ethnic and Racial Studies*, 22: 4, 629–52.

Kaldor, Mary (2003), *Global Civil Society. An Answer to War*, Cambridge: Polity Press.

Kant, Immanuel ([1781] 1998), *Critique of Pure Reason*, trans. and ed. Paul Guyer and Allan W. Wood (The Cambridge Edition of the Works of Immanuel Kant), Cambridge: Cambridge University Press.

Kant, Immanuel ([1784] 1970), 'Idea for a universal history with a cosmopolitan purpose', in Hans Reiss (ed.), *Kant's Political Writings*, Cambridge: Cambridge University Press, pp. 41–53.

Kant, Immanuel ([1786] 1991), 'What is orientation in thinking?', in H. Reiss (ed.), *Kant's Political Writings*, 2nd enlarged edn, Cambridge: Cambridge University Press, pp. 235–49.

Kant, Immanuel ([1786] 1963), 'Conjectural beginning of human history', in Lewis White Beck (ed.), *Kant on History*, Indianapolis, IN: Bobbs-Merrill, pp. 53–68.

Kant, Immanuel ([1788] 1996), *Critique of Practical Reason*, in Immanuel Kant, *Practical Philosophy*, trans. and ed. Mary J. Gregor (The Cambridge Edition of the Works of Immanuel Kant), Cambridge: Cambridge University Press, pp. 133–271.

Kant, Immanuel ([1790] 2000), *Critique of the Power of Judgement*, ed. Paul Guyer (The Cambridge Edition of the Works of Immanuel Kant), Cambridge: Cambridge University Press.

Kant, Immanuel ([1793] 1996), 'On the common saying: that may be correct in theory, but it is of no use in practice', in Immanuel Kant, *Practical Philosophy*, trans. and ed. Mary J. Gregor (The Cambridge Edition of the Works of Immanuel Kant), Cambridge: Cambridge University Press, pp. 273–309.

Kant, Immanuel (1793), 'Über den Gemeinspruch: Das mag in der Theorie richtig sein, taugt aber nicht für die Praxis', in *Kant's Gesammelte Schriften* (1910 –), ed. by the Royal Prussian (later German) Academy of Sciences, Berlin: Georg Reimer (later Walter de Gruyter & Co), vol. 8, pp. 273–313.

Kant, Immanuel ([1795] 1996), 'Toward perpetual peace', in Immanuel Kant, *Practical Philosophy*, trans. and ed. Mary J. Gregor (The Cambridge Edition of the Works of Immanuel Kant), Cambridge: Cambridge University Press, pp. 311–51.

Kant, Immanuel (1797/1974), *Anthropology, from a Pragmatic Point of View*, trans., with an introduction and notes by Mary J. Gregor, The Hague: Martinus Nijhoff.

Kant, Immanuel ([1797] 1996), 'The Metaphysics of Morals', in Immanuel Kant, *Practical Philosophy*, trans. and ed. Mary J. Gregor (The Cambridge Edition of the Works of Immanuel Kant), Cambridge: Cambridge University Press, pp. 353–603.

Kant, Immanuel ([1798] 1970), 'The Contest of the Faculties', in Hans Reiss (ed.), *Kant's Political Writings*, Cambridge: Cambridge University Press, pp. 176–90.

Kant's Gesammelte Schriften (1910–), ed. by the Royal Prussian (later German) Academy of Sciences, Berlin: Georg Reimer (later Walter de Gruyter & Co.).

Kant, Immanuel (1913), 'Reflexionen zur Anthropologie', in *Kant's Gesammelte Schriften* (1910–), vol. 15, ed. by the Royal Prussian (later German) Academy of Sciences, Berlin: Georg Reimer (later Walter de Gruyter & Co.).

Kant, Immanuel (1997), *Lectures on Ethics*, ed. Peter Heath (The Cambridge Edition of the Works of Immanuel Kant), Cambridge: Cambridge University Press.

Karl, Terry Lynn (1990), 'Dilemma of democratization in Latin America', *Comparative Politics*, 23: 1, 1–21.

Kates, Gary (1990), 'Jews into Frenchmen: nationality and representation in revolutionary France', in F. Fehér (ed.), *The French Revolution and the Birth of Modernity*, Berkeley, CA: University of California Press, pp. 103–16.

Kausikan, Bilahari (1993), 'Asia's different standard', *Foreign Policy*, Issue 92: 24–51.

Keane, John (2003), *Global Civil Society?*, Cambridge: Cambridge University Press.

Kelsen, Hans (1961), *General Theory of Law and State*, New York: Russell & Russell.

Keohane, Robert O. (1993), 'Sovereignty, interdependence, and international institutions', in Linda B. Miller and Michael Smith (eds), *Ideas and Ideals. Essays on Politics in Honor of Stanley Hoffmann*, Boulder, CO: Westview Press.

King, Preston (1974), *The Ideology of Order*, London: Allen & Unwin.

Kleingeld, Paula (1998), 'Kant's cosmopolitan law: world citizenship for a global order', *Kantian Review*, 2: 1, 72–90.

Kleingeld, Paula (2000), 'Kantian patriotism', *Philosophy and Public Affairs*, 29: 4, 313–41.

Kleingeld, Paula (2003), 'Kant's cosmopolitan patriotism', *Kant-Studien*, 94: 3, pp. 299–316.

Kleingeld, Paula (2004), 'Approaching perpetual peace: Kant's defence of a league of states and his ideal of a world federation', *European Journal of Philosophy*, 12: 3, 304–25.

Kramnick, Isaac (ed.) (1987), *The Federalist Papers*, London: Penguin Books.

Krasner, Stephen D. (1999), *Sovereignty. Organized Hypocrisy*, Princeton, NJ: Princeton University Press.

Krasner, Stephen D. (2004a), 'The hole in the whole: sovereignty, shared sovereignty, and international law', *Michigan Journal of International Law*, 25: 4, 1075–101.

Krasner, Stephen D. (2004b), 'Sharing sovereignty. New institutions for collapsed and failing states', *International Security*, 29: 2, 85–120.

Krasner, Stephen D. (2005), 'The case for shared sovereignty', *Journal of Democracy*, 16: 1, 69–83.

Krawietz, Werner (1988), 'Kontraktualism oder Konsozialismus? Grundlagen und Grenzen des Gemeinschaftsdenkens in der politischen Theorie des Johannes Althusius', in Karl-Wilhelm Dahm (ed.), *Politische Theorie des Johannes Althusius*, Berlin: Duncker & Humblot, pp. 391–23.

Kukathas, Chandran (1995), 'Are there any cultural rights?', in W. Kymlicka (ed.), *The Rights of Minority Cultures*, Oxford: Oxford University Press, pp. 228–56.

Kuper, Andrew (2000), 'Rawlsian global justice: beyond the Law of Peoples to a cosmopolitan law of persons', *Ethics*, 110: 4, 640–74.

Kurasawa, Fuyuki (2004), 'A cosmopolitanism from below: alternative globalization and the creation of a solidarity without bounds', *Arch. europ. social.*, 45: 2: 233–55.

Kymlicka, Will (1990), *Contemporary Political Philosophy. An Introduction*, Oxford: Clarendon Press.

Kymlicka, Will (1995), *Multicultural Citizenship. A Liberal Theory of Minority Rights*, Oxford: Clarendon Press.

Kymlicka, Will (2000), 'American multiculturalism and the "nations within"', in Duncan Ivison, Paul Patton, and Will Sanders (eds), *Political Theory and the Rights of Indigenous Peoples*, Cambridge: Cambridge University Press, pp. 216–36.

Lal, Deepak (1983), *The Poverty of 'Development Economics'*, London: Institute of Economic Affairs (Hobart paperback, vol. 16).

Lal, Deepak (1994), 'Participation, markets, and democracy', Human Resources Development and Operations Policy, *HRO Working Papers 20*, Washington, DC: The World Bank.

Lauterpacht, Hersch (1947), *Recognition in International Law*, Cambridge: Cambridge University Press.

Leftwich, Adrian (1996), 'Two cheers for democracy?', *Political Quarterly*, 67: 4, 334–9.

Levitsky, Steven and Lucian A. Way (2002), 'The rise of competitive authoritarianism', *Journal of Democracy*, 13: 2, 51–65.

Levitsky, Steven and Lucian A. Way (2005), 'International linkage and democratization', *Journal of Democracy*, 16: 3, 20–34.

Lewis, J. U. (1968), 'Jean Bodin's "Logic of Sovereignty"', *Political Studies*, 16: 2, 206–22.

Lijphart, Arend (1977), *Democracy in Plural Societies: A Comparative Exploration*, New Haven, CT: Yale University Press.

Linklater, Andrew (1996), 'Citizenship and sovereignty in the post-Westphalian state', *European Journal of International Relations*, 2:1, 77–103.

Linklater, Andrew (1998a), 'Cosmopolitan citizenship', *Citizenship Studies*, 2:1, 23–41.

Linklater, Andrew (1998b), *The Transformation of Political Community*, Cambridge: Polity Press.

Linklater, Andrew (1999), 'The evolving spheres of international justice', *International Affairs*, 5:3, 473–82.

Linz, Juan J. (1990), 'Transitions to democracy', *Washington Quarterly*, 13: 3, 143–64.

Lipset, Seymour M. (1959), 'Some social requisites of democracy: economic development and political legitimacy', *American Political Science Review*, 53: 1, 69–105.

Lipset, Seymour M. (1983), *Political Man: The Social Bases of Politics*, London; Heinemann (2nd edn; 1st edn published in 1959/1960).

Lipset, S. M. (1994), 'The social prerequisites of democracy revisited', *American Sociological Review*, 59: 1, 1–22.

Lipson, Charles (2003), *Reliable Partners. How Democracies Have Made a Separate Peace*, Princeton, NJ: Princeton University Press.

Locke, John ([1689] 1989), *Two Treatises of Government*, ed. with an introduction and notes by Peter Laslett, Cambridge: Cambridge University Press.

Locke, John ([1690] 1975), *An Essay Concerning Understanding*, ed. H. Nidditch, Oxford: Clarendon Press.

Loughlin, Martin (2000), *Sword and Scales. An Examination of the Relationship between Law and Politics*, Oxford: Hart Publishing.

Lutz-Bachmann, Matthias (1997), 'Kant's idea of peace and the philosophical conception of a world republic', in James Bohman and Matthias Lutz-Bachmann (eds), *Perpetual Peace. Essays on Kant's Cosmopolitan Ideal*, Cambridge, MA: MIT Press, pp. 59–77.

Maaka Roger and Augie Fleras (2000), 'Engaging indigeneity: Tino Rangatiratanga in Aotearoa', in Duncan Ivison, Paul Patton, and Will Sanders (eds), *Political Theory and the Rights of Indigenous Peoples*, Cambridge: Cambridge University Press, pp. 89–109.

MacCormack, Neil (1993), 'Constitutionalism and democracy', in Richard

Bellamy (ed.), *Theories and Concepts of Politics*, Manchester: Manchester University Press, pp.124–47.

MacFarlane, S. Neil, Carolin J. Thielking, and Thomas G. Weiss (2004), 'The *Responsibility to Protect*: anyone interested in humanitarian intervention?', *Third World Quarterly*, 25: 5, 977–92.

Macklem, Patrick (1993), 'Distributing sovereignty: Indian nations and equality of peoples', *Stanford Law Review*, 45: 5, 1, 311–67.

Makumbe, John Mw (1998), 'Is there a civil society in Africa?', *International Affairs*, 74: 2, 305–17.

Markell, Patchen (2000), 'Making affect safe for democracy? On "constitutional patriotism"', *Political Theory*, 28: 1, 38–63.

Marks, Susan (2000), *The Riddle of all Constitutions. International Law, Democracy, and the Critique of Ideology*, Oxford: Oxford University Press.

Marshall, T. H. (1963), 'Citizenship and social class', in T. H. Marshall, *Sociology at the Crossroads. And Other Essays*, London: Heinemann, pp. 67–127.

Maus, Ingeborg (1992), *Zur Aufklärung der Demokratietheorie. Rechts- und demokratietheoretische Überlegungen im Anschluss an Kant*, Frankfurt a. M.: Suhrkamp.

McDonald, Michael (1991), 'Should communities have rights? Reflections on liberal individualism', *Canadian Journal of Law and Jurisprudence*, 4:2, 217–37.

McFaul, Michael (2002), 'The fourth wave of democracy *and* dictatorship', *World Politics*, 54: 4, 212–44.

McFaul, Michael (2004), 'Democracy promotion as a world value', *Washington Quarterly*, 28: 1, 147–63.

McGinnis, John and Mark L. Movsesian (2004), 'Against global governance in the WTO', *Harvard International Law Journal*, 45: 2, 353–65.

McIlwain, Charles Howard (1947), *Constitutionalism: Ancient and Modern*, revised edn, Ithaca, NY: Cornell University Press.

McIlwaine, Cathy (1998), 'Contesting civil society: reflections from El Salvador', *Third World Quarterly*, 19: 4, 651–72.

McMaster, John Bach, and Frederick D. Stone (eds) (1970), *Pennsylvania and the Federal Constitution*, 1787–1788, Da Capo Press Reprint, New York: De Capo Press, 2 vols.

Mercer, Claire (2002), 'NGOs, civil society and democratization: a critical review of the literature', *Progress in Development Studies*, 2: 1, 5–22.

Mercer, Claire (2003), 'Performing partnership: civil society and the illusions of good governance in Tanzania', *Political Geography*, 22: 7, 741–63.

Mill, John Stuart ([1861] 1991), 'Considerations on representative government', in J. St. Mill, *On Liberty and Other Essays*, ed. John Gray, Oxford: Oxford University Press, pp. 205–467.

Miller, David (1995), *On Nationality*, Oxford: Oxford University Press.

Miller, David (1999), 'Bounded citizenship', in K. Hutchings and R. Dann-reuther (eds), *Cosmopolitan Citizenship*, Basingstoke: Macmillan, pp. 60–80.

Mohan, Giles (2002), 'The disappointments of civil society: the politics of NGO intervention in northern Ghana', *Political Geography*, 21: 1, 125–54.

Montesquieu, Charles-Louis de Secondat ([1748] 1989), *The Spirit of the Laws*, trans. and ed. Anne M. Cohler, Basia Carolyn Miller and Harold Samuel Stone, Cambridge: Cambridge University Press.

Moore, Barrington (1966), *The Social Origins of Democracy and Dictatorship*, Boston, MA: Beacon Press).

Morison, Samuel Eliot (ed.) (1965), *Sources and Documents illustrating the American Revolution, 1764–1788 and the Formation of the Federal Constitution*, 2nd edn, New York: Oxford University Press.

Musgrave, Thomas D. (1997), *Self-Determination and National Minorities* (Oxford Monographs in International Law), Oxford: Oxford University Press.

Muthu, Sankar (2003), *Enlightenment against Empire*, Princeton, NJ: Princeton University Press.

Nakano, Takeshi (2006), 'A critique of Held's cosmopolitan democracy', *Contemporary Political Theory*, 5: 1, 33–51.

Nanda, Ved. P. (2006), 'The 'Good Governance' concept revisited', *Annals of the American Academy*, 603: 269–83.

National Security Strategy of the United States of America (2002), at www.whitehouse/gov/nsc/nss.pdf.

Neumayer, Eric (2006), 'Qualified ratification: explaining reservations to international human rights treaties' (July 2006), available at Social Science Research Network at http://ssrn.com/abstract=822165.

Nicholson, Peter P. (1990), *Studies in the Political Thought of the British Idealists*, Cambridge: Cambridge University Press.

Nickel, James W. (2006), 'Are human rights mainly implemented by intervention?', in Rex Martin and David A. Reidy (eds), *Rawls's Law of Peoples: A Realistic Utopia?*, Oxford: Blackwell, pp. 263–77.

Nussbaum, Martha (1996a), 'Patriotism and cosmopolitanism', in Joshua Cohen (ed.), *For Love of Country. Debating the Limits of Patriotism*, Boston, MA: Beacon Press, pp. 3–17.

Nussbaum, Martha (1996b), 'Reply', in Joshua Cohen (ed.), *For Love of Country. Debating the Limits of Patriotism*, Boston, MA: Beacon Press, pp. 131–44.

Nussbaum, Martha (1997), 'Kant and cosmopolitanism', in James Bohman and Matthias Lutz-Bachmann (eds), *Perpetual Peace. Essays on Kant's Cosmopolitan Ideal*, Cambridge, MA: MIT Press, pp. 25–57.

Nyers, Peter (2006), 'The accidental citizen: acts of sovereignty and (un)-making of citizenship', *Economy and Society*, 35:1, 22–41.

Oestreich, Gerhard (1982), *Neostoicism and the Early Modern State*, Cambridge: Cambridge University Press.

Offe, Claus (1985), 'Challenging the boundaries of institutional politics: social movements since the 1960s', in Charles Maier (ed.), *Changing Boundaries of the Political*, Cambridge: Cambridge University Press, pp. 63–105.

Oppenheim, Lassa (1905), *International Law. A Treatise. Vol. 1: Peace*, London: Longman, Green.

Oppenheim, Lassa (1920), *International Law*, 3rd edn, ed. R. Roxburgh, London: Heinemann.

Otto, Dianne (1997/98), 'Rethinking the "universality" of human rights law', *Columbia Human Rights Law Review*, 29: 1, 1–46.

Owen, John M., IV (2002), 'The foreign imposition of domestic institutions', *International Organization*, 56: 2, 375–409.

Paine, Thomas ([1791] 1985), *Rights of Man*, Harmondsworth: Penguin Classics.

Parekh, Bhikhu (1994), 'Minority rights, majority values', in D. Milliband (ed.), *Reinventing the Left*, Cambridge: Cambridge University Press, pp. 101–9.

Parekh, Bhikhu (2000), *Rethinking Multiculturalism. Cultural Diversity and Political Theory*, Basingstoke: Macmillan.

Parekh, Bhikhu (2003), 'Cosmopolitanism and global citizenship', *Review of International Studies*, 29: 1, 3–17.

Passerin d'Entrèves, Alexander (1967), *The Notion of the State: An Introduction to Political Theory*, Oxford: Clarendon Press.

Patterson, Thomas E. (2004), *The Vanishing Voter. Public Involvement in an Age of Uncertainty*, New York: Vintage Books.

Peters, Ronald M. (1978), *The Massachusetts Constitution of 1780. A Social Compact*, Amherst, MA: University of Massachusetts Press.

Petras, James (1997), 'Imperialism and NGOs in Latin America', *Monthly Review*, 49: 7, 10–27.

Pitkin, Hanna Fenichel (1967), *The Concept of Representation*, Berkeley, CA: University of California Press.

Plant, Raymond (1992), 'Citizenship and rights', in D. Milligan and William Watts Miller (eds), *Liberalism, Citizenship, and Autonomy*, Aldershot: Avebury, pp. 108–33.

Plato (1983), *The Republic*, trans. Robin Waterfield, Oxford: Oxford University Press.

Pollis, Adamantia (1996), 'Cultural relativism revisited: through a state prism', *Human Rights Quarterly*, 18: 2, 316–44.

Porta, D. della et al. (eds) (1999), *Social Movements in a Globalizing World*, Basingstoke: Macmillan.

Potter, David (1997), 'Explaining democratization', in D. Potter, D. Goldblatt, M. Kiloh, and P. Lewis (eds), *Democratization*, Cambridge: Polity Press, pp. 1–40.

Przeworski, Adam and Fernando Limongi (1997), 'Modernization: theories and facts', *World Politics*, 49: 1, 155–83.

Pufendorf, Samuel ([1672] 1994), 'On the law of nature and of nations', in

Craig L. Carr (ed.), *The Political Writings of Samuel Pufendorf*, trans. Michael J. Seidler, New York and Oxford: Oxford University Press, pp. 95–268.

Pufendorf, Samuel ([1673] 1991), *On the Duty of Man and Citizen according to Natural Law*, ed. James Tully, trans. Michael Silverthorne, Cambridge: Cambridge University Press.

Putnam, Hilary (1996), 'Must we choose between patriotism and universal reason?', in Joshua Cohen (ed.), *For Love of Country. Debating the Limits of Patriotism*, Boston, MA: Beacon Press, pp. 91–7.

Quaritsch, Helmut (1970), *Staat und Souveränität: Vol. 1: Die Grundlagen*, Frankfurt a. M.: Athenäum Verlag.

Rajagopal, Balakrishnan (2003), *International Law From Below: Development, Social Movements, and Third World Resistance*, Cambridge: Cambridge University Press.

Rao, V. (1984/85), 'Democracy and economic development', *Studies in Comparative International Development*, 19: 4, 67–81.

Rawls, John ([1993] (2005), *Political Liberalism*, expanded edn (Columbia Classics in Philosophy), New York: Columbia University Press.

Rawls, John (1999), *The Law of Peoples*, Cambridge, MA: Harvard University Press.

Raz, Joseph (1994), 'Multiculturalism: a liberal perspective', *Dissent*, 41: 1, 67–79.

Reisman, W. Michael (2000), 'Sovereignty and human rights in contemporary international law', in Gregory H. Fox and Brad R. Roth (eds), *Democratic Governance and International Law*, Cambridge: Cambridge University Press, pp. 239–58.

Resnick, Philip (1998), 'Global democracy: ideals and reality', in R. Axtmann (ed.), *Globalisation and Europe*, London: Pinter, pp. 126–43.

Rich, Roland (2001), 'Bringing democracy into international law', *Journal of Democracy*, 12: 3, 20–34.

Robertson, Roland and J. Chirico, (1985), 'Humanity, globalization and worldwide religious resurgence: a theoretical exploration', *Sociological Analysis*, 46: 3, 219–42.

Roeck, Bern (1984), *Reichssystem und Reichsherkommen*, Stuttgart: Franz Steiner Verlag.

Roper, Jon (1989), *Democracy and Its Critics. Anglo-American Democratic Thought in the Nineteenth Century*, London: Unwin Hyman.

Rosenau, James (1997), *Along the Domestic–Foreign Frontier: Exploring Governance in a Turbulent World*, Cambridge: Cambridge University Press.

Rosenau, James (1998), 'Governance and democracy in a globalizing world', in Daniele Archibugi, David Held, and Martin Köhler (eds), *Re-imagining Political Community. Studies in Cosmopolitan Democracy*, Cambridge: Polity Press, pp. 28–57.

Roth, Brad R. (1993), 'Governmental illegitimacy revisited: "pro-democratic" armed intervention in the post-bipolar world', *Transnational Law and Contemporary Problems*, 3: 2, 481–513.

Roth, Brad R. (1999), *Governmental Illegitimacy in International Law*, Oxford: Oxford University Press.

Roth, Brad R. (1999/2000), 'Governmental illegitimacy and neo-colonialism: response to review by James Thuo Gathii', *Michigan Law Review*, 98: 6, 2056–71.

Rousseau, Jean-Jacques ([1762] 1968), *The Social Contract*, ed. Maurice Cranston, London: Penguin Books.

Rousseau, Jean-Jacques ([1772] 1953), 'Considération sur le gouvernement de Pologne', in Jean-Jacques Rousseau, *Political Writings*, ed. and trans. Frederick Watson, London: Nelson.

Rueschemeyer, Dietrich, Evelyne Huber Stephens, and John D. Stephens (1992), *Capitalist Development and Democracy*, Cambridge: Polity Press.

Salmon, J. H. H. (1996), 'The legacy of Jean Bodin: absolutism, populism or constitutionalism', *History of Political Thought*, 17: 4, 499–522.

Sandel, Michael, J. (1982), *Liberalism and the Limits of Justice*, Cambridge: Cambridge University Press.

Sandel, Michael, J. (1993–4), 'Political liberalism', *Harvard Law Review*, 107: 7, 1765–94.

Sassen, Saskia (1996), *Losing Control? Sovereignty in an Age of Globalization*, New York: Columbia University Press.

Sassen, Saskia (2003), 'The participation of states and citizens in global governance', *Indiana Journal of Global Legal Studies*, 10: 5, 5–28.

Schmitter, Philippe (1995), 'Democracy's future: more liberal, preliberal or postliberal?', *Journal of Democracy*, 6: 1, 15–22.

Schmitter, Philippe (2000), *How to Democratize the European Union . . . And Why Bother?*, Lanham, MD: Rowman and Littlefield.

Schmitz, Heinz-Gerd (2003), 'Kants Lehre vom *hostis iniustus* und Carl Schmitts Kritik dieser Konzeption', *Archiv für Rechts- und Sozialphilosophie*, 89: 3, 399–417.

Schofield, Malcolm (1999), 'Cicero's definition of *Res Publica*', in M. Schofield, *Saving the City: Philosopher-Kings and other Classical Paradigms*, London: Routledge, pp. 178–94.

Scholte, Jan Aart (2000), *Globalization: A Critical Introduction*, Basingstoke: Palgrave.

Schumpeter, Joseph A. ([1976] 1942), *Capitalism, Socialism and Democracy*, London: Allen & Unwin.

Scupin, Hans Ulrich (1965), 'Der Begriff der Souveräntität bei Johannes Althusius und bei Jean Bodin', *Der Staat*, 1: 1, 1–26.

Scupin, Hans Ulrich (1988), 'Gemeinsamkeiten und Unterschiede der Theorien von Gesellschaft und Staat des Johannes Althusius und des Jean Bodin', in Karl-Wilhelm Dahm (ed.), *Politische Theorie des Johannes Althusius*, Berlin: Duncker & Humblot, pp. 301–11.

Sieyès, Emmanuel Joseph ([1789] 1963), *What is the Third Estate?*, London: Pall Mall.

Simpson, Gerry (2001), 'Two liberalisms', *European Journal of International Law*, 12: 3, 537–71.

Simpson, Gerry (2004), *Great Powers and Outlaw States. Unequal Sovereigns in the International Legal Order*, Cambridge: Cambridge University Press.

Singer, Brian C. J. (1986), *Society, Theory and the French Revolution. Studies in the Revolutionary Imaginary*, Basingstoke: Macmillan.

Skinner, Quentin (1990), 'The republican ideal of political liberty', in G. Bock, Quentin Skinner and Maurizio Viroli (eds), *Machiavelli and Republicanism*, Cambridge: Cambridge University Press, pp. 293–309.

Skinner, Quentin (2005), 'Hobbes on representation', *European Journal of Philosophy*, 13: 2, 155–84.

Slaughter, Anne-Marie (1995), 'International law in a world of liberal states', *European Journal of International Law*, 6: 4, 503–38.

Slaughter, Anne-Marie (2004a), *A New World Order*, Princeton, NJ: Princeton University Press.

Slaughter, Anne-Marie (2004b), 'Sovereignty and power in a networked world order', *Stanford Journal of International Law*, 40: 2, 283–327.

Smith, Jackie, Charles Chatfield and Ron Pagnucco (eds) (1997), *Transnational Social Movements and Global Politics: Solidarity beyond the State*, Syracuse, NY: Syracuse University Press.

Soysal, Yasemin N. (1994), *Limits of Citizenship: Migrants and Postnational Membership in Europe*, Chicago, IL: University of Chicago Press.

Soysal, Yasemin N. (2000), 'Citizenship and identity: living in diasporas in postwar Europe?', *Ethnic and Racial Studies*, 23: 1, 1–15.

State of the Union Address (2006) at www.whitehouse.gov/stateoftheunion/2006/print/index.html

Stepan, Alfred (1986), 'Paths towards redemocratization: theoretical and comparative considerations', in G. O'Donnell, P. Schmitter, and L. Whitehead (eds), *Transitions from Authoritarian Rule*, Baltimore, MD: Johns Hopkins University Press, vol. 3, pp. 64–84.

Storing, Herbert (ed.) (1981), *The Complete Anti-Federalist*, edited with commentary and notes by Herbert J. Storing, Chicago, IL: Chicago University Press.

Teson, Fernando R. (1985), 'International human rights and cultural relativism', *Virginia Journal of International Law*, 25: 4, 869–98.

Teson, Fernando R. (1992), 'The Kantian theory of international law', *Columbia Law Review*, 92: 1, 53–102.

Thirkell-White, Ben (2004a), 'The International Monetary Fund and civil society', *New Political Economy*, 9: 2, 251–70.

Thirkell-White, Ben (2004b), *The International Monetary Fund and the Politics of Financial Globalisation*, London: Palgrave.

Bibliography

Thompson, Mark R. (2001), 'Was ist mit den "asiatischen Werten" geschehen?', *Leviathan*, 29: 2, 218–36.

Thucydides (1972), *History of the Peloponnesian War*, trans. Rex Warner, London: Penguin Books.

Tuck, Richard (1999), *The Rights of War and Peace: Political Thought and the International Order from Grotius to Kant*, Oxford: Oxford University Press.

Tully, James (1995), *Strange Multiplicity. Constitutionalism in an Age of Diversity*, Cambridge: Cambridge University Press.

Tully, James (2000), 'The struggles of indigenous peoples for and of freedom', in Duncan Ivison, Paul Patton, and Will Sanders (eds), *Political Theory and the Rights of Indigenous Peoples*, Cambridge: Cambridge University Press, pp. 36–59.

Tully, James (2001), 'Introduction', in Alain-G. Gagnon and James Tully (eds), *Multinational Democracies*, Cambridge: Cambridge University Press, pp. 1–33.

Turner, Bryan S. (2002), 'Cosmopolitan virtue, globalization and patriotism', *Theory, Culture and Society*, 19: 1–2, 46–63.

Urbinati, Nadia (2003), 'Can cosmopolitan democracy be democratic?', in Daniele Archibugi (ed.), *Debating Cosmopolitics*, London: Verso, pp. 67–85.

Urwin, Derek (2001), 'Nationalism, territoriality and democracy', in Roland Axtmann (ed.), *Balancing Democracy*, London: Continuum, pp. 57–75.

Vattel, Emer de (1852), *The Law of Nations; or, Principles of the Law of Nature, applied to the Conduct and Affairs of Nations and Sovereigns*, trans. Joseph Chitty, Philadelphia: T. & J. W. Johnson.

Vienna Convention on the Law of Treaties, at www.walter.gehr.net/wvkengl.html

Vigilantius (1997), *Kant on the metaphysics of morals: Vigiliantius's lecture notes*, in Kant, Immanuel (1997), *Lectures on Ethics*, ed. Peter Heath, (The Cambridge Edition of the Works of Immanuel Kant), Cambridge: Cambridge University Press, pp. 249–452.

Vincent, Andrew and Raymond Plant (1984), *Philosophy, Politics, and Citizenship: The Life and Thought of the British Idealists*, Oxford: Blackwell.

Waldron, Jeremy (2000), 'What is cosmopolitan?', *Journal of Political Philosophy*, 8: 2, 227–43.

Warner, Carolyn M. (1999), 'The political economy of "quasi-statehood" and the demise of 19th century African politics', *Review of International Studies*, 25: 2, 233–55.

Warner, David (2003), 'The responsibility to protect and irresponsible, cynical engagement', *Millennium*, 32: 1, 109–21.

Weber, Heloise (2002), 'Global governance and poverty reduction: the case of microcredit', in R. Wilkinson and S. Hughes (eds), *Global Governance: Critical Perspectives*, London: Routledge, pp. 132–81.

Weiss, Thomas G. (2004), 'The sunset of humanitarian intervention? The responsibility to protect in a unipolar era', *Security Dialogue*, 35: 2, 135–53.

Welsh, Jennifer M. (ed.) (2004), *Humanitarian Intervention and International Relations*, Oxford: Oxford University Press.

Welsh, Jennifer (2002), 'From right to responsibility: humanitarian intervention and international society', *Global Governance*, 8: 4, 503–21.

Wheatley, Steven (2002), 'Democracy in international law: a European perspective', *International and Comparative Law Quarterly*, 51: 2, 225–47.

Williams David G. (1996), 'Governance and the discipline of development', *European Journal of Development Research*, 8: 2, 157–77.

Williams, Howard (1983), *Kant's Political Philosophy*, Oxford: Blackwell.

Williams, Paul R., Michael P. Scharf, and James R. Hooper (2002/2003), 'Resolving sovereignty-based conflicts: the emerging approach of earned sovereignty', *Denver Journal of International Law and Policy*, 31: 3, 349–53.

Williams, Paul R. and Francesca Jannotti Pecci (2004), 'Earned sovereignty: bridging the gap between sovereignty and self-determination', *Stanford Journal of International Law*, 40: 2, 347–86.

Wood, Allan (1996). 'Kant's project', in Cheah Pheng and Bruce Robbins (eds) *Cosmopolitics: Thinking and Feeling Beyond the Nation*, Minneapolis, MN: University of Minnesota Press, pp. 59–76.

World Bank (1989), 'Sub-Saharan Africa, from Crisis to Sustainable Growth', Washington, DC: World Bank.

World Bank (1994), *Governance: The World Bank's Experience*, Washington, DC: World Bank.

World Bank (1998), *Development and Human Rights: The Role of the World Bank*, Washington, DC: World Bank.

Wright, M. R. (1995), 'Cicero on self-love and love of humanity in De Finibus 3', in J. G. F. Powell (ed.), *Cicero the Philosopher. Twelve Papers*, Oxford: Clarendon Press, pp. 171–95.

Yack, Bernard (2001), 'Popular sovereignty and nationalism', *Political Theory*, 29: 4, 517–36.

Yale, D. E. C. (1972), 'Hobbes and Hale on law, legislation and the sovereign', *Cambridge Law Journal*, 31: 1, 121–56.

Young, Iris Marion (2000), 'Hybrid democracy: Iroquois federalism and the postcolonial project', in Duncan Ivison, Paul Patton, and Will Sanders (eds), *Political Theory and the Rights of Indigenous Peoples*, Cambridge: Cambridge University Press, pp. 237–58.

Zolo, D. (1997), *Cosmopolis. Prospects for World Government*, Cambridge: Polity Press.

Zolo, Danilo (2002), *Invoking Humanity. War, Law and Global Order*, London: Continuum.

Index

Index

Index

Index

moral conversation, 72
moral powers, 209
moral theology
  Catholic, 55
multiculturalism, 77, 195–231
multi-nation state, 205
multinational corporations, 216
Muslims, 207

Napoleonic wars, 148
national security, 53
national solidarity, 53
nationalism, 196, 199
  civic, 196
  liberal, 196
  post-ethnic, 196
nation-state, x, 34, 192–3, 218–19, 221, 228–
  30
  constitutional, 34
  democratic, 229–30
  European, 213
  liberal-democratic, 33
  multi-ethnic, 196
  multinational, 196
  sovereign, 216, 218
NATO, 213
natural law theory, 54
Nazi Germany, 121
neo-colonialism, 48–9
Netherlands, 121, 154, 161
New Zealand, 196
Nicaragua, 124, 131
Nicaragua v. *United States*, 80
Nigeria, 149
non-democratic regimes, 113
non-democratic states, 134, 150
non-governmental organisations, 51, 55–6,
  86, 89, 94, 104–6, 130, 146, 214, 216–
  18, 220, 222, 228
  accountability of, 106
  Asian, 57, 59
  indigenous, 105
  transparency of, 106
non-interference, 49, 68, 81, 99, 165
  right of, 10, 138
non-intervention, 27, 33, 35, 83, 89, 141, 143,
  151–2, 165
  Kant's principle of, 13
  principle of, 87, 135, 144
North America, 200
North American Free Trade Agreement, 227
North Korea, 140
Northern Ireland, 46, 196
Norway, 121
nuclear weapons, 140, 215, 222
Nuremburg tribunals, 33

Nussbaum, Martha, 17–18, 25–6

OECD, 102–3 200–1
  Report on Participatory Development and
    Good Governance (1997), 101
Old Testament, 125
Oppenheim, Lassa, 79, 135, 149
Organization for Security and Cooperation in
    Europe, 90
Organization of American States, 83, 90
Ottoman Empire, 108
outlaw states, ix–x, 30–1, 36, 134, 138–9,
  150, 152, 193
  military coercion of, 31
Owen, John, 148–9
Oxfam, 217, 231

Paine, Thomas, 169–70, 178
Pakistan, 49
Palestine, 50
Palestine Liberation Movement, 49
Parekh, Bhikhu, xi, 76, 198, 231
parliament(s), 43, 95, 108, 177, 186, 190,
  221, 223–4
  as a deliberative assembly, 185
  constitutional, 43
  regional, 82
paternalism, 2
patriotic cosmopolitanism, 231
patriotism, 19–20, 25
  civic, 20, 25
  constitutional, 210
  global, 19, 25, 231
  local, 19, 200
peace, perpetual, 14, 17, 31
  principles of, 11
Peloponnesian War, 173
Pericles, 23, 172–3
Persian Gulf, 34
Peru, 122, 125
Philippines, 49
Plant, Raymond, 67–8
Plato, 20–1
pluralism, 18, 94, 103, 128, 151, 204, 208
  and international order, 150
  liberal, 151
  liberal limitation to, 208
  political, 84, 86, 106
  tolerable, 31
Poland, 122, 124
polis, 23
political authority, 43–4
political injustice, 215
political leadership
  civilianised, 122–3
political liberalism, 208–9

Index